Karen Brown's
England, Wales & Scotland
Charming Hotels & Itineraries

Written by

JUNE EVELEIGH BROWN and KAREN BROWN

Illustrations by Barbara Maclurcan Tapp
Cover Painting by Jann Pollard

Karen Brown's Guides, San Mateo, California

Karen Brown Titles

Austria: Charming Inns & Itineraries
California: Charming Inns & Itineraries
England: Charming Bed & Breakfasts
England, Wales & Scotland: Charming Hotels & Itineraries
France: Charming Bed & Breakfasts
France: Charming Inns & Itineraries
Germany: Charming Inns & Itineraries
Ireland: Charming Inns & Itineraries
Italy: Charming Bed & Breakfasts
Italy: Charming Inns & Itineraries
Mexico: Charming Inns & Itineraries
Mid-Atlantic: Charming Inns & Itineraries
New England: Charming Inns & Itineraries
Pacific Northwest: Charming Inns & Itineraries
Portugal: Charming Inns & Itineraries
Spain: Charming Inns & Itineraries
Switzerland: Charming Inns & Itineraries

To Simon and Clare
in the hope that they will
discover Britain for themselves

Cover painting: Dunain Park Hotel, Inverness

Editors: Anthony Brown, Karen Brown, June Eveleigh Brown, Clare Brown, Iris Sandilands, Lorena Aburto Ramirez, Debbie Tokumoto, Yvonne Sartain.

Illustrations: Barbara Maclurcan Tapp.

Maps: Michael Fiegel.

Technical support: Michael Fiegel, Gary Meisner.

Copyright © 2005 by Karen Brown's Guides.

This book or parts thereof may not be reproduced in any form without obtaining written permission from the publisher: Karen Brown's Guides, P.O. Box 70, San Mateo, CA 94401, USA, email: karen@karenbrown.com.

Distributed by Fodor's Travel Publications, Inc., 1745 Broadway, New York, NY 10019, USA., tel: 212-751-2600, fax: 212-940-7352.

Distributed in Canada by Random House Canada Ltd., 2775 Matheson Boulevard, East, Mississauga, Ontario, Canada L4W 4P7, tel: 888-523-9292, fax: 888-562-9924.

Distributed in the United Kingdom, Ireland and Europe by Random House UK, 20 Vauxhall Bridge Road, London, SW1V 2SA, England, tel: 44 20 7840 8400, fax: 44 20 7233 8791.

Distributed in Australia by Random House Australia, 20 Alfred Street, Milsons Point, Sydney NSW 2061, Australia, tel: 61 2 9954 9966, fax: 61 2 9954 4562.

Distributed in New Zealand by Random House New Zealand, 18 Poland Road, Glenfield, Auckland 10, New Zealand, tel: 64 9 444 7197, fax: 64 9 444 7524.

Distributed in South Africa by Random House South Africa, Endulani, East Wing, 5A Jubilee Road, Parktown 2193, South Africa, tel: 27 11 484 3538, fax: 27 11 484 6180.

A catalog record for this book is available from the British Library.

ISSN 1535-7333

Contents

We are proud to present
for our 2005 cover painting
Dunain Park Hotel
Inverness

Introduction

This guide falls into three sections: practical information useful in planning your trip; driving itineraries that take you deep into the countryside through idyllic villages full of thatched-roofed cottages and flower-filled gardens, exploring ancient castles and traversing vast purple moorlands; and lastly, but most importantly, our personal recommendations for outstanding hotels in England, Scotland, and Wales. Every hotel included in this guide is one that we have seen and enjoyed—our personal recommendation written with the sincere belief that where you lay your head each night makes the difference between a good and a great vacation. If you prefer to travel the bed and breakfast way, you may prefer to select places to stay from our companion guide, *England: Charming Bed & Breakfasts*. We encourage you to buy new editions of our guides and throw away old ones—you will be glad you did because we add new listings, update prices, phone and fax numbers, and delete places that have not maintained standards.

About England, Wales & Scotland

The following pointers are given in alphabetical order, not in order of importance.

AIRFARE

Karen Brown's Guides have long recommended Auto Europe for their excellent car rental services. Their air travel division, Destination Europe, an airline broker working with major American and European carriers, offers deeply discounted coach- and business-class fares to over 200 European gateway cities. It also gives Karen Brown travelers an additional 5% discount off its already highly competitive prices (cannot be combined with any other offers or promotions). You can make reservations online via our website, *www.karenbrown.com*, (click on *Discount Airfares* on our home page) or by phone at (800) 223-5555. When phoning, be sure to use the Karen Brown ID number 99006187 to secure your discount.

CAR RENTAL

If you are coming from overseas, it is frequently less expensive to arrange and prepay a car rental before arriving in Britain. If you plan on a visit to London, we strongly recommend that you make it either at the beginning or end of your trip. One option is to fly into London, pick your car up at the airport, tour the countryside, drop the car back at the airport, and take public transportation or a taxi into the city. If you are starting your vacation with sightseeing in London, collect your car from the airport at the end of your stay in the city. The trick is to avoid driving in London. *Cars are rented only to persons under 75.*

Readers frequently ask our advice on car rental companies. We always use Auto Europe—a car rental broker that works with the major car rental companies to find the lowest possible price. They also offer motor homes and chauffeur services. Auto Europe's toll-free phone service, from every European country, connects you to their U.S.-based, 24-hour reservation center (ask for the Europe Phone Numbers Card to be mailed to you). Auto Europe offers our readers a 5% discount (cannot be combined with any other offers or promotions) and, occasionally, free upgrades. Be sure to use the Karen Brown ID number 99006187 to receive your discount and any special offers. You can make your own reservations online via our website, *www.karenbrown.com* (select *Auto Europe* from the home page), or by phone (800-223-5555).

CURRENCY

The pound sterling (£) is the official currency of Great Britain. An increasingly popular and convenient way to obtain pounds is simply to use your bankcard at an ATM machine. You pay a fixed fee for this but, depending on the amount you withdraw, it is usually less than the percentage-based fee charged to exchange currency or travelers' checks. Be sure to check with your bank or credit card company about fees and necessary pin numbers prior to departure. Visit our website (*www.karenbrown.com*) for an easy-to-use online currency converter.

DRIVING

Just about the time overseas visitors board their return flight home, they will have adjusted to driving on the "right" side which is the left side in England. You must contend with such things as roundabouts (circular intersections); flyovers (overpasses); ring roads (peripheral roads whose purpose is to bypass city traffic); lorries (trucks); lay-bys (turn-outs); boots (trunks); and bonnets (hoods). Pedestrians are permitted to cross the road anywhere and always have the right of way. Seat belts must be worn at all times.

MOTORWAYS: The letter "M" precedes these convenient routes for covering long distances. With three or more lanes of traffic either side of a central divider, you should stay in the left-hand lane except for passing. Motorway exits are numbered and correspond to numbering on major road maps. Service areas supply petrol (gas), cafeterias, and "bathrooms" (the word "bathroom" is used in the American sense—in Britain "bathroom" means a room with a shower or bathtub, not a toilet—"loo" is the most commonly used term for an American bathroom).

"A" ROADS: The letter "A" precedes the road number. All major roads fall into this category. They vary from three lanes either side of a dividing barrier to single carriageways with an unbroken white line in the middle indicating that passing is not permitted. These roads have the rather alarming habit of changing from dual to single carriageways at a moment's notice.

"B" ROADS AND COUNTRY ROADS: The letter "B" preceding the road number, or the lack of any lettering or numbering, indicates that it belongs to the maze of country roads that crisscross Britain. These are the roads for people who have the luxury of time to enjoy the scenery en route and they require your arming yourself with a good map (although getting lost is part of the adventure). Driving these narrow roads is terrifying at first but exhilarating after a while. Meandering down these roads, you can expect to spend time crawling behind a tractor or cows being herded to the farmyard. Some lanes are so narrow that there is room for only one car.

ELECTRICITY

The voltage is 240. Most bathrooms have razor points (American style) for 110 volts. If you are coming from overseas, it is recommended that you take only dual-voltage appliances and a kit of electrical plugs. Often your host can loan you a hairdryer and an iron.

INFORMATION

The British Tourist Authority is an invaluable source of information. You can visit their website at *www.visitbritain.com*. Its major offices are located as follows:

AUSTRALIA–SYDNEY: VisitBritain, Level 2, 15 Blue Street, North Sydney NSW 2060, freephone: 300 858 589, email: visitbritainaus@visitbritain.org

CANADA–TORONTO: VisitBritain, 5915 Airport Road, Suite 120, Mississauga, Ontario L4V 1T1, freephone: (888) 847 4885, email: travelinfo@visitbritain.org

FRANCE–PARIS: VisitBritain, 5th Floor, 22 Avenue Franklin Roosevelt, 75008 Paris, tel: 01 58 36 50 50, email: gbinfo@visitbritain.org

GERMANY–BERLIN: VisitBritain, Hackescher Markt, 10178 Berlin, tel: (030) 315 7190, email: gb-info@visitbritain.org

NEW ZEALAND–AUCKLAND: VisitBritain, NZI House, 17th Floor, 151 Queen Street, Auckland 1, freephone: 0800 700 741, email: newzealand@visitbritain.org

USA–NEW YORK: VisitBritain, 551 Fifth Avenue, Suite 701, New York, NY 10176, freephone: 1 800 462 2748, email: travelinfo@visitbritain.org

If you need additional information while you are in Britain, there are more than 700 official Tourist Information Centres identified by a blue-and-white letter "I" and "Tourist Information" signs. Many information centers will make reservations for local accommodation and larger ones will "book a bed ahead" in a different locality.

In London at the British Visitor Centre at 1 Regent Street, London SW1Y 4PQ (near Piccadilly Circus tube station) you can book a room, hire a car, or pay for a coach tour or theatre tickets. It is open 9 am to 6:30 pm, Monday to Friday; 10 am to 4 pm, Saturday and Sunday, with extended hours from mid-May to September.

THE NATIONAL TRUST

The National Trust is dedicated to the preservation of places of historic interest or national beauty in England, Wales, Northern Ireland, and Scotland. Its care extends to stately homes, barns, historic houses, castles, gardens, Roman antiquities, moors, fells, woods, and even whole villages. During the course of a driving itinerary, whenever a property is under the care of the National Trust we state (NT). You can check when a property is open in the current edition of *The National Trust Handbook,* available from many National Trust shops and overseas from the British Tourist Authority, or utilize their website, *www.nationaltrust.org.uk.* If you are traveling to Scotland, you will need a copy of *The National Trust for Scotland Guide* or log on to *www.nts.org.uk.* A great many National Trust properties have excellent shops and tearooms. If you are planning on visiting several sites, consider joining the National Trust as a member, thus obtaining free entry into all properties. In the UK contact: The National Trust, PO Box 39, Bromley, Kent BR1 3XL, tel: (020) 7315-1111. In the USA contact: The Royal Oak Foundation, 26 Broadway, Suite 950, New York, NY 10004, tel: (800) 913-6565.

SHOPPING

Visitors from non-EU countries can reclaim the VAT (Value Added Tax) that they pay on the goods they purchase. Not all stores participate in the refund scheme and there is often a minimum purchase price. Stores that do participate will ask to see your passport before completing the VAT form. This form must be presented *with the goods* to the customs officer at the point of departure from Britain within three months of purchase. The customs officer will certify the form. After having the receipts validated by customs you can receive a refund in cash from the tax-free refund counter. Alternatively, you can mail your validated receipts to the store where you bought the goods. The store will then send you a check in sterling for the refund.

WEATHER

Britain has a tendency to be moist at all times of the year. The cold in winter is rarely severe; however, the farther north you go, the greater the possibility of being snowed in. Spring can be wet but it is a lovely time to travel: the summer crowds have not descended, daffodils and bluebells fill the woodlands, and the hedgerows are filled with wildflowers. Summer offers the best chance of sunshine but also the largest crowds. Schools are usually closed the last two weeks of July and all of August—this is the time when most families take their summer holidays. Travel is especially hectic on the weekends in summer—try to avoid major routes and airports at these times. Autumn is also an ideal touring time: the weather tends to be drier than in spring and the woodlands are decked in their golden fall finery.

Overview Map of Driving Itineraries

Scotland

Edinburgh

The Lake District

The Dales and Moors of North Yorkshire

York

Chester

Chesterfield

Ashbourne

Derbyshire Dales and Villages

Cambridge and East Anglia

Wales

Coventry

Cambridge

Oxford

In and Around the Cotswolds

Bath

LONDON

Southwest England

Winchester

Exeter

Portsmouth

Southeast England

Introduction–About Itineraries

About Itineraries

Nine driving itineraries map a route through the various regions of England, Wales, and Scotland. At the beginning of each itinerary, we suggest our recommended pacing to help you decide the amount of time to allocate to each region. Often all, or a large portion, of an itinerary can be enjoyed using one hotel as a base and staying for several days.

Most sightseeing venues operate a summer and a winter opening schedule, changing over around late March/early April and late October/early November. If you happen to be visiting at the changeover times, be sure to check whether your chosen destination is open before making plans. We try to give an indication of opening times, but there is every possibility that these dates and times will have changed by the time you take your trip, so before you embark on an excursion, check the dates and hours of opening.

MAPS

Each of our driving itineraries is preceded by a map showing the route, and each hotel listing is referenced to a map at the back of the book. These are drawn by an artist and are not intended to replace commercial maps. Our suggestion is to purchase a large-scale road atlas of England where an inch equals 10 miles. We use the Michelin Tourist and Motoring Atlas of Great Britain–1122. To outline your trip you might want to consider the one-page map of Britain, Michelin Map 986. We sell these and regional Michelin Green Guides in our website store at *www.karenbrown.com*.

About Hotels

The third section of this guide contains our recommendations for outstanding places to stay in England, Scotland, and Wales. Each listing is very different and occasionally the owners have their eccentricities, which all adds to the allure of these special hotels. We have tried to be candid and honest in our appraisals and attempted to convey each hotel's special flavor, so that you know what to expect and will not be disappointed. All hotels are places that we have inspected, or stayed in—places that we enjoy. Our recommendations cover a wide range: please do not expect the same standard of luxury at, for example, the lovely Hotel du Vin in Harrogate as at the luxurious Chewton Glen—there is no comparison—yet each is outstanding in what it offers. We have tried to mention major sightseeing attractions near each countryside listing to encourage you to spend several nights in each location. Few countries have as much to offer as Great Britain—within a few miles of most listings there are places of interest to visit and explore:lofty cathedrals, quaint churches, museums, and grand country houses.

CHILDREN

Places that welcome children have a "children welcome" icon 🐾. The majority of listings in this guide do not "welcome" children but find they become tolerable at different ages over 5 or, more often than not, over 12. On our website (*www.karenbrown.com*) you can put your cursor over the 🐾 to see at what specific age children are welcome. These indications of children's acceptability are not cast in stone, so, for example, if you have your heart set on staying at a listing that accepts children over 12: and you have an 8-year-old, call them, explain your situation, and they may well take you. Ideally, we would like to see all properties welcoming children and all parents doing their bit by making sure that children do not run wild.

CHRISTMAS PROGRAMS

Several listings offer Christmas getaways. If the information section indicates that the hotel is open during the Christmas season, there is a very good chance that it offers a festive Christmas package.

CREDIT CARDS

Whether or not an establishment accepts credit cards is indicated in the list of icons at the bottom of each description by the symbol ▆. We have also specified in the bottom details which cards are accepted as follows: none, AX–American Express, MC–MasterCard, VS–Visa, or simply, all major.

FINDING HOTELS

At the back of the book is a key map of Great Britain plus regional maps showing each recommended hotel's location. The pertinent regional map number is given at the right on the top line of each hotel's description. Also, we give concise driving directions to guide you to the listing, which is often in a more out-of-the-way place than the town or village in the address. We would be very grateful if you would let us know of cases where our directions have proved inadequate.

HANDICAP FACILITIES

If there is *at least* one guestroom that is accessible by wheelchair, it is noted with the symbol ♿. This is not the same as saying it meets full disability standards. In reality, it can be anything from a basic, ground-floor room to a fully equipped facility. Please discuss your requirements when you call your chosen place to stay to determine if they have accommodation that is suitable for you.

ICONS

We use these icons in the guidebooks and more on our website, *www.karenbrown.com*. ❄ Air conditioning in rooms, ☕ Breakfast included in room rate, ⚗ Children welcome (age given on website), ♨ Cooking classes offered, [CREDIT] Credit cards accepted, ⛑ Dinner served upon request, ☎ Direct-dial telephone in room, ⌂ Dogs by special request, ⊞ Elevator, ⅄ Exercise room, ⊞ Gift shop, @ Internet access, ⅄ Mini-refrigerator in room, ⊗ Non-smoking rooms, P Parking available, ⅋ Restaurant, ⅄ Room Service, ⋓ Sauna, ⚘ Spa, ⊷ Swimming pool, ⅄ Tennis, ⛫ TV in bedrooms, ⚐ Wedding facilities, ♿ Wheelchair accessible, ⊥ Beach nearby, ⌂ Archaeological site nearby, ⅄ Golf course nearby, ⅄⅄ Hiking trails nearby, ⅄ Horseback riding nearby, ⋌ Skiing nearby, ⅄ Water sports nearby, ⅄ Wineries nearby. Icons allow us to provide additional information about our recommended properties. When using our website to supplement the guides, positioning the cursor over an icon will, in many cases, give you further details. For easy reference an icon key can be found on the last page of this book.

RATES

Rates are those quoted to us for the 2005 summer season. We have tried to keep rates uniform by quoting the 2005 rate for a standard double room and for a suite. Not all places conform, so where dinner is included, or the listing quotes only per-person rates, we have made a note of this. Prices are usually quoted to include breakfast (except in London where breakfast is not usually included in the rate), Value Added Tax (VAT), and service (if these are applicable). Please use the figures printed as a guideline and be certain to ask what the rate is at the time of booking. Many listings offer special terms, below their normal prices, for "short breaks" of two or more nights.

RELAIS & CHÂTEAUX

Several of the hotels we recommend are members of Relais & Châteaux, in which case we note *Relais & Châteaux* at the bottom of the descriptions.

RESERVATIONS

When making your reservations, be sure to identify yourself as a "Karen Brown Traveler." The hoteliers appreciate your visit, value their inclusion in our guide, and frequently tell us they take special care of our readers, and many offer special rates to Karen Brown members (visit our website at *www.karenbrown.com*). We hear over and over again that the people who use our guides are such wonderful guests!

It is important to understand that once reservations for accommodation are confirmed, whether verbally, by phone or in writing, you are under contract. This means that the proprietor is obligated to provide the accommodation that was promised and that you are obligated to pay for it. If you cannot, you are liable for a portion of the accommodation charges plus your deposit. Although some proprietors do not strictly enforce a cancellation policy many, particularly the owners of the smaller properties in our book, simply cannot afford not to do so. Similarly, many airline tickets cannot be changed or refunded without penalty. We recommend insurance to cover these types of additional expenses arising from cancellation due to unforeseen circumstances. A link on our website (*www.karenbrown.com*) will connect you to a variety of insurance policies that can be purchased online.

Reservations can be confining and usually must be guaranteed with a deposit. July and August are the busiest times and it is advisable to make reservations during this period. When making a reservation be specific as to what your needs are, such as a ground-floor room, en suite shower, twin beds, or family room. Check the prices, which may well have changed from the guidelines given in the book (summer 2005). Ask what deposit to send or give your credit card number. Tell them about what time you intend to arrive and request dinner if you want it. Ask for a confirmation letter with brochure and map to be sent to you. There are several options for making reservations:

EMAIL: This is our preferred way of making a reservation. All hotels featured on the Karen Brown website that have email addresses also have those addresses listed on their web pages. This information is constantly kept updated and correct. You can link directly to a property from its page on our website using its email hyperlink. *Always spell out the month as the British reverse the American month/day numbering system.*

FAX: If you have access to a fax machine, this is a very quick way to reach a hotel. If the place to stay has a fax, we have included the number in the listing. (See comment above about spelling out the month.)

LETTER: If you write for reservations, you will usually receive your confirmation and a map. You should then send your deposit. (Be sure to spell out the month.)

TELEPHONE: By telephoning you have your answer immediately, so if space is not available, you can then decide on an alternative. If calling from the United States, allow for the time difference (Britain is five hours ahead of New York) so that you can call during their business day. Dial 011 (the international code), 44 (Britain's code), then the city code (dropping the 0), and the telephone number.

WEBSITE

Please visit the Karen Brown website (*www.karenbrown.com*) in conjunction with this book. It provides comments and discoveries from you, our readers, information on our latest finds, post-press updates, the opportunity to purchase goods and services that we recommend (airline tickets, rail tickets, car rental, travel insurance), and one-stop shopping for our guides and associated maps. Most of our favorite places to stay participate in our website, where you can find color photos and direct links to their own websites and email.

In & Around The Cotswolds

Coventry

M6

M69

M6

M1

M40

M42

Warwick

Stratford-
upon-Avon

A40

Worcester

M5

A429

M40

Hidcote

Broad
Campden

Broadway

Chipping
Campden

Moreton
in Marsh

Buckland

Snowshill

The Swells

Upper
Slaughter

Lower Slaughter

Stow-on-
the-Wold

Bourton-on-
the-Water

Great
Barrington

A44

Woodstock/Blenheim Palace

A40

A40

Burford

Minster
Lovell

Witney

A4095

A40

Oxford

A40

M5

A429

M40

● Orientation/Sightseeing
▪▪ Itinerary Route

In & Around The Cotswolds

From the gracious university town of Oxford through the quintessentially English Cotswold villages to Shakespearean Stratford and the grand fortress of Warwick Castle, this itinerary covers famous attractions and idyllic countryside nooks and crannies. The Cotswolds is a region of one sleepy village after another clad in the local soft-gray limestone or creamy-golden ironstone, where mellow stone walls, manor houses, and churches cluster along riverbanks, perch on steep-sided hills, or scatter independently in a pocket of a pretty valley. In Shakespeare's day this was sheep country and the center of England's wool industry. By the mid-1800s the area had fallen into decline, its wool trade usurped by Australia and New Zealand. Thus the area slept, by-passed by the factories and cities of the Industrial Revolution. Now tourists flock to the Cotswolds and yet the region remains remarkably unspoilt: in fact, it appears to thrive on the attention.

Lower Slaughter

Recommended Pacing: Spend a night in Oxford or in nearby Woodstock. Follow this with two nights in a countryside hotel as a base for exploring the beautiful Cotswold villages (consider going into Stratford one night to see a play).

Oxford is a beautiful university town graced by spacious lawns, pretty parks, lacy spires, honey-colored Cotswold stones, romantic pathways, and two picturesque rivers—the Cherwell and the Thames. Follow signs for the city center, park in any of the well-signposted, multi-story car parks, and foray on foot to explore. You may want to make your first stop the **Oxford Information Centre** on Gloucester Green, off George Street, to obtain a map. Walking tours of the town start from here. Much of the sightseeing in this the oldest university town centers on its colleges whose open times depend on whether the students are "up" (there) or "down" (not there). Particularly worth visiting are **Christ Church College** with its superb quad and tower designed by Christopher Wren to hold the bell Great Tom; **Magdalen College**, the most beautiful college, with its huge gardens making you feel as if you are in the countryside; and **Merton College**, whose chapel contains 13th- to 14th-century glass. Apart from the colleges, visit **St. Mary's Church** where you can climb the spire for a marvelous view of the city; the **Radcliffe Camera** and adjacent **Ashmolean Museum** with its remarkable collection of paintings, tapestries, and sculptures; the riverside **Botanical Gardens** opposite Magdalen College; **Blackwell's**, the most famous of Oxford's many bookstores; and **The Bear**, on Alfred Street, a tiny old pub dating from 1242. **Punts** can be rented on the River Cherwell beside Magdalen Bridge.

Leaving Oxford, take the A44 (Stratford-upon-Avon) to **Woodstock**, one of England's prettiest country towns. On the outskirts of Woodstock are the famous gates of **Blenheim Palace**, Sir John Vanbrugh's masterpiece, which was built for John Churchill, the 1st Duke of Marlborough. The construction of the house was a gift from Queen Anne to the Duke after his victory over the French and Bavarians at Blenheim in 1704. However, before its completion, Queen Anne's gratitude had waned and the Marlborough family had to pay to have the house finished. The gardens and parklike grounds were landscaped by Capability Brown. Sir Winston Churchill, the grandson of the 7th Duke, was born here on November 30, 1874, and associations with him have accentuated the historical interest of the palace. (Winston Churchill, his wife, father, Lord Randolph Churchill, and mother, Jenny Jerome, the beautiful daughter of an American newspaper owner, are buried in St. Martin's churchyard in Bladon, 2 miles away.) You drive through the grounds to the house, park on the grass, and either tour the sumptuous rooms with a group or wander independently. A narrow-gauge railway takes you through the park to the butterfly farm and plant center. In contrast to the immense palace and spacious grounds are the compact streets of the little town of Woodstock with its coaching inns and interesting shops.

Blenheim Palace

In & Around The Cotswolds

Retrace your steps for a short distance on the A44 in the direction of Oxford and take the A4095 for 7 miles to the mellow-stone town of **Witney** where blankets have been made for over a thousand years and which still preserves its Cotswold market-town atmosphere. The 18th-century **Blanket Hall** was used for weighing blankets and has an unusual one-handed clock.

Minster Lovell is a few miles to the west along the B4047: to reach the old part of the village, follow the brown signs for **Minster Lovell Hall**. Park at the end of the lane and walk through the churchyard to see the ruined home of the Lovell family in a field by the river's edge. Leave the village by the road to the side of the prettiest building in the village, The Swan, following signs through Astall Leigh and Astall to the A40, which you take in the direction of Cheltenham for a short distance to Burford.

Follow Tourist Information signs down the hill into the lovely old-world Cotswold town of **Burford**. The broad High Street sweeps down the hillside, bordered by numerous antique and gift shops, to the bridge spanning the River Windrush. Branching off are delightful, narrow residential streets with flower-filled cottage gardens. In the days when the horse-drawn coach was the main form of transport, Burford was a way station. The coaches are long gone but the lovely inns remain: two with the most atmosphere are **The Bay Tree** and the adjacent **Lamb Inn**.

Explore Burford and leave town following the road over the River Windrush. Go left at the mini-roundabout, directing yourself down country lanes to **Taynton** with its adorable thatched and golden-stone cottages and on up the valley to Great Barrington and **Little Barrington**, a village of quaint cottages. Turn right along the A40 towards Cheltenham and first right to Windrush where you pick up signs for the drive down country lanes through Sherbourne to Bourton-on-the-Water. (When you come to the A429 turn right and then right into Bourton-on-the-Water.)

Bourton-on-the-Water is a lovely village with a number of riverside greens and low bridges spanning the River Windrush. Go early in the morning, just before sunset, or in the winter to avoid the crowds that overrun this peaceful (albeit somewhat over-commercialized) spot.

Leave Bourton-on-the-Water by going down the main street and turning right for a very short distance on the A429 (in the direction of Cheltenham) to a left-hand turn that directs you down country lanes to the more peaceful side of the Cotswolds. This is typified by the outstandingly lovely villages of **Lower and Upper Slaughter** with their honey-colored stone cottages beside peaceful streams—just the names on the signposts are enough to lure you down their lanes. From Upper Slaughter follow signs for Stow-on-the-Wold down country lanes through "the Swells," **Lower and Upper Swell**, further picturesque examples of villages with whimsical names.

Stow-on-the-Wold, its market square lined by mellow, old, gray-stone buildings, was one of the most prosperous wool towns in England. Most of the 17th-century buildings around the square now house interesting shops. Two of Stow's main thoroughfares—Sheep Street and Shepherds Way—are reminders that selling sheep was once the town's main livelihood. Cromwell converted the 12th-century church into a prison and used it to hold 1,000 Royalists captive after a Civil War battle in 1646.

Nearby **Moreton in Marsh's** broad main street, once part of the Roman road known as the Fosse Way, is lined with interesting shops. At the crossroads take the A44 towards Evesham to **Bourton-on-the-Hill**, an appropriately named village whose houses climb a steep hillside. At the top of the hill turn right for Blockley and follow signs for the village center until you pick up signs for Broad Campden and **Chipping Campden**, its High Street lined with gabled cottages and shops topped by steep tile roofs.

Leave Chipping Campden in the direction of Evesham (a small side road off the High Street that takes you past chocolate-box cottages to the A44, which you cross for the short drive through lavender-lined lanes past **Snowshill Lavender** to **Snowshill** and **Snowshill Manor** (NT), a Tudor manor packed with collections of musical instruments, clocks, toys, and bicycles, and surrounded by lovely cottage gardens.

In & Around The Cotswolds

Just down the lane, flowers dress the picutesque weathered-stone houses of **Broadway**, a town that is often described as the perfection of Cotswold beauty. The **Lygon Arms** is as famous as the town, a magnificent 14th- to 16th-century hotel whose public rooms are exquisitely furnished with antiques. In summer the town is thronged with tourists so it is best to visit early or late in the day.

Turn right up the main street and first left on the B4632 (signposted Stratford), through peaceful **Willersey,** where ducks sail serenely on the village mere, and Weston-sub-Edge, to the outskirts of Mickleton where you turn right for **Hidcote Manor Gardens** (NT), one of the most delightful gardens in England. Created early this century by Major Lawrence Johnston, it is a series of individual gardens each bounded by sculpted hedges and linked by paths and terraces. Each "mini-garden" focuses on a specific theme or flower. There are stunning displays of old roses and in summer the perennials are a blaze of color. Next door, another outstanding garden, **Kiftsgate Court**, has exquisite displays of roses.

Leaving Hidcote, the 9-mile drive to Stratford-upon-Avon down country lanes is well-signposted. As you enter the town look for signposts directing you **Anne Hathaway's Cottage.** Anne married William Shakespeare in 1582, but until then she lived in a darling thatched cottage at **Shottery**, a small village just a stone's throw from Stratford-upon-Avon. You see paintings and photographs of this picture-book cottage all over the world.

Stratford-upon-Avon is the birthplace of the greatest poet in the English language, William Shakespeare. Stratford-upon-Avon is always impossibly crowded with visitors—if crowds are not to your liking, give it a miss. William Shakespeare was born in 1564 in a half-timbered house on Henley Street (**Shakespeare's Birthplace**, now a museum), educated at the King's New Grammar School and, in 1597, six years before his death, retired to **New Place**, one of the finest and largest houses in Stratford. Simply engraved stones in front of the altar of the **Holy Trinity Church** mark the burial spot of Shakespeare and some other members of his family. It is a fairly large town, with beautifully renovated timbered buildings and lovely shops. The town's glory, however, is brought expertly to the stage at the **Royal Shakespeare Theatre** and at its associate theatre, **The Other Place**.

Leave Stratford on the A46 for Warwick. **Warwick Castle** is a magnificent 14th-century fortress of formidable towers and turrets. The fortress dominates a choice spot on the riverbank and its striking structure is beautifully preserved. Climb the towers, explore the armory and torture chamber below, then visit the Manor House. As you walk through the house you see what it was like to attend a house party given by the Earl and Countess of Warwick in 1898. The house has retained its period furniture and Madame Tussaud's has populated the rooms with wax figures from the past. Here a servant pours water into a bath for a guest while downstairs visitors listen to a recital being given by Dame Clara Butt. The gardens are decorated by arrogant, strutting peacocks.

Wander into **Warwick** with its mixture of Georgian and old timber-framed houses. At the town's west gate stands the **Leycester Hospital**, for 400 years an almshouse for crippled soldiers. In the **Beauchamp Chapel** lies the tomb of Elizabeth I's favorite, the Earl of Leicester.

From Warwick fast motorways will connect you to all parts of Britain.

Warwick Castle

In & Around The Cotswolds

 23

Southwest England

Boscastle
Tintagel
Padstow
Lostwithiel
The Eden Project
St Austell
Truro
Lost Gardens of Heligan
Mevagissey
Veryan
Trelissick Gardens
Portloe
Portscatho
St Just in Roseland
St Mawes
Falmouth
St Ives
Marazion
Cape Cornwall
St Just
St Michael's Mount
Lands End
Penzance

● Orientation/Sightseeing
-- Itinerary Route

A39
A30
A30
A390
A394

25

Southwest England

Scenery changes noticeably as this itinerary traverses England southwest from Bath through Somerset and along its unspoilt coast, outlining Cornwall, into the heart of Devon. Wild ponies gallop across the expanses of Exmoor. Along the northern coastline, the scenery changes dramatically from wooded inlets dropping to the sea to wild rollers crashing on granite cliffs, giving credence to old tales of wreckers luring ships onto rocky shorelines. Picturesque villages surround sheltered harbors, their quays strewn with nets and lobster pots. Southern ports present a gentler scene: bobbing yachts dot wooded estuaries and gentle waves lap the shoreline. Hedgerow-lined lanes meander inland across Dartmoor's heather-clad moorlands to picturesque towns nestling at her edge. Relax and enjoy your explorations of this westernmost spur of land jutting out into the Atlantic Ocean.

St. Michael's Mount

Recommended Pacing: Spend two full days in Bath to give you time to appreciate the flavor of this lovely city. We suggest that you use Rock as a base for exploring the northern coast of the peninsula, and Penzance, St. Mawes, Fowey, or Talland-by-Looe as a base for exploring the south of Cornwall. Complete the itinerary with a couple of nights in south Devon to enable you to enjoy the wild beauties of Dartmoor.

The elegant city of **Bath** with its graceful, honey-colored buildings, interesting museums, and delightful shopping area is best explored on foot over a period of several days. Bath, founded by the Romans in the 1st century around the gushing mineral hot springs, reached its peak of popularity in the early 1700s with the arrival of Beau Nash, who opened the first Pump Room where people could take the water and socialize. Architects John Wood, father and son, used the local honey-colored stone to build the elegant streets and crescents in neoclassical Palladian style.

Maps are available from the Tourist Information Centre near the abbey (corner of Cheap and Stall streets). Entry into the **Roman Baths** is via the **Pump Room,** which was the place to gather in the 18th and 19th centuries. The Great Bath, a large warm swimming pool built around a natural hot spring, now open to the sky, was once covered. Mosaics, monuments, and many interesting artifacts from the town can be seen in the adjacent museum.

Nearby, tucked into a narrow passageway between Abbey Green and North Parade, is **Sally Lunn's House**, a museum and a teashop. The museum, in the cellar, has the kitchen preserved much as it was in the 1680s when Sally's buns and other baked goods were the favorites of Bath society. Upstairs you can try a freshly baked Sally Lunn bun.

Eighteenth-century society came to be seen at balls and gatherings at the **Assembly Rooms** and authors such as Austen, Smolett, and Fielding captured the social importance of these events. The **Museum of Costume**, in the Assembly Rooms basement, should not be missed.

From the Museum of Costume it is an easy walk via **The Circus**, a tight circle lined with splendid houses designed by John Wood I, and Brock Street to the **Royal Crescent**, a great arc of 30 terraced houses that epitomize the Georgian elegance of Bath. **One Royal Crescent** has been authentically restored to the 18th-century style and contains an interesting kitchen museum and a gift shop.

Bath has some wonderful restaurants and delightful shops and boutiques: whether you are in the market for antiques or high fashion, you will find shopping here a real joy.

While our itinerary takes us south and west from Bath, there are a great many interesting places to the east, listed below, that can easily be visited as day trips from this lovely city.

The village of **Avebury** (NT), made up of a church, several houses, shops, and an old pub, lies within a vast circle of standing stones surrounded by earthworks. The site covers 28 acres. Unlike Stonehenge, where the stones are larger, the site smaller and the crowds sometimes overwhelming, Avebury is a peaceful spot. Here, armed with a map, you can wander amongst the stones and wonder why 4,000 years ago Bronze Age man spent what has been estimated at 1½ million man-hours to construct such a temple. (Just off the A4 between Calne and Marlborough.)

Castle Combe is a most photogenic collection of warm, honey-stone cottages snuggled along a stream's edge. (Just south of the M4 motorway between exits 17 and 18.)

Claverton Manor is the American museum in the United Kingdom. Furniture, household equipment, and period rooms show home life in the United States from the 17th to 19th centuries. (3 miles east of Bath.)

Lacock (NT) is an exquisite village where no building dates from later than the 18th century, many dating from much earlier. Be sure to visit the **Fox Talbot Museum** of early photographs and **Lacock Abbey**. The abbey was converted to a manor house in the 16th century but retains its 13th-century cloisters. **At The Sign of The Angel** is a delightful 15th-century inn, easily distinguished by being the only black-and-white building in the village. (Between Chippenham and Melksham on the A350.)

Salisbury has been a prosperous Hampshire market town since the 13th century. Park your car in one of the large car parks on the edge of town and wander through the bustling town center to **Salisbury Cathedral**, the only ancient English cathedral built to a single design. Completed in 1258, it sits gracefully isolated from the busy town, surrounded by a large green field.

Salisbury Cathedral

Britain's most famous ancient monument is **Stonehenge**. Built over a period of almost 1,000 years up to 1250 B.C., this circular arrangement of towering stone slabs was probably meant either to mark the seasons or to be used as a symbol of worship. It is intriguing to ponder what prompted a society thousands of years ago to drag these immense stones many miles and erect them in just such a formation, isolated in the middle of flat Salisbury Plain. Understandably, Stonehenge attracts many visitors. Your visit will be more enjoyable if you are prepared for coachloads of tourists. (On the A303 about 10 miles from Salisbury.)

When it is time to leave Bath, take the A4 following signs for Bristol until you come to the A39 Wells road. **Wells** is England's smallest cathedral city and the cathedral is glorious. Park your car in one of the well-signposted car parks on the edge of town and walk through the bustling streets to **Wells Cathedral**. The cathedral's west front is magnificently adorned with 400 statues of saints, angels, and prophets. The interior is lovely and on every hour the Great Clock comes alive as figures of four knights joust and one is unseated. From the cathedral you come to Vicars Close, a cobbled street of tall-chimneyed cottages with little cottage gardens, built over 500 years ago as housing for the clerical community. On the other side of the cathedral regal swans swim lazily in the moat beneath the Bishop's Palace where at one time they rang a bell when they wanted to be fed—now visitors' picnics provide easier meals.

Nearby **Glastonbury** is an ancient market town steeped in legends. As the story goes, Joseph of Arimathea traveled here and leaned on his staff, which rooted and flowered, a symbol that he should build a church. There may well have been a primitive church here but the ruins of **Glastonbury Abbey** that you see are those of the enormous abbey complex that was begun in the 13th century and closed by Henry VIII just as it was completed. The abbey is in the center of town. Legend also has it that Glastonbury (at that time surrounded by marshes and lakes) was the Arthurian Isle of Avalon. Arthur and Guinevere are reputedly buried here and it is said that Arthur only sleeps and will arise when England needs him.

Cross the M5 near Bridgwater, detouring around the town, and follow the A39, Minehead road, to **Dunster**, a medieval town dominated by the battlements and towers of **Dunster Castle** (NT). Constructed by a Norman baron, it has been inhabited by the Luttrell family since 1376. While much of the castle was reconstructed in the last century, it has a superb staircase, halls, and dining room. Park before you enter the town and explore the shops and ancient buildings (including a dormered Yarn Market) on the High Street. On Mill

Lane you can tour 18th-century **Dunster Watermill** (NT), which was restored to working order in 1979.

Continue your drive along the A39, watching for a sign directing you to your right to the hamlet of **Selworthy** (NT). Its pretty green, surrounded by elaborate thatched cottages, makes this a very picturesque spot. The National Trust has a small visitors' center and excellent teashop.

Porlock is a large, quaint, bustling village with narrow streets. As the road bends down to the sea, the hamlet of **Porlock Weir** appears as a few picturesque cottages, the Ship Inn facing a pebble beach and a tiny harbor dotted with boats.

Retrace your steps towards Porlock for a short distance and take the first road to the right, a private toll road that rises steeply out of Porlock Weir. It is a pretty, forested drive along a narrow lane with views of Porlock Bay. The toll road returns you to the A39, which you take for a short distance before turning left for the village of **Oare**. R. D. Blackmore who wrote about the people, moods, and landscape of Exmoor used the little church that you see in the valley below for Lorna Doone's marriage to John Ridd. Continue into the village where you can park your car near the village shop and take a 3-mile walk along the river to Badgworthy Valley, the home of the cutthroat outlaw Doone family.

Continue to Brenden where you turn right, signposted Lynton and Lynmouth, and regain the A39. A short drive through squat red and green hills brings you to the coast where the road dips steeply and you see the neighboring villages of **Lynton** and **Lynmouth.** Victorian Lynton stands at the top of the cliff and Lynmouth, a fishing village of old-style houses, nestles at its foot. Park by the harbor and take the funky old cliff railway, which connects the two villages.

Leaving Lynmouth, proceed up the hill into Lynton, and follow signs for the alternative route for light vehicles to Valley of the Rocks. Wend your way through the town and continue straight. Beyond the suburbs the road tapers and you find yourself in a narrow valley with large, rugged rock formations separating you from the sea, then in a more pastoral area with seascapes at every dip and turn.

Deposit your road toll in the honesty box and follow signs along narrow lanes for **Hunters Inn**, a lovely old pub set in a peaceful valley. From here direct yourself back towards the A39, which bends inland across the western stretches of Exmoor and south through **Barnstaple**, a market center for the area. Continue along the A39 to Bideford where a bridge sweeps you high above the old harbor.

Just beyond Bucks Cross you see a small signpost for **Clovelly**, an impossibly beautiful spot, its whitewashed cottages tumbling down cobblestone lanes to boats bobbing in the harbor far below. However, to be able to walk through this picturebook village you have to pay an entrance fee at the visitors' center, which rankles but also preserves this lovely place.

Leave the A39 at the B3263 and detour on narrow country lanes leading to the picturesque little village of **Boscastle**. Braced in a valley 400 feet above a little harbor, the town was named after the Boscastle family who once lived there, rather than an actual castle.

Nearby, **Tintagel Castle** clings to a wild headland, exposed to coastal winds, claiming the honor of being King Arthur's legendary birthplace. The sea has cut deeply into the slate cliffs, isolating the castle. Climb the steep steps to the castle and gaze down at the sea far below. Prince Charles, as Duke of Cornwall, owns the castle whose interior is more attractive than the exterior. The town itself, while it is quite touristy, has charm and the most adorable, and certainly most photographed, **Post Office** (NT) in Britain.

Leaving Tintagel, follow signs for the A39, in the direction of Truro, to the A30, which takes you around Redruth, Cambourne, and Hayle to the A3074 to **St. Ives**, about an hour-and-a-half's journey if the roads are not too busy. Stay on the A3074 until the road is signposted sharp right to the harbor. Go left and follow parking signs to the Recreation Centre. Park your car here and walk down into town. Your destination is Fore Street with its galleries, restaurants, and interesting shops. Fore Street leads you to the quaint harbor while a left on Digbey will bring you to the **Tate Gallery** on Porthmeor Beach. Whistler and Sickert discovered St. Ives while sculptress Barbara Hepworth and painter Ben Nicholson made it famous. Admission to the Tate also includes admission to Barbara Hepworth's garden filled with her sculptures. If you are not a fan of modern art, just ask for a pass to visit the rooftop café and enjoy the spectacular views.

Leaving St. Ives, follow signposts to St. Just, which brings you the most attractive, windswept stretch of Cornwall's coastline. Stone farm villages hug the bare expanse of land and are cooled by Atlantic Ocean breezes that waft up over the cliff edges. Abandoned old tin mine towers stand in ruins and regularly dot the horizon. On the western outskirts of **St. Just** lies **Cape Cornwall**. Rather than visit over-commercialized Land's End, visit here to enjoy a less crowded, more pastoral western view. Pull into **Sennen Cove** with its long, curving crescent of golden sand and the powerful Atlantic surf rolling and pounding.

The expression "from John O'Groats to Land's End" signifies the length of Britain from its northeasternmost point in Scotland to England's rocky promontory, **Land's End**, in the southwest. Many visitors to Cornwall visit Land's End, but be prepared to be disappointed—you have to pay to enter a compound of refreshment stands, exhibits, and children's rides to get to the viewpoint.

As the road rounds the peninsula from Land's End, it is exposed to the calmer Channel waters, far different from the Atlantic rollers. Mount's Bay is just around the bend from Land's End with the pretty village of **Mousehole** (pronounced "mowzle") tucked into a nicht on its shores. With color-washed cottages crowded into a steep valley and multicolored fishing boats moored at its feet, this adorable village is crowded in summer but worth the aggravation endured in finding a parking spot.

Pirates from France and the Barbary Coast used to raid the flourishing port town of **Penzance** until the mid-18th century. Now it is quite a large town, a real mishmash of styles from quaint fishermen's cottages to '60s housing estates, where long, peaceful, sandy beaches contrast with the clamor and activity of dry-dock harbors.

Leave Penzance on the A30 following the graceful sweep of Mount's Bay and turn right onto a minor road that brings you to **St. Michael's Mount** (NT). Its resemblance to the more famous mount in France is not coincidental, for it was founded by monks from Mont St. Michel in 1044. A 19th-century castle and the ruins of the monastery crown the island, which is reached at low tide on foot from the town of Marazion. If you cannot coincide your arrival with low tide, do not worry—small boats ferry you the short distance to the island. The steep climb to the top of this fairy-tale mount is well worth the effort.

To the east lies **Falmouth**. Overlooking the holiday resort, yachting center, and ancient port are the ruins of **Pendennis Castle**. Built in 1540 to guard the harbor entrance, it was held during the Civil War by the Royalists and withstood six months of siege before being the last castle to surrender to Cromwell's troops in 1646. Falmouth is a bustling town whose narrow, shop-lined streets have a complex one-way system—parking is an additional problem. Unless you have shopping to do, avoid the congestion of the town center and follow signposts for Truro.

The road from Falmouth to St. Mawes winds around the river estuary by way of Truro. A faster and more scenic route is to take the **King Harry Ferry** across the river estuary. If you love wandering around gardens, you will enjoy **Trelissick Gardens** (NT), filled with subtropical plants, located on the Falmouth side of the estuary.

St. Mawes is a charming, unspoilt fishing harbor at the head of the Roseland Peninsula. Its castle was built by Henry VIII to defend the estuary. The 20 miles or so of coastline to the east of St. Mawes hide several beautiful villages located down narrow, winding country lanes. **Portscatho** is a lovely fishing village that has not been overrun with tourists. **Veryan** is a quaint village where thatched circular houses were built so that "the devil had nowhere to hide." **Portloe** is a pretty fishing hamlet. The most easterly village is **Mevagissey** whose beauty attracts writers, artists, and throngs of tourists.

Overlooking this quaint port lie the expansive estates of the Tremayne family, centered at one time on Heligan House and its vast acres of gardens and woodlands. There used to be

20 staff in the house and 22 in the garden but all this ended in the 1914–18 war when two-thirds of the gardeners died fighting in Flanders. After that the garden went into decline and when the Tremaynes sold the house, in 1970, for conversion to apartments it simply went to sleep—a sleep from which it emerged in the 1990s when two professional gardeners hacked their way through the undergrowth and were inspired to begin the largest garden restoration project in Europe. Evoking images of *The Secret Garden,* the **Lost Gardens of Heligan** have emerged from their slumber. A magnificent complex of walled gardens, vegetable gardens, and melon yards shows how pineapples and melons were grown in Victorian times. To the south of the main garden are vast acres of palms and tree ferns know as The Jungle, which leads to the Lost Valley with its woodland walks.

Drive through St. Austell on the A390 and turn left up into the hills above the town, following signs to **The Eden Project**, set in a former china clay pit. The aim of this project is to promote the understanding and responsible management of the vital relationship between plants, people, and resources. At the bottom of the giant crater are the world's largest greenhouses clinging onto the cliffs like huge soap bubbles. In the space of a day you can walk from the scented warmth of the Mediterranean to the steaminess of a rainforest. You'll find plenty of convenient parking and enough hands-on exhibits and restaurants to make this a fun visit rather than an academic experience.

Your next destination, **Lanhydrock** (NT), lies just a short distance away. Follow signs to Bodmin and take the dual carriageway (A30) to the first exit signed Lanhydrock. Set in a vast estate and surrounded by formal gardens, Llanydrock showcases what was the very latest in contemporary living in 1881—there's even central heating. It looks as though the family has just stepped out, leaving the dining table laid for an elaborate party, toys in the nursery waiting to be played with, the schoolroom all set for lessons, afternoon tea set up in the mistress's sitting room, and desserts all ready to be served from the kitchen.

Returning to the A30, drive northeast to **Lostwithiel**, the 13th-century capital of Cornwall. Twenty miles to the east, **Liskeard** is crowded in summer, but fortunately much of the traffic has been diverted around the town. Between Liskeard and Tavistock you find **Cotehele** (NT), built between 1485 and 1627, the home of the Edgecumbe family. The house contains original furniture, armor, and needlework. A highlight is the kitchen with all its wonderful old implements. The gardens terrace steeply down to the lovely River Tamar.

The A390 crosses the River Tay and brings you into Tavistock. Turn right at the first roundabout in town signposted B3357 Princetown (then the B3212 Mortenhampstead road), which brings you up, over a cattle grid, and into **Dartmoor National Park**. Vast expanses of moorland rise to rocky outcrops (tors and crags) where ponies and sheep graze intently among the bracken and heather, falling to picturesque wooded valleys where villages shelter beneath the moor. From Mortenhampstead it's a half-hour drive to Exeter and the motorway. But, saving the best for last, linger on Dartmoor and enjoy some of the following sights.

The view from atop **Haytor Crags** on the Bovey to Widecombe road is a spectacular one—there is a feel of *The Hound of the Baskervilles* to the place. Softer and prettier is the walk down wooded **Lydford Gorge** (NT) to White Lady Waterfall (between Tavistock and Okehampton). A cluster of cottages and a tall church steeple make up **Widecombe in the Moor**, the village made famous by the *Uncle Tom Cobbleigh* song. The famous fair is still held on the second Tuesday in September. The pretty town of **Chagford** at the edge of the moor has attractive houses and hostelries grouped round the market square. **Buckland-in-the-Moor** is full of picturesque thatched cottages. **Buckland Abbey** (NT), once a Cistercian abbey and home of Sir Francis Drake, is now a museum with scale model ships from Drake's time to today among its exhibits At **Buckfastleigh** you can take a steam train 7 miles alongside the river Dart. **Castle Drogo** (NT) is a fanciful, castlelike home designed by Edward Lutyens overlooking the moor near Drewsteignton.

Leaving Dartmoor National Park, A roads quickly bring you to **Exeter**. The old town towards the River Exe has many fine old buildings including the Custom House and a maze of little streets with old inns and quaint shops. The center is a modern shopping complex. From Exeter the M5 will connect you to all parts of Britain.

Southeast England

Legend:
- ● Orientation/Sightseeing
- ▬ ▬ Itinerary Route
- ◉ Highway Exit

London
Westerham
Exit 6
Chartwell
Penshurst Place
Hever Castle
Scotney Castle Gardens
Sissinghurst Castle
Tunbridge Wells
Canterbury
Winchester
Bodiam Castle
Southampton
Weald & Downland Museum
Midhurst
Petworth
Rye
Chichester
Arundel
Hastings
Brighton
Eastbourne
Portsmouth
Alfriston

M25
M20
M2
M3
M23
M27
A27
A259

Southeast England

Southeast from London, through Kent and Sussex to England's southern coast, the land is fertile and the climate mild. Scores of narrow country lanes twist and turn among the gentle slopes of the pleasant countryside, leading you from Chartwell, Churchill's home, through castles, manors, and some of the most exquisitely beautiful gardens in England to Rye, a town full of history and rich in smugglers' tales. Along the busy, crowded coast you come to Brighton, where seaside honky-tonk contrasts with the vivid spectacle of the onion domes of the Royal Pavilion, Arundel with its mighty fortress, and Portsmouth with its historic boats.

Rye

Recommended Pacing: Spend two nights in southeast England to enable you to accomplish the first part of this itinerary. Allow a day's drive, with sightseeing, along the coast and into Winchester. Spend two nights in Winchester to give you a complete day for sightseeing.

Chartwell, your first sightseeing destination, lies 9 miles from exit 6 of the M25, through Westerham and onto country lanes. Chartwell was the home of Winston Churchill from 1924 until his death in 1965, when Lady Churchill gave the house and its contents to the nation. To visit this large home and Churchill's studio, full of his mementos and paintings, is to have a glimpse into the family life of one of Britain's most famous politicians.

Leave Chartwell to the left following the country road a short distance to **Hever Castle**, a small 13th-century moated castle that was at one time home to the Boleyn family. Anne Boleyn was Henry VIII's second wife and Elizabeth I's mother. At the turn of the last century vast amounts of money were poured into the castle's restoration by William Waldorf Astor, an extremely wealthy American who forsook his native country and became a naturalized British citizen. Because the castle was far too small to provide accommodation for his family and friends, Mr Astor built an adjacent village of snug, Tudor-style cottages and joined it to the castle. While the village is not open to the public, the restored castle, its rooms full of antiques that span the last 800 years, and the parklike grounds are open to visitors.

Leave the castle heading left in the direction of Tunbridge Wells, turning left down a small country road to **Chiddingstone**, a National Trust village, whose short main street has several 16th- and 17th-century, half-timbered houses, a church, and a teashop. Park by the old houses and follow a footpath behind the cottages to the Chiding Stone, from which the village gets its name: nagging wives were brought here to be chided by the villagers.

Just beyond the village, branch left at the oast house for Penshurst Station and **Penshurst Place**, a 14th-century manor house with an Elizabethan front surrounded by magnificent parkland and gorgeous gardens. Here Sir Philip Sidney—poet, soldier, and statesman—was born and his descendant, Viscount de l'Isle, lives today. The enormous, 14th-century great hall with its stone floor and lofty, ornate, beamed ceiling contrasts by its austerity with the sumptuously furnished state rooms. There is also a fascinating collection of old toys. The gardens are a delight, full of hedges and walls that divide them into flower-filled alleyways and rooms—each garden with a very different character.

Tunbridge Wells lies about 7 miles to the south. In its heyday Royal Tunbridge Wells rivaled Bath as a spa town. The Regency meeting place, The Pantiles, a terraced walk with shops behind a colonnade, is still there as are the elegant Regency parades and houses designed by Decimus Burton. Central parking is well signposted to the rear of the Corn Exchange, which contains an exhibit, *Day at the Wells*, which traces the town's growth from the time the spring water became fashionable for its curative powers to its popularity with wealthy Victorians.

Leave Tunbridge Wells on the A267 following signposts for Eastbourne till you are directed to the left through Bells Yew Green to cross the A21 (Hastings road) and enter **Scotney Castle Gardens** (NT), a gorgeous, romantic garden surrounding the moated ruins of a 14th-century castle.

Leave Scotney Castle Gardens to the left, taking the A21 (Hastings road) for a short distance to Flimwell where you turn left on the A268 to Hawkshurst and from here left on the A229 Maidstone road to **Cranbrook**. While it is not necessary to go through Cranbrook to get to Sissinghurst Gardens, it makes a very worthwhile detour because it is a delightful town whose High Street has many lovely, white-board houses and shops, a fine medieval church, and a huge, white-board windmill with enormous sails. On the other side of town you come to the A262 where you turn right for the short drive to Sissinghurst Castle Gardens.

Sissinghurst Castle (NT) was a jail for 3,000 French prisoners in the Seven Years' War. Its ruined remains were bought by Vita Sackville-West and her husband, Harold Nicolson, in 1930 and together they created the most gorgeous gardens with areas divided off like rooms, each with a distinctly different, beautiful garden. They also rescued part of the derelict castle where you can climb the tower in which Vita wrote her books. At the entrance to the garden an old barn has been tastefully converted into a tearoom and shop.

Scotney Castle Gardens

Continue along the A262 to Biddenden and take the A28 through **Tenterden** with its broad High Street of tiled and weather-boarded houses to the A268 (Hawkshurst road) where you turn right for the short drive to the village of Sandhurst. Here you turn left onto country lanes to **Bodiam Castle** (NT), a small, picturesque, squat fortress with crenelated turrets surrounded by a wide moat and pastoral countryside. Richard II ordered the castle built as a defensive position to secure the upper reaches of the Rother against French raiders who had ravaged nearby towns, but an attack never came.

Turn left as you leave the castle, following a country lane to Staple Cross where you turn left on the B2165, which brings you into **Rye**, a fortified seaport that was often attacked by French raiders. However, the sea has long since retreated, leaving the town marooned 2 miles inland. Find the quaintest street in Rye, **Mermaid Street**, with its weatherboard and tile-hung houses and up one cobblestoned block you find yourself on the doorstep of **The Mermaid Inn**. Opened in 1420, The Mermaid Inn is a fascinating relic of the past. As late as Georgian days, smugglers frequented this strikingly timbered inn and used to sit drinking in the pub with their pistols on the table, unchallenged by the law. Near the Norman Church is the 13th-century **Ypres Tower**—formerly a castle and prison, it is now a museum of local history. **Lamb House** (NT) (on West Street near the church) was the home of American novelist Henry James from 1898 to 1916. To learn more about Rye's fascinating history attend the sound and light show at the **Rye Town Model**.

Leave Rye on the A259, taking this fast road around Hastings and Bexhill to **Eastbourne** where you follow signs for the seafront of this old-fashioned holiday resort and continue on to the B2103, which brings you up and onto the vast chalk promontory, **Beachy Head**, rising above the town. It is a glorious, windswept place of soaring seagulls and springy turf, which ends abruptly as the earth drops away to giant chalk cliffs plummeting into the foaming sea. This is the starting point for the **South Downs Way**, a popular walking path. Passing the Belle Tout Lighthouse, you come to **Birling Gap**, a beach once popular with smugglers but now favored by bathers. The most dramatic scenery, the **Seven Sisters**, giant, white, windswept cliffs, are an invigorating walk from the visitors' center.

Your next destination is **Alfriston**, an adorable village on the South Downs Way which traces its origins back to Saxon times. Behind the main village street in a little cottage garden facing the village green sits the **Clergy House** (NT) with its deep thatched roof, the first building acquired by the National Trust, in 1896.

Either the fast A27 or the slower coastal road (A259) will bring you into **Brighton**, a onetime sleepy fishing town transformed into a fashionable resort at the beginning of the 19th century when the Prince Regent built the fanciful, extravagant **Royal Pavilion** with its onion domes and gaudy paintwork. Follow signs for the town center and park near the pavilion, an extravaganza of colorful, rather overpowering decor. Very near the Royal Pavilion are **The Lanes**, narrow streets of former fishermen's cottages now filled with restaurants and antique and gift shops. The seafront is lined by an almost 3-mile-long promenade with the beach below and gardens and tall terraces above. Many of the once-fashionable townhouses are now boarding houses and small hotels but this does not detract from the old-fashioned seaside atmosphere of the town. Stretching out into the sea, the white, wooden **Palace Pier** harks back to an earlier age. At the end is a delightful, old-fashioned funfair with a helter-skelter and carousel horses along with other rides.

Leave Brighton along the seafront in the direction of Hove to join the A27 at Shoreham-by-Sea. This section of the A27 passes through suburb after suburb and is the least interesting part of this itinerary. On the outskirts of **Arundel** the massive keep and towers of **Arundel Castle** rise above the town. Built just after the Norman Conquest to protect this area from sea pirates and raiders, the castle contains a collection of armor, tapestries, and other interesting artifacts.

From Arundel take the A284 inland towards Pulborough and then follow signs through the narrow, winding old streets of **Petworth**, proffering several antique stores, to **Petworth House** (NT), an enormous, 17th-century house in a vast deer park with landscaping by Capability Brown. The house, completed by the 6th Duke of Somerset in 1696, retains the 13th-century chapel of an earlier mansion and houses a proud art collection, which includes a series of landscapes by Turner and also paintings by Holbein, Rembrandt, Van Dyck, Gainsborough, Titian, Rubens, and Reynolds.

Retrace your route the short distance into Petworth and take the A272 through Midhurst to reach the A286 (Chichester road). **Midhurst** has some fine old houses and attractive inns. Knockhundred Row leads from North Street to Red Lion Street and the old timbered market. Curfew is faithfully rung each evening at 8 pm in the parish church. Legend has it that a rider, lost in darkness, followed the sound of the church bells and found his way to the town. To show his gratitude he purchased a piece of land in

Midhurst, now called Curfew Garden, which he presented to the town as a gift and made money available for the nightly ringing of the bells.

Across the South Downs the A286 brings you to the **Weald and Downland Museum**, an assortment of old, humble buildings such as farmhouses and barns brought to and restored on this site after their loss to demolition was inevitable. Inside several of the structures are displays showing the development of buildings through the ages.

Leaving the museum, take the A286 around Chichester to the A27 Portsmouth road, which leads you onto the M275 to the historic center of **Portsmouth** and your goal, the *H.M.S. Victory* and *Mary Rose*. The **H.M.S. Victory**, Nelson's flagship at the Battle of Trafalgar in 1805, has been restored to show what life was like on board. Nearby, the **Mary Rose**, Henry VIII's flagship, is housed in a humidified building that preserves its remains, which were raised from the seabed several years ago. The **Naval Museum** has a display of model ships, figureheads, and a panorama depicting the Battle of Trafalgar.

Retrace your steps up the M275 and onto the M27, which quickly brings you to the A33/M3 and **Winchester** where a magnificent **cathedral** stands at the center of the city. Park in one of the car parks on the edge of town and walk into the pedestrian heart of the city, which was the capital of England in King Alfred's reign during the 9th century and stayed so for 200 years. Construction of the 556-foot-long cathedral began in 1079 and finished in 1404. Treasures include a memorial window to Izaak Walton, a black marble font, seven chancery chapels for special masses, medieval wall paintings, stained glass, and tombs of ancient kings including King Canute. Close by is **Winchester College**, founded in 1382, one of the oldest public (i.e., private) schools in England. At the top of the High Street is a fascinating area that has formed an important part of the city's defenses since Roman times. Here you find the 13th-century **Great Hall**, the only surviving part of Winchester Castle and home to the legendary Round Table which has hung on the wall here for 600 years. Military history buffs will enjoy the five **military museums**, which offer guided tours by arrangement.

Leaving Winchester, the M3 will quickly take you back to London.

Cambridge & East Anglia

Holkham Hall
Morston
Wells-next-the-Sea
Holt
Caley Mill
Sandringham
Blickling Hall
King's Lynn
Norwich
A146
Beccles
A10
A145
Southwold
Ely
Walberswick
Dunwich
Framlingham
A45
Snape
Bury St Edmunds
Aldeburgh
Cambridge
A12
Kersey
Lavenham
Long Melford
Hadleigh
Ipswich
East Bergholt
Dedham
M11
To London
A12
To London
M25

● Orientation/Sightseeing
▬ ▬ Itinerary Route

45

Cambridge & East Anglia

Many visit the famous university town of Cambridge, but few travelers venture beyond to explore the bulge of England's eastern coastline with its sky-wide landscapes, stunning sunsets, lofty windmills, and unspoilt villages. This itinerary takes you from the vast fenlands, drained by the Dutch in the 17th century, along the pancake-flat Norfolk coastline with the sea often just out of sight beyond fields and marshes, into Norwich with its ancient streets and vast cathedral, through sleepy Suffolk villages full of quaint cottages to "Constable Country" where John Constable painted so many of his famous works. Be sure to visit Cambridge, but expand your trip to explore this quiet corner of Britain.

Kersey

Recommended Pacing: Spend one night in Norfolk, two if you have the luxury of time, and two in Suffolk, which gives you ample time to explore its quaint villages.

Leaving London, navigate yourself onto the M11 for the fast, two-hour drive to **Cambridge**, a city with much new building, but at whose heart is a fascinating university complex whose history spans over 700 years. Park your car in one of the well-marked car parks near the town center, buy a guidebook, and set out to explore, for this is a city for strolling and browsing.

At most times visitors can go into college courtyards, chapels, dining halls, and certain gardens. **King's College Chapel** is one of the finest buildings in England, with Rubens' masterpiece, the *Adoration of the Magi*, framing the altar. Be sure not to miss **Clare College**, **Trinity College**, and **St. John's College**, which backs onto the enclosed stone "Bridge of Sighs." Explore the various alleys and streets on foot, row, or punt, drifting under the willow trees that line the River Cam. **Punts** can be rented at Silver Street Bridge and Quayside.

Leaving Cambridge on the A10 towards **Ely**, you come to open countryside offering sky-wide horizons of flat farmland that are soon punctuated by the soaring mass of **Ely Cathedral**, a building so large that it seems to dwarf the little market town that surrounds it. Until the surrounding fens were drained, Ely was an island, surrounded by water, and the cathedral must have appeared even more magnificent than it does today. This awesome structure was built in 1083, awesome not only for its sheer size but because it is an amazing piece of engineering, its huge tower held up by eight massive oak timbers each more than 60 feet in length.

Leaving Ely, regain the A10, following it around Downham Market to **King's Lynn**, a large, bustling town with a well-marked historic core. A market is held every Saturday and Tuesday and the port has several fine old buildings: the **Customs House** (1683) by the harbor, now the tourist office, the **Guildhall** (1421), and the adjacent **St. Margaret's Church**. The father of George Vancouver, who explored the northwestern coast of North

America and after whom the Canadian city and island are named, was a customs officer here.

Leaving King's Lynn, follow signs for the A149 in the direction of Hunstanton. After several miles turn right for **Sandringham**, one of the Royal Family's homes, and almost immediately first left to take you on a scenic drive through the woodlands that surround it. Edward VII, at that time Prince of Wales, bought this huge Victorian house in 1861 because he did not like Osborne House on the Isle of Wight. From mid-April to the end of September from 11 am (all week except Fridays and Saturdays) the grounds and several rooms in the house are open to the public—provided that the Royal Family is not in residence.

Leave the car park to your left, and passing the main gates (the Norwich gates, a wedding gift to Edward from the city of Norwich), go left through Dersingham to regain the A149. In summer the air is heavy with the scent of lavender and the fields surrounding **Caley Mill** are a brilliant purple for this is one of the country's centers for the cultivation of lavender. There is a gift shop selling every imaginable lavender product.

After bypassing Hunstanton, the A149 becomes narrower, pottering along through attractive villages of pebble-and-red-brick cottages (Thornham, Titchwell, Brancaster, Staithe, and Overy Staithe) as it traces the flat Norfolk coast with the sea often just out of sight beyond fields and marshes. This is not a coastline of dramatic cliffs and headlands—the land merely ends and the sea begins.

On the outskirts of **Holkham** you follow the wall surrounding **Holkham Hall** to its driveway. This magnificent, 18th-century Palladian mansion, the seat of the "modern" Earls of Leicester, contains paintings by Rubens, Van Dyck, Poussin, and Gainsborough; 17th- and 18th-century tapestry and furniture; thousands of items of bygone days, such as steam engines, kitchen equipment, smithy tools, ploughs, and fire engines; and Greek and Roman statuary. Detour into **Wells-next-the-Sea**, one of the few villages along this coast to have a waterfront. Leave the coast behind and turn inland following the B1156 into Holt then continuing in the direction of Norwich (B1354) to **Blickling Hall** (NT), a grand, 17th-century red-brick house set in acres of parkland. The house if full of fine pictures, tapestries, and gracious furniture.

Following signs for Norwich, join the A140, which takes you to the heart of this sprawling city. **Norwich** is rich in historic treasures including a beautiful Norman cathedral, topped by a 15th-century spire, with a huge close running down to the River Wensum. The castle, built by one of William the Conqueror's supporters, is now the **Castle Museum**. **Elm Hill** is a cobbled street with shops and houses from the 14th to the 18th centuries. **Colman's Mustard Shop** in Royal Arcade is a big tourist attraction. Norwich has an interesting market and some very nice shops and restaurants.

From the ring road surrounding Norwich take the A146 in the direction of Lowestoft. Turn on the A145 through Beccles to the A12 where you turn left and first right on the A1095 into **Southwold**, a quiet, sedate Victorian/Edwardian seaside resort, with most attractive houses lining the seafront and narrow rows of shops forming the town center. Across the river estuary lies **Walberswick**, a pretty little fishing/holiday village of cottages and a pub, reached by a little ferry that plies back and forth (or the longer road route that traces the estuary).

Regaining the A12, turn left, towards Ipswich, for a short distance to the village of **Blythburgh** and visit its church, so imposing in size that hereabouts it is referred to as **Blythburgh Cathedral**. The size of the church is indicative of the community's importance in years gone by when it was a thriving port, with its own mint, on the estuary of the River Blyth. Its prosperity declined and the church was neglected until it was restored this century. Carvings of the Seven Deadly Sins decorate the pew-ends and the rare, wooden Jack-o'-the-Clock.

A short distance farther along the A12 you come to the left-hand turn for **Dunwich**— cross the heathlands and go through the village to the car park in front of the **Flora Tea Rooms**, which serves excellent fish and chips, beneath the pebbly bank which separates it from the sea. The fish comes fresh from the fishermen who draw their boats up on the beach. Along the headlands lie the few remains of the medieval port of Dunwich, which was almost completely swept out to sea in 1326 by a great storm. What was left has continued to be eroded by the sea. Local legend has it that before a storm the bells of Dunwich's 15 submerged churches can be heard ringing.

A short drive brings you to **Minsmere Nature Reserve**, a celebrated place for birdwatching, and through Westleton to **Aldeburgh**, a charming town whose streets are lined with Georgian houses and whose High Street has antique and other interesting shops. The local council still meets in the half-timbered **Moot Hall** (1512). Benjamin Britten, who directed the Aldeburgh music festival for 30 years until his death in 1976, based his opera, *Peter Grimes,* on a poem by local poet George Crabbe.

Head inland on the A1094, turning left onto the B1069 into **Snape** to arrive at **Snape Maltings**, a collection of red-brick granaries and old malthouses, which has been converted into a riverside center with interesting garden and craft shops, art galleries, tearooms, and a concert hall, home of the Aldeburgh music festival every June. From here you can take a boat trip on the River Alde, which meanders through the marshes to the sea.

Continue inland and map a quiet country route through sleepy Suffolk villages and rolling farmland to **Framlingham**, a quiet market town where Mary Tudor was proclaimed queen of England in 1553. The town is dominated by 12th-century **Framlingham Castle** with tall, gray-stone walls linking its towers.

Two miles away at **Saxtead Green** a 200-year-old **Post Mill**, one of Suffolk's few remaining windmills, stands guard over the green.

From Saxtead Green follow the A1120 towards Ipswich and the A14 as it skirts Ipswich and joins the A12 (in the Colchester direction) at a large roundabout (busy dual carriageways like these keep the small roads quiet and peaceful). Leave the A12 at the third exit, following signs to your left for **Dedham**, a pretty village settled along the banks of the lazy River Stour made famous by John Constable who painted its mill and church spire on several occasions. (Even though it is just a river bend away from East Bergholt, Constable's birthplace, today you have to go between the two villages by way of the busy A12.) Sir Alfred Munnings, the painter of horses, lived in **Castle House**, which is now a museum containing examples of his work.

Retrace your steps to the A12 and return in the direction of Ipswich, following signs for **Flatford** and **East Bergholt** where John Constable was born in 1776, the son of the miller of Flatford Mill. The little hamlet of Flatford, now a National Trust property, is signposted in East Bergholt. A one-way lane directs you to the car park above the hamlet (it is not well signposted and you may have to stop and ask the way). The collection of cottages has been restored to the way it was in Constable's time and a tearoom serves scrumptious afternoon teas and sandwiches. If the weather is fine, you can take a picnic, hire a rowing boat, or simply while away an afternoon on the river. The National Trust shop sells a packet that includes a map identifying where Constable painted some of his most famous pictures and postcards of the paintings so you can wander along the riverbank and pinpoint the very spot where he painted his father's mill, Willy Lott's cottage, or the boatbuilders at work. The scene has changed little since those times—apart from the tourists. Constable said of the area, "Those scenes made me a painter."

Leaving the Constable complex, the road returns you to East Bergholt where you turn right to go through the village and take the B1070 to **Hadleigh**, a large market town whose High Street has some lovely old houses. On the edge of the town cross the A1071 and then take the first left and first right to bring you onto the main street of **Kersey**, the most picture-book-perfect of all Suffolk villages. Its narrow main street is lined with ancient weavers' cottages, grand merchants' houses, and old pubs, all jostling one another for roadside space and each colorwashed a different color. In the middle of the village a stream runs across the road and drivers must take care to avoid the local ducks.

Join the A1141 for a short drive through **Monks Eleigh** with its thatched cottages and large craft shop selling traditional corn dollies to **Lavenham**, which in Tudor times was one of England's wealthiest towns. Now it is a sleepy village where leaning timbered houses line its quiet street. Continue into the market square with its 16th-century cross and **Guildhall** (NT), which houses displays of local history and the medieval wool industry.

Country lanes take you the 5 miles to **Long Melford** whose long, broad, tree-lined main street houses many antique shops and leads to the village green, which is overshadowed by the magnificent, 15th-century Holy Trinity Church. A short walk away, the redbrick, turreted **Melford Hall** (NT) contains a wealth of porcelain, paintings, and antiques and a display of Beatrix Potter's paintings—she was a frequent visitor here.

Leaving Long Melford, you can go south to the A12 or west to the M11, which quickly return you to London.

Cycling through Suffolk

The Lake District

Carlisle

M6

Cockermouth

Bassenthwaite Lake

A66

Keswick

A5091

Crummock Water

Derwent Water

Ullswater

Buttermere

A591

Rosthwaite

Thirlmere

M6

Grasmere

Little Langdale

Ambleside

A593

Troutbeck

Coniston

Windermere

Hawkshead

Far Sawrey

Coniston Water

Sizergh Castle

Windermere

A5074

A590

Levens Hall

● Orientation/Sightseeing

▬▬ Itinerary Route

The Lake District

For generations the beauty of the Lake District has inspired poets, authors, and artists. It is a land of tranquil lakes of all shapes and sizes, quiet wooded valleys, and awesome bleak mountains, a land where much of the natural beauty is protected by the National Trust who work hard to keep this a working community of sheep farmers and to keep man in harmony with nature. One of the most determined preservers of the Lake District was Beatrix Potter, who used much of her royalties from her famous children's books to purchase vast tracts of land and donate them to the nation. It is a region to be explored not only during the summer when the roads are more heavily traveled and the towns crowded, but also in the early spring when the famous daffodils brighten the landscape and well into the autumn when the leaves turn to gold and dark storm clouds shadow the lakes.

Dove Cottage, Grasmere

Recommended Pacing: Base yourself at one of the hotels we recommend in the Lake District. If you cover all of our sightseeing recommendations, you will need four nights, though three might just suffice.

From junction 36 on the M6 motorway take the A590 in the direction of Barrow then a few minutes' drive along the A591 brings you into the grounds of **Sizergh Castle** (NT), not a mighty fortress but a lovely, mostly Tudor house, the home of the Strickland family for over 700 years. The house is fully furnished—just as though the family has gone out for the day and you are a visitor to their home. There is an excellent teashop in the old cellar and a portion of the grounds presents an impressive rock garden.

Return to the A590 and in just a minute you are at another fine Tudor manor house, **Levens Hall**. The property is most famous for its topiary gardens, which have remarkably remained unchanged since 1690, when they were landscaped by a Frenchman, Guillaume Beaumont.

Join the A5074 Windermere road and on the outskirts of the town follow signs to the ferry, which takes you across the broad expanse of **Windermere** for the short drive to the tiny villages of **Near Sawrey** and **Far Sawrey**, discovered by Beatrix Potter on childhood holidays. She was so charmed by the villages that out of the royalties from *Peter Rabbit* she bought **Hill Top Farm** (NT) in Near Sawrey. It was here in a vine-covered stone cottage set among trees and a garden of flowers that she dreamed up childhood playmates such as Jemima Puddleduck, Mrs Tiggy Winkle, the Flopsy Bunnies, Cousin Ribby, and Benjamin Bunny. Because of its popularity the house is open on a very limited basis, but the National Trust shop by the roadside is open more often and you can walk through the garden to the front door.

In nearby **Hawkshead**, a pretty village with a pedestrian center, there is a delightful **Beatrix Potter Gallery** (NT) containing an exhibition of her original drawings and illustrations of her children's books, together with a display of her life as author, farmer, and preserver of her beloved Lake District. A short drive brings you to **Coniston**, a delightful village of gray-stone buildings at the head of **Coniston Water**. John Ruskin, the eloquent 19th-century scholar, lived on the east side of the lake at **Brantwood.** His home contains many mementos and pictures. You will find a small **Ruskin Museum** with drawings and manuscripts in the village.

Travel a short distance along the A593 Ambleside road and turn left to wind along a country lane up into a quiet, less touristy part of the Lake District. Stop for refreshment in **Little Langdale** at the **Three Shires**, a delightful walkers' pub that also offers accommodation. Leaving the village, you enter a wild, bleak, and beautiful area. The lane brings you to Blea Tarn and just as you think you are in the absolute midst of nowhere and contemplate turning around, you come to a cattle grid and a fork in the road. Take the right-hand fork signposted Great Langdale and follow the narrow road through wild and lonely countryside, down a steep pass, and through a lush valley into **Great Langdale**, another off-the-beaten-path village popular with walkers. Leaving the village, the road winds you up onto the moor and drops you back onto the A593 where a left-hand turn quickly brings you into Ambleside.

Ambleside is a bustling, busy town at the head of Lake Windermere with lots of shops selling walking equipment and outdoor wear, and gray Victorian row houses huddling along its streets. Leave town in the direction of Keswick (A591), watching for a right-hand turn to **Rydal Mount**, the home of William Wordsworth, the poet, from 1813 to his death in 1850. The house is furnished and contains many family portraits and possessions. A keen gardener, Wordsworth laid out the 4½ acres of informal gardens.

Wordsworth fans will also want to stop at **Dove Cottage** where Wordsworth lived from 1799 to 1808 and the adjacent **Wordsworth Museum**. Park by the tearoom on the main road and walk up to the museum to buy your ticket. Try to visit early in the day as they restrict a tour to the number of people who can comfortably fit into Wordsworth's tiny living room. As you tour the few meager rooms, which housed six adults and three children, it is hard to believe that this was home to one of the leading poets of the era. Poet laureates write poems on royal events, but not Wordsworth: he was the only poet laureate to write not a word on such occasions—but he relished the royal stipend. Just off the busy main road, the adjacent village of **Grasmere** is full of charming shops and galleries.

The A591 is a delightful drive into Keswick through in turn wild, rugged, and pastoral scenery. Take small roads to the west of **Thirlmere** as the views from the west of the lake are much better than from the A591. The lively market town of **Keswick**, cozily placed at the northern end of **Derwent Water**, is full of bakeries, sweet shops (selling fudge and Kendal mint cake), pubs, restaurants, and outdoor equipment suppliers. There are plenty of car parks near the town center, though on a busy summer afternoon you may have to drive around for a while before you secure a spot. The **Moot** (meeting) **Hall** at the center of the square is now the National Park Information Centre—full of maps, books, and good advice.

Returning to your car, head towards Derwent Water, taking the B5289 to Borrowdale for a spectacular drive between Keswick and Cockermouth, a journey not to be undertaken in bad weather. Follow Derwent Water to **Grange** where inviting woodlands beckon you to tarry awhile and walk, but desist because the most spectacular walking country lies ahead. Passing through the village of Rosthwaite, the narrow road begins to climb, curving you upwards alongside a tumbling stream to the high, treeless fells before suddenly tipping you over the crest of the mountain and snaking you down into the valley to **Buttermere** and **Crummock Water** whose placid surfaces mirror the jagged peaks surrounding this wooded, green valley. The mountains here are over 500 million years old—among the oldest in the world. Walking paths beckon in every direction—though these are not paths to be trod without equipment and maps, for the fickle weather can turn from sun to storm in just a short while. Leaving this lovely spot, the narrow road quickly brings you into the center of bustling **Cockermouth** where Wordsworthians have the opportunity to visit **Wordsworth House**, his birthplace on Main Street.

From Cockermouth follow signs for the A66 and Keswick along a country road that parallels the A66 to the head of **Bassenthwaite Lake**. At the junction cross the busy A66 onto a quiet country road to visit **The Pheasant**, a superb example of the very best of traditional pubs. From here the A66 quickly speeds you alongside Bassenthwaite Lake, around Keswick, and to the M6 motorway. However, if you have time for one more idyllic lake, take the A5091 through Troutbeck to **Ullswater** where you turn left to trace the lake to **Aira Force** (NT), a landscaped Victorian park with dramatic waterfalls, arboretum, and rock gardens (there is also a café). After a walk along the shores of Ullswater Wordsworth wrote his poem *Daffodils*. The dramatic scenery is still very much as it was in his day. Leaving Ullswater, return to the A66 and join the M6 at junction 40, with convenient connections to all parts of Britain.

The Lake District

Derbyshire Dales & Villages

Edale

Castleton

Hope

A625

Hathersage

Sheffield

M1

M18

A623

Eyam

Tideswell

Buxton

A6

Ashford-in-the-Water

Baslow

A619

Chesterfield

A6

Chatsworth

A515

Bakewell

Haddon Hall

Monyash & Arbor Low

Rowsley

A617

M1

Parsley Hay

A53

Hartington

A515

A6

Matlock

Alstonfield

Dovedale

Ilam

Tissington

Ashbourne

● Orientation/Sightseeing

▪▪ Itinerary Route

Derbyshire Dales & Villages

Every structure in this itinerary—manor houses, churches, cottages, farmhouses, shops, even the walls that edge the fields, making a patchwork of the landscape—is built of gray stone. This is the Peak District, a National Park, where you can enjoy the beauty of a wild landscape of rolling rocky pastures, sheltered valleys, and windswept moors laced by swift rivers tumbling through deep dales—Monks Dale, Monsal Dale, Miller Dale, and, the most beautiful of all, Dovedale where the River Dove flows through a rocky, wooded ravine and is crossed by stepping stones. While this is a driving itinerary, to really appreciate the wild beauty of this area you have to forsake your car and proceed on foot—on the many miles of well-marked footpaths—or rent a bike and pedal the cycle routes that travel disused railway lines and quiet country lanes.

Chatsworth House
Derbyshire Dales & Villages

Recommended Pacing: Select a base for this itinerary. To cover all our sightseeing suggestions will take two full days.

This itinerary begins in **Ashbourne**, a small market town just south of the Peak District National Park where on Thursdays and Saturdays market stalls crowd the town square. Close by, on St. John Street, visit the **Gingerbread Shop**, which sells aromatic Ashbourne gingerbread and baked goods from a restored 15th-century timber-framed shop that gives you a glimpse of how beautiful Ashbourne must have been during its heyday.

Leave Ashbourne on the A515, Buxton road, and watch for a discreetly signposted right-hand turn that brings you through a broad avenue of trees to **Tissington** with its Jacobean manor house, Norman church, limestone cottages, and ducks swimming on the village pond. Tissington is reputedly the birthplace of the Derbyshire village tradition of well dressing, giving thanks for the unfailing supply of fresh water that the village wells provided by creating intricate, large mosaic pictures from flower petals and placing them beside the village wells. These spectacular displays are very interesting to visit, so in the course of this itinerary, the dates that villages dress their wells is mentioned in parentheses, for example, "Tissington (*wells dressed for Ascension day*)." If you carry on through the village and across open farmland, you come to a ford where the road splashes through a brook.

Retrace your steps to the A515 and cross it, heading through **Thorpe** village and down into **Dovedale**. Dr. Johnston gave it a glowing testimonial: "He who has seen Dovedale has no need to visit the Highlands." Cars can go no farther than the car park whence you walk into the dale, cross the River Dove on stepping stones and enter a rocky ravine. The farther you walk into the dale the more you are tempted to continue as round each river bend beautiful scenery unfolds—fantastic rock formations, steeply wooded hillsides, and the noisy, tumbling water. The length of the dale is a delightful 4-mile walk. Walkers can be dropped at the car park and picked up in Milldale by Viators Bridge.

At a bend in the road sits **Ilam** (pronounced "I lamb"), a picture-postcard estate village, built to house the workers on what was once a shipping magnate's vast holdings. On to **Alstonfield** (pronounced "Alstonfeld") and the **Post Office Teashop**, which serves scrumptious scones and cream. (Turn right here if you are picking walkers up in nearby Milldale.)

Well Dressing

Drive into **Hartington** (*wells dressed on second Saturday in September*) with its white limestone cottages, shops, and pubs. Admire the mallards waddling by the village pond and visit the **cheese shop**, an outlet for the last of Derbyshire's cheese factories producing Hartington Stilton and Buxton Blue.

Leave Hartington on the B5054, Ashbourne road, and take the first left, signposted Crowdicote, following the narrow dale. As the dale widens, turn right to **Parsley Hay**.

From here you can cycle the **Tissington Trail** towards Ashbourne or the **High Peak Trail** to Cromford. At the main road turn left (towards Buxton) and immediately right towards Monyash then right again following discreet signposts for **Arbor Low**, Derbyshire's answer to Stonehenge. The huge monoliths have all fallen to the ground and you will probably be one of only a few visitors. The stones are set atop a bare hill, swept by cold winds, and reached by tramping across fields from a lonely farm. Pause and wonder why man built here 4,000 years ago.

Retrace your path to the Monyash road, turning right in the village onto the B5055, which leads you into **Bakewell** (*wells dressed on last Saturday in June*), a lovely market town ringed by wooded hills where a picturesque, 700-year-old arched and buttressed bridge spans the swiftly flowing River Wye. The Tourist Information Centre in the splendid, 17th-century **market hall** has displays on the Peak District and information pamphlets. Behind it are set the market stalls where every Monday a farmers' market is held—offering everything from lengths of dress fabric to underwear and pigs. You can buy the original Bakewell tarts (known as puddings in Bakewell) from **Ye Olde Original Pudding Shop** and the splendid **Bakewell Pudding Factory** on Granby Arcade. The town has some excellent shops (china, antiques, clothing, and hardware). Up the hill, just behind the church, is **The Old House Museum**, a folk museum displaying kitchen and farm equipment.

Three miles along the A6 in the direction of Matlock lies **Haddon Hall**, a 14th-century manor, home of the Duke of Rutland. In my opinion, this house is more interesting to tour than the opulent Chatsworth House (your next stop) because it lacks the vastness and grandeur of Chatsworth and you can really imagine people living in these aged rooms hung with threadbare tapestries and decorated with magnificent woodcarvings. Parts of the chapel walls are covered with barely discernible frescos that date back to the 11th century. In summer the gardens are a fragrant haven, with a profusion of climbing roses and clematis decorating the house and the stone walls of the terraces.

Continue along the A6 to **Rowsley** where you can tour **Caudwell's Mill**, a water-powered flour mill and visit the craft shops. Leaving Rowsley, take the first left (B6012).

Pass the edge of Beeley, cross the River Derwent on a narrow humpbacked bridge, and enter the vast Chatsworth estate. Immediately on your left is the **Chatsworth Garden Centre,** which, in addition to an expansive array of all things garden, has a gift and coffee shop. The road leads you through rolling green parkland to **Chatsworth House**, the enormous home (the roof alone covers 1.3 acres) of the Duke and Duchess of Devonshire. While the Duke and Duchess occupy a portion of the house, you can walk through the opulent halls admiring priceless paintings, furnishings, silver plate, and china. Best of all, though, are the acres and acres of landscaped gardens: vast lawns laid down in 1760 and groomed ever since (except in wartime); the maze; the gardens (rock, kitchen, rose, cottage, and sensory). Water pours down the steps of the 1st Duke's water cascade (take off your shoes and climb its broad steps to the fountains at the top of the hill), shoots from the willow tree (known as the squirting tree), and spills from Revelation, the water-operated sculpture. There are 5 miles of walks with trees, shrubs, fountains, and ponds. There is also access to the excavated coal tunnel. The gift and teashop are a must. If you are traveling with children, they will enjoy a visit to the farm and the adventure playground.

The picturesque village of **Edensor** (pronounced "Ensor"), mentioned in the Doomsday Book of 1086, was much rebuilt and moved here in the 19th century by a duke who did not want to see it from his park. Kathleen Kennedy, JFK's sister, lies buried near the handsome old church.

Leave the estate in the direction of Baslow and take the first left, B6048, to **Pilsley** where the farm shop sells an interesting variety of nifty gifts and produce from the Chatsworth estate. As the B6048 merges with the main road take the first right on the A6020 (Ashford) following it to **Ashford-in-the-Water** and cross the river into this picturesque village strung along the River Wye. "Sheepwash" is the oldest and quaintest of the village's bridges. Built for packhorses and now closed to traffic, it gets its name from the adjacent stone enclosure in which sheep used to be washed.

Follow the narrow lanes upwards to **Monsal Head** where the ground seemingly falls away and opens up to a magnificent vista of the River Wye running through **Monsal**

Dale. Go straight across, alongside the Monsal Head car park, and follow the road as it winds down into and along the dale to **Cressbrook Mill**, where the road climbs steeply past the terraces of mill cottages clinging precariously to the hillsides. The first terrace is where pauper apprentices lived and higher up are the more opulent foremen's houses. Emerging from the dale, the narrow road skirts stone-walled fields to **Litton** (*wells dressed in June*), a delightful stone village round a green where you turn left for Tideswell.

The magnificent, spacious, 14th-century church at **Tideswell** (*wells dressed on Saturday nearest John the Baptist day, June 24th*) is so impressive that it is often described as "the cathedral of the Peak." It was built between 1300 and 1370 when Tideswell was an affluent place and it is fortunate that Tideswell fell upon hard times so that parishioners could not afford to update their church as ecclesiastical fashions changed.

Leaving Tideswell, you come to the A623 and turn left in the direction of Chapel-en-le-Frith to Sparrowpit where you turn right at the Wanted Inn. Passing an enormous quarry, you see that half the mountain is missing—gone to build all the lovely stone houses and cottages. When you come to a brown-and-white country sign stating "Castleton Caverns, Peveril Castle, light traffic only," turn right into Winnats Pass, which drops you down a steep ravine between high limestone cliffs.

As the ravine opens up to the valley, **Speedwell Cavern** presents itself. This is one of several famous caverns (mixtures of natural cavities and lead-mine workings resplendent with stalagmites and stalactites) found around Castleton. Speedwell is reached by a 105-step descent to a motorboat that takes you along an underground canal to a cavern which was the working face of the former Speedwell Mine. Blue John (a corruption of the French *bleue-jaune,* blue-yellow), a translucent blue variety of fluorspar found only in this area, was mined here.

Before you head off to explore other nearby caves (Blue John, Treak Cliff, and Peak), head into **Castleton**, a village huddled far below the brooding ruins of Norman **Peveril Castle** where Henry II accepted the submission of Malcolm of Scotland in 1157.

Castleton

Below the castle is the huge mouth of **Peak Cavern**, an enormous cave that once sheltered ropemakers' cottages. The soot from the chimneys of this subterranean village can be seen on the cave's roof. Regrettably, the entrance to the cave has been marred by the erection of a high wooden barrier giving access to the cave only to those willing to pay an entrance fee. In the village's streets you will find cafés, pubs, and several shops selling the polished Blue John set into bracelets, rings, and the like.

This is walking country and you might consider walking up **Mam Tor** (the big bulky mountain beside Winnats Pass) known hereabouts as "Shivering Mountain" because its layers of soft shale set between harder beds of rock are constantly crumbling. Those in search of a longer walk may wish to go to nearby **Edale** where the **Pennine Way** starts its 250-mile path north.

Leave Castleton on the A625 traveling along the broad Hope valley through **Hope** (*wells dressed last Saturday in June*) and Bamford to **Hathersage**, a thriving, non-traditional Derbyshire village strung out along the main road. Its tourist attractions center on its 14th-century church, St. Michael and All Angels, built by a knight named Robert Eyre. Memorial brasses to the Eyre family are in the church and Charlotte Brontë used the village as "Morton" in *Jane Eyre*. In the graveyard is the reputed grave of Little John, the friend and lieutenant of Robin Hood.

Leaving the churchyard, backtrack on the A625 for a short distance, taking the first left (B6001), signposted Bakewell, beyond the village where you turn right, opposite The Plough, up a narrow country lane signposted "Gliding Club." This country lane takes you through the hamlet of **Abney** past the gliding club and the historic **Barrel Inn** (offering views of the valley, good pub food, and refreshing ale) and brings you, via Foolow, into **Eyam** (pronounced "Eem") (*wells dressed last Saturday in August*).

This large mining and quarrying village was made famous by its self-imposed quarantine when plague hit the village in 1665. It was thought that the virus arrived in a box of cloth from London brought by a visiting tailor. The rector persuaded the community to quarantine themselves to prevent the plague spreading to outlying villages. For over a year the village was supplied by neighboring villagers who left food and supplies at outlying points. Tragically 259 people from 76 families perished—little plaques on Eyam's cottages give the names of the victims who lived there. The church has a plague register and just inside the door is the letter written by the young rector when his wife succumbed (Katherine Mompesson is buried near the Saxon cross in the churchyard). The most poignant reminder of these grim days lies in a field about ½ mile from the village where within a solitary little enclosure, known as the **Riley Graves**, are the memorials to a father and his six children, all of whom died within eight days of each other.

Leave Eyam in the direction of Bakewell, traveling down a steeply wooded gorge that brings you to the A623. Following signs for Chesterfield, you drive down narrow **Middleton Dale**, whose limestone cliffs are so sheer they almost block the sunlight from the road, to **Stoney Middleton**, an appropriately named village huddling beneath the cliffs. It does not look at all inviting from the main road but its quiet side streets and pretty church are full of character.

Driving a few miles farther along the A623 brings you to the winding lanes of **Baslow** where the River Derwent flows past tidy houses on the northern edge of the Chatsworth estate. From here fast roads will bring you to **Chesterfield** (visit the leaning spire and if it is a Monday, Friday, or Saturday, you will enjoy the interesting open-air market) where you can join the M1 at junction 29.

The Dales & Moors of
North Yorkshire

NORTH SEA

Whitby

Grosmont

Robin Hood's
Bay

Egton

Richmond

Gunnerside

Swaledale

Muker

Reeth

Rosedale
Abbey

Askrigg

A1068

Hutton-
le-hole

Hawes

Leyburn

A684

Rievaulx
Abbey

A170

Wensleydale

A1

Bolton Castle

Middleham

Thirsk

A170

Helmsley

Pickering

A169

Coverdale

Woodale

Kilburn

Kettlewell

Castle Howard

Arncliffe

Wharfedale

Kilnsey

Ripon

Malham

Grassington

Fountains
Abbey

A64

Pateley
Bridge

York

● Orientation/Sightseeing
■-■ Itinerary Route
╫╫╫╫ Railway

69

The Dales & Moors of North Yorkshire

After exploring historic York, this itinerary samples the wild and beautiful countryside of two National Parks: the North York Moors and the Yorkshire Dales. This is an area of rugged, untamed, harsh beauty in its landscape and its stout stone villages. With seemingly endless miles of heather-covered moorlands, few roads, and even fewer sturdy villages sheltering in green valleys, the North York Moors appear vast and untamed, dipping to the sea to embrace the villages and towns of the east coast. Across the flat expanse of the Vale of York lie the Yorkshire Dales, characterized by sleepy rivers weaving through peaceful valleys and by gray-stone walls bounding the fields and tracing patterns on the countryside to the moorlands above. Here every valley has a name and a very different character—Swaledale, Littondale, Coverdale, and Wharfedale. Scattered throughout Yorkshire are small gray-stoned villages with a cluster of stone houses, a hump-backed bridge, a friendly pub, and an ancient church.

Recommended Pacing: Spend two nights in York to appreciate the flavor of this historic city. Follow this with a minimum of one night on or near the North York Moors (Helmsley or Lastingham) and two nights in the Yorkshire Dales.

If you delight in historic towns, you will love **York**, a compact city brimful of history, encircled by 700-year-old walls with great imposing gates known as "bars." There has been a settlement here since Roman times and by the time of the Norman Conquest it was, after London, the principal city of England.

Your first stop in York should be the Tourist Information Centre on St. Leonards, near Bootham Bar. Avail yourself of a detailed city map and ask about walking tours that will, in the space of several hours, orient you to this historic city.

Walk the narrow, cobblestoned streets with appealing names such as The Shambles, Stonegate, and Goodramgate past timbered buildings whose upper stories lean out, almost forming a bridge over the streets. While interesting shops abound, the **National Trust Shop** on Goodramgate and **Betty's Bakery and Tearooms** on St. Helen's Square are ones to target.

York's magnificent cathedral is known simply as **The Minster**, a huge structure that towers above the skyline and dwarfs everything else around it. It was begun in 1220 and you can quickly appreciate why it took over 250 years to complete. Entering through the Great West Door, you see the vast nave stretching out in front of you and fluted pillars rising to flying buttresses reaching high above. There are more than 100 stained-glass windows and the huge east window is almost the size of a tennis court. Guided tours leave at regular intervals. Nearby the **Treasurer's House** (NT), a 17th/18th-century townhouse on the site of the former residence of the Treasurers of York Minster, has a fine collection of beautiful furniture.

The **Jorvik Viking Centre**, Coppergate, is set below ground amidst the most complete Viking dig in England. Electric cars take you on a Disneyland ride backwards through history to a re-created Viking village—complete with sounds and smells of Viking

Jorvik. Then they move you forward to the dig itself and a display of the artifacts that have been recovered.

Enjoy another trip back in time at York's outstanding **Castle Museum**. One section of the museum is a reconstructed Victorian cobbled street, with houses, shops, jail, and a hansom cab in recognition of inventor Joseph Hansom who was born in Mickelgate. Opposite the museum you can climb to the ramparts of **Clifford's Tower**, a stubby, 13th-century keep set high on a mound. From its ramparts you have a panoramic view of York.

Located beyond York's walls, just a short walk from the magnificent Victorian railway station, is the **National Railway Museum**, on Leeman Road, crammed with famous steam locomotives including the world's fastest (202 mph), *Mallard*, and a wealth of railway items.

Depart York on the A64 Scarborough road for the fast drive to **Castle Howard**, which is well signposted to your left just 4 miles from Malton. Designed by Sir John Vanbrugh for the 3rd Earl of Carlisle, a member of the Howard family, Castle Howard was built between 1699 and 1726—one glimpse of this majestic building and you understand why it took 27 years to complete. Its immense façade reflects in a broad lake and it is surrounded by a vast parkland and approached down a long, tree-lined avenue. It isn't really a castle at all but one of England's grandest homes, as impressive inside as out, full of fine furniture and paintings. This grand setting is better known to many visitors as "Brideshead" from the television dramatization of Evelyn Waugh's *Brideshead Revisited*. It is still owned by the Howard family.

From nearby Malton take the A169 through Pickering and across the vast expanse of the North York moors to **Robin Hood's Bay**, the most picturesque of villages situated beneath a cliff top, a maze of huddled houses clinging to the precipitous cliff. Park in the large car park above the village and follow the long, steep street down to the shoreline, peeping into little alleyways and following narrow byways until you emerge at the slipway. Pieces of Robin Hood's Bay have been washed away, and in an attempt to minimize further damage to this little fishing village, much of the cliff has been reinforced by a large sea wall.

The ruins of **Whitby Abbey** face the cold North Sea and the old seaside town of **Whitby**, built on either side of the River Esk. It's a lovely sight: majestic ruins high on a bleak, windy headland; rows of cottages climbing up the hillsides; and, gazing over the scene, a statue of the town's most famous mariner, Captain Cook. Cook circled the world twice, explored the coasts of Australia and New Zealand, and charted Newfoundland and the North American Pacific coast before being killed by natives in Hawaii. His home on Grape Lane is a small museum. Near Cook's statue is a whalebone arch commemorating this photogenic old town's importance as a whaling port. The whaling ships are a thing of the distant past: now just a few fishing boats bob in this large, sheltered harbor. Explore the area of the town that lies below the abbey, for this is the quaintest, most historic portion of Whitby. During the summer the town is filled with holidaymakers.

Leave Whitby on the A169, Pickering road, and follow signs to the right for the **North York Railway**, a road that winds you to **Grosmont**, the terminus of a glorious, 18-mile steam railway that runs to and from Pickering. The railway opened in 1863 with horse-drawn carriages—steam engines came 11 years later. The line was closed by British Rail in 1965 and reopened by train enthusiasts. The railway shed is full of steam locomotives of all colors. You can see engines being prepared for their daily shift and watch restoration from the viewing gallery.

From nearby Egton a narrow road leads you up from a lush valley and onto acres of gently rolling moorland, with a mass of purple heather stretching into the distance, a dramatically empty, isolated spot. It then drops you into another green valley where stone walls separate a patchwork of fields around the tiny village of Rosedale Abbey. Go straight across the crossroads, up the steep bank, and across another stretch of vast moorland. Keep to your right at the fork in the road, and you arrive in the most picturesque village on the North York Moors, **Hutton-le-Hole**. A tumbling stream cuts through the village and children play on close-cropped grassy banks between the sturdy stone houses. At the heart of the village lies **Ryedale Folk Museum** where paths lead from a museum of domestic bygones through a collection of ancient Yorkshire buildings (from simple cottages to an elaborate cruck-framed house) rescued from demise and restored on this site.

Farther on from Hutton-le-Hole you join the A170, which brings you to **Helmsley**, a pretty market town beneath the southern rim of the moors. Around the market square (*market day Friday*) are interesting shops and the lovely **Black Swan** hotel. At the edge of town sits a ruined castle enclosed by Norman earthworks.

About 4 miles beyond Helmsley (take the B1257 towards Stokesley) lie the ruins of **Rievaulx Abbey** (pronounced "Ree-voh"), the delicate and beautiful remnants of York's first Cistercian abbey, standing quietly beside a picturesque group of thatched cottages. The abbey fell into debt and declined until Henry VIII ordered its dissolution. Today it is a graceful, ghostly ruin, often shrouded in mist. Follow the narrow lane beside the cottages, turn right over the little humpbacked bridge, proceed through Scrawton, and turn right on the A170 (Thirsk road) for a short distance to a left-hand turn that zigzags you down **Sutton Bank**. On a clear day park in the car park at the top and enjoy the sky-wide view of the Vale of York before descending down the Hambleton Hills escarpment.

A delightful side trip can by taken by turning left at the bottom of the escarpment and following the narrow lane that brings you to **Kilburn**, a village known for its fine oak furniture. Quality oak furniture found all over the world can easily be traced back here to the workshop of Robert Thompson. He died in 1955, but craftsmen he trained still use his carved signature, a small church mouse, signifying "poor as a church mouse" to identify their work. It is fun to tour the workshops and watch skilled craftsmen quietly hand-carving beautiful oaken objects with a wavy, adzed surface.

Returning to the main road, you soon come to **Thirsk**, its very pleasant cobbled market square overlooked by shops (*market day Monday*). Here you can visit the **Herriot Centre**, onetime veterinary surgery of James Herriot, quiet local vet-turned-author.

From Thirsk the A61 traverses rich farmland, crosses the A1 and meanders you through **Ripon** to the market square (*market day Thursday*) where you follow well-marked signs for Fountains Abbey.

Cistercian monks arrived in sheltered **Fountains Abbey** (NT) in 1132, at about the same time they came to Rievaulx, but, unlike Rievaulx, this abbey prospered, so that by the end of the 13th century it had acquired vast estates and the abbey was home to over 500 monks. However, its prosperity did not save it from the axe of Henry VIII who sold the monastery, leaving the abbey to fall into majestic ruin. Considering that for hundreds of years it was used as a quarry for precut stone, the complex is remarkably intact. Wander over the closely cropped grass to the soaring walls of the church. Examine the few remaining floor tiles, gaze at the flying buttresses soaring high above, wander through the cloisters, and wonder at the glory that was Fountains Abbey so many years ago. Walking paths abound: a particularly pretty path leads you across grassy meadows to the adjacent National Trust property of **Studley Royal**, an 18th-century deer park and water garden.

Turn west (B6265) through Pateley Bridge and climb higher and higher onto bleak moorlands through Greenhow and down the fellside through fields trimmed with white stone walls to Hebden and into **Grassington**, a neat village of narrow streets and cobbled squares full of shops and cafés. It's this itinerary's introduction to the Dales National Park which is very crowded in summer, so you may want to park at the National Park Information Centre (useful for maps and information) and walk into town.

To experience some magnificent scenery, take a breathtaking circular drive from Grassington and back again through Littondale, over the fells to Malham Cove, and back to the B6160 on the outskirts of town. Leave Grassington on the B6265, cross the River Wharfe, and turn right onto the B6160, which leads you up **Wharfedale** towards Kettlewell. Just after passing the huge crags that hang above Kilnsey, turn left up a narrow lane for Arncliffe. The road meanders deep into **Littondale**, a narrow, steep-sided, very pretty dale. At the cluster of cottages that make up Arncliffe turn left for Malham and follow the narrow road as it zigzags you up the side of the dale. As the road reaches the top, there is a spectacular view back into Littondale. The high, bleak moorland suddenly ends and to your left lie immense curving cliffs that drop 240 feet into a green valley. This is **Malham Cove**, one of Yorkshire's most celebrated natural features. Huddled in the valley below lies the village of **Malham**. Country lanes take you through Kirby Malham, Airton, Winterburn, Hetton, and Threshfield to rejoin the B6160, which takes you back into Wharfedale.

Retrace your steps and head north to **Kettlewell**, a pretty village at the foot of Great Whernside. In the 8th century this was an Anglican settlement, then after the Norman Conquest formed part of the estates of the powerful Percy family. A small road leads you to the right over Great Whernside and into quiet **Coverdale** through **Woodale**, **Horsehouse**, and **Carlton**, little villages that shelter in this pretty valley with the moors looming above. Horses are a feature of **Middleham** for there are many famous racing stables in this attractive town of gray-stone houses beneath the ruins of Middleham Castle.

Cross the River Ure and follow the A6108 into Leyburn then turn left on the A648 and right on country lanes through Redmire to the crumbling ruins of **Bolton Castle**, which stands grim and square, dwarfing the adjacent village, overlooking distant Wensleydale. You can tour several restored rooms. The castle's most famous visitor was Mary, Queen of Scots, who was held prisoner here for six months in 1568.

Minor roads take you up Wharfedale through Carperby (detour into **Aysgarth** if you would like to walk to **Aysgarth Falls**, a series of spectacular waterfalls where the River Ure cascades down a rocky gorge) and Woodhall to the picturesque Dales village of Askrigg. Cross the river to Bainbridge and take the A648 into **Hawes**, a bustling village whose narrow streets abound with interesting shops, good pubs, and cafés. You can visit the **Wensleydale Creamery** to watch cheese being produced. After exploring, leave town in the direction of Muker. As the road climbs from the valley go right, following signs for Muker via **Buttertubs**. This is one of the highest mountain passes in England (1,682 feet), rising steeply from Wensleydale, crossing dramatic high moorlands, and depositing you in narrower, wilder **Swaledale**. The road gets its name "Buttertubs" from the deep, menacing, limestone pits some distance from the road near the summit.

At the T-junction follow the road to the right and cross the little bridge into **Muker**, the most charming of Swaledale's little villages—just the place to stop for a refreshing cuppa.

As you travel down Swaledale, there's a feeling of remoteness: sturdy, gray-stone barns dot the stone-walled fields that checker the valley floor and rise to the green fells. **Gunnerside**, Norse for "Gunner's pasture," where a Viking chieftain herded his cattle long ago, is now an appealing village.

Through Low Row, Feetham, and Healaugh the enchantment of being in a narrow, secluded valley continues till at **Reeth** the landscape opens up and the feeling of being in a wild and lonely place is gone. On the village green you will find **The Burgoyne Hotel**. You continue on to Richmond through pretty countryside.

Richmond sits at the foot of Swaledale, a network of cobbled alleys and streets stretching from its cobbled square. At its center sits an ancient church with shops set into its walls. Overhanging the River Swale, **Richmond Castle** was built by Norman lords within 20 years of the Norman Conquest. Over the years only a few Scottish raiders tested the defenses of this guardian of North Yorkshire. Sweeping views across dales down to the Vale of York can be enjoyed from the top of its 11th-century ruins.

The nearby A1 will quickly guide you north into Scotland or return you south towards York.

Scotland

Inverewe Gardens

Ullapool

A835

Torridon

A832

Portree

A855

Shieldaig

Dunvegan

Kyle of Lochalsh

A87

Sleat

A851

Mallaig

Genfinnan

A830

Fort William

Glencoe

A82

A85

Bunchrew

Nairn

Culloden

A96

Auldearn

Inverness

Cawdor Castle

A82

Loch Ness

A4

Dufftown

A96

Kildrummy Castle

A941

Castle Fraser

Grantown-on-Spey

A97

Aberdeen

Craigievar Castle

A93

Banchory

Braemar

Ballater

A9

Balmoral Castle

A93

Fort Augustus

Pitlochry

A924

A9

A984

Blairgowrie

Dunkeld

Kinclaven

Perth

A93

Callander

A84

M90

Stirling

Glasgow

M74

Edinburgh

● Orientation/Sightseeing
▪- Itinerary Route

Scotland

This itinerary begins in Scotland's capital, Edinburgh, journeys to Inverness via Pitlochry, samples magnificent castles and portions of "The Whisky Trail," traces the shore of Scotland's most famous lake, Loch Ness, wends through the glens, and travels over the sea to Skye. It then takes you up into the beauties of Wester Ross where the gardens at Inverewe blossom in a harsh landscape then on to Fort William, Callander, and Glasgow with its magnificent Burrell Collection. At every turn there are echoes of history and romance—Nessie the legendary monster of Loch Ness, homes that sheltered Bonnie Prince Charlie and Flora Macdonald, and the lands where Rob Roy MacGregor roamed. The roads are few and often narrow and the long distances between villages and small towns add to the feeling of isolation. The fickle Scottish weather offers no guarantee that the dramatic scenery will be revealed, but what you can be assured of is a warm, friendly welcome from the hospitable Scots.

Edinburgh Castle

Scotland

Recommended Pacing: Spend a full day (two if possible) sightseeing in Edinburgh. With an early-morning start you will find yourself at Kildrummy Castle by nightfall (skip Perth sightseeing). If you prefer a more leisurely pace, also include an overnight in Pitlochry. Stay overnight around Inverness because it's an all-day drive from Inverness to the Isle of Skye, then spend two nights on Skye—more if you prefer a more leisurely pace. If you are venturing up Wester Ross, plan on spending two nights there. A day-long drive from Skye will find you in Glasgow by nightfall. If you are not a cities person, skip Glasgow and stay instead in or around Callander.

Edinburgh is Scotland's beautiful capital, dominated by Edinburgh Castle sitting high above the city. Before the castle lies the long green band of gardens that separates Edinburgh's Old Town, with its narrow streets crowded with ancient buildings, and New Town where Edinburgh's shopping street, Princes Street, is backed by wide roads of elegant Georgian houses. The city's principal sights are easily explored on foot, but as an introduction to Edinburgh take one of the double-decker sightseeing buses from Waverley Bridge opposite the Tourist Information Office and railway station. The tours run every ten minutes and wind a circular route through the city with a commentary on the significance of the buildings along the route. Your ticket is valid for the whole day and the bus makes several stops so you can take the entire tour for an overview of what there is to see and then later use it as transportation between the sights, hopping on and off to visit the places that interest you. Several guided walking tours are offered, some exploring the city's ancient underground chambers—purported to be haunted!

The most popular time to visit Scotland's capital is during the **Edinburgh Festival**. The city glows for the last three weeks of August: pipers dance down the streets and kilts are worn almost as a uniform. The hum of bagpipes sets the stage, and parades, flags, presentations, floodlights, and color appear everywhere. The Military Tattoo provides tradition, The Fringe offers everything from the avant-garde to the eccentric along with jugglers, mimes, and buskers, making this the most comprehensive international arts festival in the world.

Some of Edinburgh's major sights are:

Princes Street, the elegant main thoroughfare, its north side lined by shops and its south side bordered by gardens.

Majestically perched on the edge of the city atop an extinct volcanic outcrop, **Edinburgh Castle** looms against the skyline. There has been a castle here throughout the city's history, with today's comprising a collection of buildings from the little 11th-century St. Margaret's chapel, through medieval apartments to more modern army barracks and the Scottish United Services Museum. A dramatically staged exhibition tells the tale of the Scottish Crown Jewels, the "Honours of Scotland," which dazzle the visitor from their glass case. From the castle ramparts the view over Edinburgh is spectacular.

From the castle gates you enter a famous sequence of ancient streets, referred to as The Royal Mile, where you find **Gladstone's Land** (NT), a building which typifies the more pleasant side of what life must have been like in the crowded tenements of Old Town Edinburgh. The house is arranged as a 17th-century merchant's house with the ground floor set up as a cloth merchant's booth and the upstairs as a home.

On the High Street is the great **St. Giles' Cathedral**, founded in the 1100s, whose role has been so important in the history of the Presbyterian Church. John Knox preached from its pulpit from 1561 until his death in 1572, hurling attacks at the "idolatry" of the Catholic Church.

John Knox's home is just a little farther down the High Street.

At the end of The Royal Mile lies **The Palace of Holyroodhouse**, the historic home of the Stuarts, to which Mary, Queen of Scots came from France at the age of 18. The six years of her reign and stay at Holyrood made a tragic impact on her life. Shortly after marriage to a meek Lord Darnley, the happiness of the couple dissolved and their quarrels became bitter. Lord Darnley was jealous of Mary's secretary and constant companion, David Rizzio, and conspired to have him stabbed at Holyrood in the presence of the queen. Just a year later, Lord Darnley himself was mysteriously murdered and gossip blamed the Earl of Bothwell. Mary, however, married the Earl promptly after Lord Darnley's death and rumors still question the queen's personal involvement in the murder. Conspiracies continued and Scotland's young queen fled to the safety of the English court. However, considering her a threat to the English Crown, Queen Elizabeth I welcomed her with imprisonment and had her beheaded 19 years later. Bonnie Prince Charlie was the last Stuart king to hold court at Holyrood in 1745. Today Holyrood, whose apartments are lavishly furnished with French and Flemish tapestries and fine works of art from the Royal Collection, is used by the British monarch as an official residence in Scotland.

Not far from the palace, on Holyrood Road, **Our Dynamic Earth** takes you on a fantastic journey of discovery from the very beginning of time to the unknown future of Planet Earth. The special effects and dioramas are amazing.

The **Museum of Scotland** on Chambers Street chronicles the variety and richness of Scotland's long and exciting history, bringing it all to life with the fascinating stories each object and every gallery has to tell. An added bonus is the spectacular view from its rooftop garden.

The Georgian House (NT), at 7 Charlotte Square, is typical of the elegant Georgian homes found in New Town. From the kitchen through the drawing room to the bedrooms, the house is furnished and decorated much as it would have been when it was first occupied in 1796 and gives you an insight into the way the family and servants of the house lived.

Just outside the city, at the historic port of Leith, you can visit the royal yacht *Britannia*, which traveled to every corner of the globe as a floating residence for the royal family. A visitors' center and audio-visual presentation introduce you to the yacht's history then you can take a self-guided tour to every part of the ship. If you are driving, follow signs to Leith (North Edinburgh) and *Britannia*. There is a direct bus service from Waverley Bridge, next to the railway station.

Leaving Edinburgh, follow signs for the **Firth of Forth Bridge** and Perth. After crossing the Firth of Forth, the M90 takes you through hilly farmland to the outskirts of Perth where you take the A93 following signs for Scone Palace.

Before reaching the palace you can detour off the main road to visit the city of **Perth**, known as the "Fair City," which straddles the banks of the Tay. A lovely city, it was the capital of Scotland until 1437 and the murder of James I. Following his death, his widow and young son, James II, moved the court to Edinburgh. One of Perth's most important historic buildings is **St. John's Kirk**, a fine medieval church that has been attended by many members of English and Scottish royalty. Also of interest are the **Perth Museum and Art Gallery** and the **Museum of the Black Watch**, which is housed in **Ballhousie Castle**.

Scone Palace is a 19th-century mansion that stands on the site of the Abbey of Scone, the coronation palace of all Scottish kings up to James I. By tradition, the kings were crowned on a stone that was taken from the abbey in 1297 and placed under the Coronation Chair in Westminster Abbey. This token of conquest did nothing to improve relations between Scotland and England. The present mansion is the home of the Earl of Mansfield and houses a collection of china and ivory statuettes.

Continuing along the A93, shortly after leaving the abbey you pass through **Old Scone**. This was once a thriving village but was removed in 1805 by the Earl of Mansfield to improve the landscape and only the village cross and graveyard remain to mark the site.

Continue through Guildtown to **Stobhall**, a picturesque group of buildings grouped round a courtyard. Once the home of the Drummond family, much of the structure dates back to the 15th century.

Cross the River Isla and continue alongside the enormous beech hedge that was planted in 1746 as the boundary of the Meikleour estate. At the end of the hedge turn left to the village of **Meikleour**. The focal point of the village is the 1698 mercat cross, opposite which is an old place of punishment known as the Jougs Stone. Driving through the village you join the A984 Dunkeld road.

Continue through Caputh to **Dunkeld**. Telford spanned the Tay with a fine bridge in 1809, but this picturesque town is best known for the lovely ruins of its ancient cathedral. Founded in the 9th century, it was desecrated in 1560 and further damaged in the 17th-century Battle of Dunkeld. The choir has been restored. Stroll to **Dunkeld Cathedral** by way of Cathedral Street where the National Trust has restored the little 17th- and 18th-century houses.

Leaving the town, cross Telford's bridge and take the A9 for the 11-mile drive to **Pitlochry** where the Highlands meet the Lowlands of Scotland. The town owes its ornate Victorian appearance to its popularity in the 19th century as a Highland health resort. Now it is better known for its **Festival Theatre** whose season lasts from May to October and attracts some 70,000 theatergoers each year.

In the 1940s the local electricity company built a hydroelectric station and dam across the salmon-rich River Tummel on the outskirts of town. It is hard to imagine a power station being an asset to the town but this is certainly the case here. From the observation room at the dam you can watch fish as they climb the 1,000-foot **fish ladder** around the dam and fight their way upstream to spawn in the upper reaches of the river. A special exhibition is devoted to their life cycle and the efforts being made to conserve them.

The drive from Pitlochry to Braemar is spectacular. The A924 winds up from Pitlochry to the moorlands behind the town. Alternating lush green fields and heather-clad hills give way to heather-carpeted mountains as you approach the glorious Highland scenery of **Glen Shee** (A93). At the edge of the village of **Spittal of Glenshee** large orange gates are swung across the road when it is closed by winter storms. The road begins its steep climb across the heather up the Devil's Elbow to the ski resort at the summit and drops down to the green lush valley of the River Dee and **Braemar**.

Here in this picturesque valley the clans gather for Scotland's most famous Highland games, the **Braemar Gathering,** a brilliant spectacle of pipe bands, traditional Scottish sports, and Highland dancing. The event is usually attended by the Queen and her family.

Also in the village of Braemar is the cottage in which Robert Louis Stevenson lived the year he wrote *Treasure Island*.

Following the River Dee, a short drive brings you to **Braemar Castle**, a doll-sized castle on a little knoll surrounded by conifers—a hint of the magnificent castles that wait you. Following the rushing River Dee, a turn in the road offers a splendid view of **Balmoral Castle**, the Royal summer residence. It's a very overrated Victorian pile of a building built in 1853 in the Scottish baronial style at the request of Queen Victoria and Prince Albert. When the Royal Family are not in residence, you can visit the gardens and view the exhibition in the castle ballroom.

Craigievar Castle

Coming into the tiny hamlet of **Craithe**, park in the riverside car park and stroll up to **Craithe Church** whose foundation stone was laid by Queen Victoria in 1895. The Royal Family attend services here when in residence at Balmoral just across the river.

Continue into **Ballater**, an attractive, small town internationally famous for its Highland games held in August. These include many old Scottish sports and the arduous hill race to the summit of Craig Cailleach. Continue along the A93, watching for the signpost that directs you left for a drive of several miles to **Craigievar Castle** (NT). This single-turret, pink-washed fortress surrounded by farmland is the most appealing of fairy-tale castles. Up the narrow spiral staircase the rooms are small and familial and furnished as though the laird and his family are still in residence. Willie Forbes, better known as Danzig Willie because he made his money trading with Danzig, bought an incomplete castle here in 1610. He wanted the best that money could buy and gave the master mason free reign with the castle's beautiful design. The best plasterers were busy, so Danzig Willie waited many years for the magnificent molded plasterwork ceilings that were completed the year before his death in 1627.

Twenty miles away lies **Castle Fraser** (NT), a grander, more elaborate version of Craigievar set in parklike grounds with a formal walled garden. Begun in 1575, the castle stayed in Fraser hands until the early part of this century. It contains a splendid Great Hall and what remains of an alleged eavesdropping device known as the "Laird's Lug."

Regain the A944, which takes you through Alford and on towards Rhynie. Detour from the main road to visit the romantic ruins of **Kildrummy Castle** (A97). Overlooking the ruins and surrounded by acres and acres of beautiful gardens is **Kildrummy Castle Hotel**.

The road from Kildrummy to **Dufftown** via the little Highland villages of Lumsden, Rhynie (where you leave A97 and turn left on A941), and Cabrach takes you across broad expanses of moorland. James Duff, the 4th Earl of Fife, laid out Dufftown in the form of a right-angled cross in 1817. Turn right at the Tolbooth tower in the center of the square and you come to the **Glenfiddich Distillery**, the only distillery in the Highlands where you can see the complete whisky-making process from barley to bottling. (*Closed last two weeks of December*.)

Malt whisky is to Scotland what wine is to France. The rules for production are strict: It must be made from Highland barley dried over peat fires. Water is gathered from streams that have run through peat and over granite. Distillation is carried out in onion-shaped copper stills with the final product aged and stored in oak vats before bottling. A map is available from the tourist office in Dufftown that gives details of which distilleries are open and when.

Once a Highland fortress but now sadly in ruins, **Ballathie Castle** stands on the hill overlooking the distillery.

Four miles down the A941 you come to **Craigellachie** village and distillery (the home of White Horse Whisky). Turn left on the A95 for Grantown-on-Spey and follow the Spey valley through pleasant countryside to **Ballindalloch Castle**, the beautiful home of the Macpherson-Grants. An interesting selection of tastefully furnished rooms and a teashop are open to the public. This elegant home with its lovely gardens shows the transition from the tower house of Craigievar to the country mansion so idealized by the Victorians in the Highlands.

A short distance brings you to the **Glenlivet Distillery**.

Cross the River Spey at Advie and continue into Grantown-on-Spey on the narrow road that follows the north bank of the river. From Grantown-on-Spey the A939 leads towards the holiday resort of Nairn. After about 15 miles take a small road to the left signposted for **Cawdor Castle**. This was the castle Shakespeare had in mind when he set the scene of Duncan's death in *Macbeth*. The present-day Thane of Cawdor shares his family home and gardens with the public. Portraits, tapestries, lovely furniture, and, of course, tales of romance and mystery blend to make this an interesting tour.

An 8-mile drive brings you to the cairn that marks the site of the battle of **Culloden** (NT) where on a wet day in 1746 Bonnie Prince Charlie marched his tired, rain-soaked

Highlanders into hopeless battle with the English: 1,200 Highlanders were killed. This was the last battle fought on British soil and Charles's defeat led to the decline of the Highlands and the destruction of the clan system. After the battle the British hunted Charles for five months before he escaped to France. A museum documents this sad incident and on the surrounding moorland red flags outline the Scots battle plan while yellow flags denote the English.

Nearby **Inverness** is known as the "Capital of the Highlands." Straddling the River Ness, the town takes its name from the river and the Gaelic word "inver" meaning river mouth. Leave the town on the A82 (Fort William road) and after a mile you come to the Caledonian Canal, which links the lochs of the Great Glen together to provide passage between the Irish and the North Seas. The canal splits Scotland in two and without it boats would have to risk the dangerous passage around the northernmost stretches of Scotland.

The road then follows the northern shore of Scotland's deepest (700 feet), longest (24 miles), and most famous lake, **Loch Ness**. This is the legendary home of the Loch Ness Monster or "Nessie," as she is affectionately known. So, keep an eye on the muddy gray waters of the lake and you may see more than the wind ruffling its surface. If she doesn't happen to surface for you, visit the **Loch Ness Monster Exhibition** at **Drumnadrochit**, which documents sightings that go back to the 7th century. Photographs of eel-like loops and black heads swimming give credence to the legends.

Monster spotting is a favorite pastime around Loch Ness and visitors gaze from the ramparts of **Urquhart Castle** because some of the best sightings have been made from here. The ruined castle dates from the 14th century and has a long and violent history.

Following the shores of Loch Ness, a 19-mile drive brings you to **Fort Augustus**, a village that stands at the southwestern end of the loch. Park your car by the **Caledonian Canal** and wander along its banks to see the pleasure craft being lowered and raised through the locks. Thomas Telford, the famous engineer, spent from 1803 to 1847 building the sections of this canal that connects the North Sea and the Atlantic without boats having to navigate around the treacherous Cape Wrath.

A few miles to the southwest, the little village of **Invergarry** is framed by spectacular mountain scenery. The village was burnt to the ground after the battle of Culloden because it had sheltered Bonnie Prince Charlie before and after the battle. Turn west in the village and follow the A87, through breathtaking Highland scenery, for 50 miles to Kyle of Lochalsh. The wild, rugged scenery changes with every bend in the road as you drive high above the lochs across empty moorlands then descend into glens to follow the shores of lochs whose crystal-clear, icy waters reflect the rugged mountain peaks. Habitations are few and far between yet, until the Highland chiefs decided in the 18th century, that sheep were more profitable than tenants, the hillsides held crofts, schools, and chapels.

Eilean Donan Castle

Scotland

As you trace the shore of **Loch Duich**, on the last lap of the journey to Skye, **Eilean Donan Castle** appears, linked to the rocky shore by a bridge. The castle is named for a saint who lived here in the 7th century. It is a massive, walled keep that during subsequent centuries defended the coast against Danish and Norse invaders. More recently it has been restored and it is fascinating to go into rooms with 14-foot-thick walls and to climb to the battlements to see the loch spread out before you.

From the busy fishing port of **Kyle of Lochalsh** the toll road bridge takes you "over the sea to Skye." There is an exhilarating feel to the often mist-shrouded shores of the **Isle of Skye** where mystery and legends intermingle with dramatic scenery. Islanders still make a living crofting and fishing, though tourism is becoming ever more important. This is the home of the Scottish heroine Flora Macdonald who disguised Bonnie Prince Charlie as her maid and brought him safely to Skye after his defeat by the English at the battle of Culloden.

Set out to explore Skye's coastline where magnificent mountains rise from the rocky shore and sea lochs provide scenic sheltered harbors. Skye has very good roads, although often quite narrow, making it easy to tour portions of the island in a day. (A trip from Portree—around the northern end of Skye, west to Dunvegan, and back to Portree by the hill road from Struan—is all that you could expect to do comfortably in one day.) If the weather is inclement and mist veils the island, content yourself with a good book by the fireside, for what appears stunningly beautiful on a fine day can appear dreary when sheathed in fog.

Follow the A87 (signposted Portree) through the scattered village of Broadford set along a broad, sheltered bay. Skirting the shoreline, you pass the island of Scalpay before tracing the southern shoreline of Loch Ainort. The surrounding humped peaks of the Cullin Hills are spectacular as you follow the road through Sconser and Sligachan to Portree.

Portree, the capital of Skye, is its most attractive town. Pastel-painted houses step down to the water's edge, fishing boats bob in the harbor, and small boats arrive and depart from its pier. Climbing away from the harbor, the town's streets are lined with attractive shops. If you have not booked your ferry passage from Armadale to Mallaig, you can do so at the Caledonian MacBrayne ferry office behind the bus station. The town derives its name from *Port an Righ*, meaning "King's Haven," following the visit in 1540 of James V who made a vain attempt to reconcile the feuding MacLeod and Macdonald clans.

Leaving the town, turn right onto the A850, a narrow, single-lane road with passing places, which takes you north. As you approach the shores of Lochs Fada and Leathan, the jagged, craggy peaks of **The Storr** (mountains) come into view. Standing amongst them is the **Old Man of Storr**, one of the most challenging pinnacles for mountain climbers.

Around the island's northernmost headland the crumbling ruins of the Macdonalds' **Duntulm Castle** stand on a clifftop promontory overlooking the rocky shores of Duntulm Bay. A short drive brings you to the **Skye Croft Museum** where four traditional Highland crofts have been restored and appropriately furnished to show a family home, a smithy, a weaver's house, and a small museum. These little cottages with their thick stone walls topped by a thick straw thatch were the traditional island dwellings—very few good examples remain though, as you travel around the island, if you look very carefully, you can see several traditional cottages in various states of ruin. Flora Macdonald is buried in a nearby graveyard.

Returning to the main coastal route (A850), a short drive takes you through Kilmuir and down a steep hill into the scattered hamlet of **Uig** whose pier is used by ferries to the Outer Hebrides. It is here that Bonnie Prince Charlie and Flora Macdonald landed after fleeing the Outer Hebrides. Continue to Kensaleyre and half a mile beyond the village turn right onto the B8036. When this road meets a T-junction, turn right onto the A87 for the 22-mile drive to the village of **Dunvegan**.

Just to the north of the village is **Dunvegan Castle**, the oldest inhabited castle in Scotland and the home of the MacLeod family for over 700 years. It stands amidst hills and moorlands guarding the entrance to a sheltered bay. After parking your car walk through rhododendron-filled gardens to the fortress. The castle's 15th-century section is known as the Fairy Tower after the threadbare Fairy Flag that hangs in one of the chambers. Legend has it that this yellow silk flag with crimson spots is the consecrated banner of the Knights Templar, taken as a battle prize from the Saracens. It is said to have the magical properties to produce victory in battle, the birth of sons, and plentiful harvests. Other relics include items relating to Bonnie Prince Charlie. During the summer you can take boat excursions to view the nearby seal colonies.

The A863 winds you down the western side of Skye. If you wish to visit the island's only distillery, take the B8009 to **Talisker** where the **Talisker Distillery** offers guided tours and a tasting.

Follow the narrow, single-track A851 across open moorland to **Sleat** (pronounced "Slate"), which refers to the complete southern peninsula of Skye where most of the land is divided into two estates: Clan Donald lands to the south and those of Sir Iain Noble to the north. Sir Iain is a great promoter of Gaelic, which is undergoing a revival in the western Highlands. On a rocky spit of land almost surrounded by water, the whitewashed **Eilean Iarmain** hotel, a shop, and a huddle of cottages face **Isle Ornsay**—a postage-stamp-sized island whose lighthouse was built by Robert Louis Stephenson's grandfather. (The lighthouse cottage's most famous occupant was Gavin Maxwell.) Across the sound mountains tumble directly into the sea adding a wild, end-of-the-earth feel to this hamlet.

A few more miles of narrow roads bring you to the **Clan Donald Centre** where the stable block serves as a tearoom and gift shop whence you walk through the wooded **Armadale Castle** grounds to an exhibition on the Lords of the Isles and Gaelic culture.

SKYE TO FORT WILLIAM VIA MALLAIG

If time or weather prevents you from following this itinerary north into Wester Ross, you can board the ferry for **Mallaig** in nearby **Armadale**. The ferry sails five to six times a day during the summer months and reservations should be made before sailing—it is suggested that you purchase your tickets from the Caledonian MacBrayne ferry offices in Portree (*tel: 01478-612075*). The ferry company requires that cars arrive half an hour before sailing time. It takes 1½ hours to drive from Portree to the ferry, so unless you are an insomniac, do not book the 9 am ferry. Leaving Mallaig, you cannot get lost for there is only one narrow road, "The Road to the Isles," that leads you out of town (A830).

If the weather is fine, you may want to pause at the spectacular white beaches that fringe the rocky little bays near **Morar**. The narrow road twists and turns and passing places allow cars going in opposite directions to pass one another. The village of **Arisaig** shelters on the shores of **Loch Nan Ceal** with views, and ferries, to the little islands of **Rhum** and **Eigg**.

From Arisaig your route turns eastwards following the picturesque shores of **Loch Nan Uamh**, best known for its associations with Bonnie Prince Charlie and the Jacobite Rising of 1745. The clan leaders met in a house nearby and after his defeat the prince hid near here before being taken to the Outer Hebrides—a cairn marks the spot where he left Scotland.

More than 1,000 clansmen gathered at **Glenfinnan** at the head of **Loch Shiel** to begin the 1745 Jacobite Rising. A tall castellated tower marks the place where they are said to have hoisted the Stuart standard. You climb the tower stairs to the statue of a Highlander overlooking the icy waters of the mountain-ringed loch. At the adjacent visitors' center the prince's exploits are portrayed.

Leaving the monument to Bonnie Prince Charlie's lost cause, follow the A830 for the 15-mile drive through Kinlocheil and Corpach to **Fort William**. As you approach the town, the rounded summit of Britain's highest mountain, **Ben Nevis**, appears before you.

Plockton on Loch Carron

SKYE TO FORT WILLIAM OR INVERNESS VIA WESTER ROSS

If you love Skye with its magnificent seascapes and mountains, then you will adore the Wester Ross coastline that stretches from Kyle of Lochalsh to Ullapool and beyond. It is a long day's drive from Kyle to Ullapool and the scenery is so magnificent that you may want to break the journey and spend several days in the area. Traditionally, **Wester Ross** has most sunshine in May and June, it rains more in July and August, then brightens up in September. Scottish weather is very fickle in May: we went from seven days of glorious sunshine to seemingly endless days of lashing rain. A great deal of the drive from Kyle of Lochalsh to Ullapool is on single-track road—one lane of tarmac just a few inches wider than your car (with passing places).

From **Kyle of Lochalsh** turn left to **Plockton** to see the hardy yucca palms growing bravely in the harborside gardens in this pretty village that hugs a sheltered spot of the wooded bay. Leaving Plockton, the road traces Loch Carron and after passing the Stratcarron Hotel, at the head of the loch, you turn left on the A896 for Tornapress and on to Shieldaig.

If the weather is sunny, rather than continuing along the A896 from Tornapress to Shieldaig, take the coastal road around the headland following signposts for Applecross. You will be rewarded by a most challenging drive and spectacular scenery. The narrow road twists and turns as it climbs ever higher up the **Bealach-na-Bo** pass with the mountains rising closer and taller at every turn. Crest the summit, cross a boulder-strewn moorland dotted with tarns (tiny lakes), and drop down into **Applecross**—a few whitewashed houses set in a lush green valley with salmon-pink sandy beaches. Grazing sheep fill the coastal fields and the occasional whitewashed croft faces across the water to the Isle of Raasay and, beyond that, the misty mountains of Skye. Rounding the peninsula you come to **Ardehslaig**, a few white cottages set round a rocky inlet with boats bobbing in the tiny sheltered harbor. Turn into **Shieldaig** where little cottages line the waterfront facing a nearby island densely forested with Scotch pines. It's an idyllic, peaceful spot and **Tigh an Eilean** (House by the Island) with its shop, hotel, and pub makes an excellent place to break your journey.

A deceptive few yards of two-lane road quickly turn to single track as you travel along the south shore of **Loch Torridon** where the **Loch Torridon Hotel** sits on its bank and through Glen Torridon to turn left on the A832, an arrow-straight, two-lane highway. After half a mile you find a whitewashed visitors' center on the left. The road traces **Loch Maree** with tempting glimpses of the glassy loch between groves of birch trees. The soft lushness and straight road give way to wild moorland and a single-track road to **Gairloch** with its wide bay of pink sand, scattered houses, cemetery, and golf course.

Heading inland to cross the peninsula you come to **Inverewe Gardens** (NT). Osgood MacKenzie bought this little peninsula in 1862, a barren site exposed to Atlantic gales but with frosts prevented by the warmth of the Gulf Stream. He planted belts of trees for shelter, brought in soil, and began his garden, a lifetime project that was continued by his daughter who handed over Inverewe to the National Trust in 1952. The lushness of the gardens is a striking contrast to the miles of dramatic, barren scenery that surround it. The surprise is not so much what the garden contains as the fact that it exists at all on a latitude similar to that of Leningrad. The gardens, shop, and tearoom are a venue that will occupy several hours. The National Trust brochure outlines a suggested route along the garden's pathways, but you can wander at will down the twisting paths through the azaleas, rhododendrons, and woodlands. Colorful displays are to be found in most seasons: in mid-April to May, rhododendrons; May, azaleas; June, rock garden, flower borders, and roses; September, heather; and November, maples.

Leaving Inverewe, another 35 miles finds you at the head of **Loch Broom** at an impressive vantage point that offers magnificent views down the valley across lush farmland to the distant loch. Travel down the hill and turn left into the green valley for the 12-mile drive to Ullapool.

Ullapool has a beautiful setting: cottages line the quay and overlook a jumble of slipways, quays, vessels from huge international trawlers to small wooden fishing boats, fishing gear, and nets. On the distant shore heather-clad hills rise steeply from the waters of Loch Broom. The port is a bustle of freighters and foreign fishing boats and is the terminal for the car ferry to Stornoway on the Isle of Lewis. Summer visitors add to the throng. You can always find good food and a reviving cup of coffee at **The Ceilidh Place**.

North of Ullapool there's a lot of heart-stopping scenery but beyond the Summer Isles there are no good places to stay. Journey to the **Summer Isles** by boat to see the seals and seabirds. Travel to **Lochinver** with its breathtaking views of beautiful coastline and visit the **Inchnadamph Caves** and the ruin of **Ardvreck Castle**.

Leaving Ullapool, a 60-mile drive (A835) will return you to Inverness from where it's a three-hour drive down the A9 to Edinburgh. Or retrace your steps down the northern shore of Loch Ness and continue into Fort William (A82).

Bordering the shores of **Loch Linnhe**, **Fort William** is the largest town in the Western Highlands. While the town itself cannot be described as attractive, it is the economic hub of the area and it is always crowded with tourists during the busy summer months.

From Fort William the A82 takes you southwest along the southern shore of Loch Linnhe, then turns you inland over the pass of **Glen Coe**, notorious for the massacre of the Macdonalds by the Campbells in 1692. After accepting their hospitality, the Campbells issued an order—written on the nine of diamonds playing card—to kill their hosts, the Macdonalds. The pass of Glen Coe is barren and rocky and the road south travels across this seemingly empty land. A short detour to **Killin** with its craft shops and impressive waterfalls provides an enjoyable break on a long drive.

The area of low mountains and serene lakes around **Callander**, a most attractive town, is known as **The Trossachs**. This is the country of Sir Walter Scott's novel *Rob Roy* and his poem *Lady of the Lake*. Robert MacGregor, "Rob Roy," existed as a romanticized 17th-century Robin Hood, who stole from the rich and gave to the poor. However, some regarded him more realistically as a thief and rustler! Scott's "lady" was Ellen Douglas, and her "lake" was **Loch Katrine**. There are several lovely lakes to view in this area, such as **Loch Achray** and **Loch Venachar**.

A few miles distant lies **Stirling**, dominated by its imposing Renaissance castle. **Stirling Castle**, once the home of Scottish kings, is perched high on a sheer cliff overlooking the battleground of **Bannockburn** where the Scots turned the English back in their attempt to subdue the Highland clans.

From Stirling the M80 will quickly bring you to **Glasgow**, Scotland's most populous city. Its established tradition as a port and industrial center has in recent years been surpassed by its reputation as a cultural center.

As in many large cities, the best way to get an overview of the major sights is to take a tour bus. Open-top double-deckers leave every half hour on two routes from George Square, where you also find the **Tourist Information Centre**, and you can hop on and off wherever you like. This is a Victorian city with a particular pride in its architecture and architects of that time, notably Charles Rennie Mackintosh and Alexander "Greek" Thomson, whose buildings feature prominently on the tour. Be sure to visit the 13th-century **cathedral** with its open timber roof and splendid collection of stained-glass windows. Here you find the shrine of St. Mungo, patron saint of Glasgow who died in 603, which was an important medieval pilgrimage spot.

Glasgow is home to over 30 art galleries and museums including the **Kelvingrove Art Gallery and Museum**, the most popular in Scotland, **St. Mungo Museum of Religious Life and Art**, the only museum of its kind in the world, and **The Burrell Collection**, Scotland's most outstanding museum. The Collection is set in the delightful surroundings of Pollok Country Park, formerly the grounds of **Pollok House** (NT), and can be reached by bus, train, or car (take the M8 towards the airport to the M77). Sir William Burrell, a successful Glasgow shipping agent, amassed a magnificent collection of some 9,000 works of art, primarily in the areas of medieval European art (the tapestries are stunning), Oriental ceramics and bronzes, and European paintings. In 1944 he bequeathed his collection to the city, with the stipulation that it be housed away from the highly polluted city center and eventually, in 1983, it found the perfect setting here in a corner of the Pollok Estate in a custom-built, award-winning building.

At the other end of the social spectrum, it is fascinating to get a glimpse of what life used to be like for working-class Glaswegians, as you can in the **Tenement House Museum** (NT), a Victorian apartment re-creating the poorest living conditions in the first half of the 20th century. **The People's Palace** opened in 1898 as a cultural center for the people of the East End, one of the unhealthiest and most overcrowded parts of the city. It is now the local history museum of Glasgow, telling the story of the people from 1750 to the present.

Shopping is excellent in Glasgow and evenings are alive with every kind of entertainment from opera to nightclubs.

Wales

- Isle of Anglesey
- Beaumaris
- Conwy
- Llandudno
- Llanfair
- Bodnant Gardens
- Llanddeiniolen
- A494
- Ruthin
- Chester
- Caernarfon
- Llanberis
- A470
- Betws-y-Coed
- A5
- Blaenau Ffestiniog
- Llangollen
- Porthmadog
- Portmeirion
- Bala
- A494
- Dinas Mawddy
- Rhayader
- Elan Valley
- Builth Wells
- A470
- Hay-on-Wye
- Llyswen
- Brecon
- Blwch
- Tretower Court
- Talybont-on-Usk
- Monmouth
- Pontiscill
- Merthyr Tydfil
- A40
- Raglan Castle
- Tintern Abbey
- M4

● Orientation/Sightseeing
▬ ▬ Itinerary Route

101

Wales

Wales has myriad towns and villages with seemingly unpronounceable names, its own language, an ancient form of Celtic, and its own prince, Charles. Narrow-gauge steam railways puff contentedly through glorious scenery, and there are more castles per square mile than anywhere else in Europe. The Welsh have always been fiercely independent. Consequently, they built fortifications to defend themselves while Edward I commissioned a series of daunting fortresses from which the English could sally forth to subdue the fiery Welsh. Today these mighty fortresses are some of Wales's greatest treasures. Smaller but beloved treasures are the "Great Little Trains," narrow-gauge steam railway lines with hard-working "toy" trains that once hauled slate and still steam through gorgeous countryside. And at journey's end there is bound to be a steaming cuppa to be enjoyed with *bara brith*, a scrumptious currant bread. As the signs say, *Croeso i Cymru*—Welcome to Wales.

Conwy Castle

Wales

Recommended Pacing: One night in southern Wales is all you need to accomplish the sightseeing outlined in this itinerary. In our opinion, Wales's most magnificent scenery and stunning castles lie to the north in and around Snowdonia National Park, so allow at least two nights in northern Wales.

Leave England on the M4 crossing the Severn toll bridge. The first indication that you are in another country is that all road signs appear in two languages, Welsh first, English second. As you leave the bridge take the first left turnoff signed A466 Monmouth and the Wye Valley. The road winds a course up the steep-sided, wooded valley to **Tintern Abbey**, a romantic ruin adored by the sentimental Victorians. Drive alongside the ruin to the car park at the rear by the tourist office. Stretch your legs with a quick walk round the ruin or, if you would like to visit the prettiest spot on the 168-mile length of **Offa's Dyke**, the tourist office will provide you with a detailed instruction sheet called *Offa's Dyke and the Devil's Pulpit Viewpoint*. Offa's Dyke was a great earthwork built over 1,200 years ago at the direction of King Offa to divide England and Wales.

Follow the river as it winds into Monmouth and turn left on the A40 towards Abergavenny. Traveling this dual carriageway quickly brings into view the substantial ruins of **Raglan Castle** in a field to your right. Because it is on the opposite side of a divided highway you need to do an about-face at the first roundabout. Raglan Castle is the last of the medieval castles, dating from the later Middle Ages when its builders could afford to indulge in decorative touches. It was begun in 1431 and its Great Tower was rendered the ruin you see today by Oliver Cromwell's demolition engineers. A huge fireplace and the windows are all that remain of the Grand Hall but with imagination and the aid of a map you can picture what a splendid place this must have been. You can climb the battlements and picnic in the grassy grounds.

Stay on the ring road around Abergavenny and 2 miles after passing through **Crickhowell**, a one-time stagecoach stop for coach travelers on the way to Brecon, turn right on the A479 to **Tretower Court and Castle**. The castle, a sturdy keep, was usurped as a habitation in the 14th century by nearby Tretower Court, a grand mansion that was the home of the Vaughan family for three centuries. As you walk through the empty medieval hall and along the stone passageways, you can imagine how splendid a home it was.

Leaving Tretower, continue down the lane, beside the house, and turn right on the A40. If the weather is fine, you can enjoy an almost circular driving tour through the **Brecon Beacons** by turning left towards Llangynidr and, after crossing the river, taking a right turn to Cwm Cronon and Talybont-on-Usk. Here you turn left and follow a beautiful wooded valley alongside lakes and over the hills to Pontiscill. On a fine day it is a spectacular drive along a narrow paved road, but this is not a trip to be appreciated when the clouds hang low over the mountains and visibility is not good. From Pontiscill the road weaves down to the outskirts of Merthyr Tydfil where you turn right on the A470 along another lovely valley and climb the stark, bare escarpment over the pass to Brecon.

If you do not deviate through the Brecon Beacons, remain on the A40 where views of the Usk Valley and the mountains present themselves as the road climbs to the village of Blwch. Bypass the market town of Brecon and take the A470 (Buith Wells) to **Llyswen** where you can enjoy an overnight stay at **Llangoed Hall**. From Llyswen an 18-mile round-trip detour will afford you the chance to explore the many bookstores and antique shops of **Hay-on-Wye**.

It's a lovely drive to Buith Wells as the road follows the River Wye through soft, pretty countryside. Crossing the river, head to **Rhayader** where an opportunity to enjoy a beautiful (in fair weather) drive through wild, rugged moorlands rising from vast reservoirs is afforded by turning left in the village for the **Elan Valley**. Your first stop lies beneath the looming dam at the information center where a small display outlines the importance and history of clean drinking water and gives details on the vast reservoirs that provide 76 million gallons of drinking water a day. Returning to the road, follow it as it traces the reservoir through fern-covered mountains. A right-hand turn returns you to the center of Rhayader and the A470.

From Rhayader the A470 quickly takes you north. After the junction with the A458 be on the lookout for a small sign that directs you into the pretty roadside village of Dinas

Mawddy and along a narrow lane that climbs and climbs above the green fields into stark mountains. You crest the pass and wind down and around the lake to the outskirts of Bala. Here you make a right-hand turn then go immediately left on the A4212 (Trawsfyndd road) for a short distance to the B4501, which quickly brings you to Cerrigydrudion. There you turn left on the A5 to **Betws-y-Coed**, set in a narrow, densely wooded valley at the confluence of three rivers. Crowds of visitors come to admire this town, which was popularized by the Victorian painter David Cox.

From Betws-y-Coed take the A470, following the eastern bank of the River Conwy north as it winds its way to the sea. After passing through the village of Tal-y-Cafn, look for **Bodnant Gardens** (NT) on your right. Garden lovers will enjoy almost a hundred acres of camellias, rhododendrons, magnolias, and laburnum, which provide incredible displays of spring color. Above are terraces, lawns, and formal rose and flower beds; below, in a wooded valley, a stream runs through the secluded, wild garden.

The swell of **Conwy Bay** is flanked by high cliffs and the town of **Conwy** is unforgettable for its picturesque castle set on a promontory at the confluence of two rivers and for the town's wall—over ¾ mile in length with 22 towers and 3 original gateways. **Conwy Castle** was begun in the 13th century for Edward I and suffered the scars of the turbulent years of the Middle Ages and the Civil War. The defensive complex includes an exhibit on Edward I and his castles in Wales. On the top floor of the Chapel Tower is a scale model of how the castle and the town might have appeared in 1312.

Leaving the castle, cross the road to the quay to visit a tiny home that claims to be the smallest house in Britain, then turn onto the High Street and visit the oldest house in Wales, **Aberconwy House** (NT).

Leave Conwy and follow the A55 as it hugs the coast in the direction of Caernarfon. Rather than going directly to Caernarfon, follow signs for Bangor (A5122) and call in at **Penrhyn Castle** (NT), a fabulous sham castle built as a grand home by a local slate magnate in the 19th century. This impressive house of intricate masonry and woodwork is filled with stupendous furniture.

Cross over the Menai Straight to the **Isle of Anglesey** on the Menai suspension bridge, the first of its kind, built by the famous engineer Thomas Telford, then follow the road that hugs the coast to **Beaumaris** with its closely huddled houses painted in pastel shades strung along the road. **Beaumaris Castle**, the last of the castles built by Edward I in his attempt to control Wales, is a squat, moated fortress with grassy grounds inside thick walls facing a harbor full of sailboats.

Return to the Menai bridge and, if you are inclined to have your picture taken by the sign of the town with the longest name in the world, follow directions to **Llanfair**, the abbreviation (that fits on signposts) for Llanfairpwllgwyngyllgogerychwyndrobwyllllan-tysiliogogogoch. This translates as "St. Mary's Church by the white aspens over the whirlpool and St. Tysilio's Church by the red cave." The drab little town has little to recommend it but commercial opportunists have cleverly situated a large shopping complex directly next to the station.

The A5 (Bangor road) quickly returns you to the mainland via the Britannia road bridge where you pick up signs for **Caernarfon**. Edward I laid the foundations of **Caernarfon Castle** in 1283 after his armies had defeated the princes of North Wales. Many revolts against English rule took place in this imposing fortress and during the Civil War it was one of Cromwell's strongholds. The first English Prince of Wales was born here in 1284. The investitures of the Duke of Windsor in 1911 and of Prince Charles in 1969 as Prince of Wales both took place in this majestic setting. This is the most massive and best preserved of the fortifications in this itinerary. It takes several hours to clamber up the towers, peep through arrow slits in the massive walls, and visit the exhibitions on the Princes of Wales, Castles of Edward I, and the Museum of the Royal Welsh Fusiliers.

Caernarfon Castle

Leave the coast at Caernarfon with the beauty of Snowdonia ahead of you, following the A4086 Llanberis road. The **Snowdonia National Park** is a region of wild mountains which, while they cannot be compared in size to the Alps or the Rockies (Snowdon rises to 3,560 feet), are nevertheless dramatically beautiful with ravines and sheer cliffs whose sides plummet into glacier-cut valleys sparkling with wood-fringed lakes and cascading waterfalls.

The village of **Llanberis** is the starting point for the ascent of the highest mountain in Wales, **Mount Snowdon**. Easier than the rugged walking ascent is the two-hour round-trip journey on the **Snowdon Mountain Railway**, an adorable "toy" steam train that pushes its carriages up the mountainside on a rack-and-pinion railway. The little train winds you along the edges of precipices and up steep gradients to the mountain's summit. If the weather is fine (the train runs only in clear weather) and especially if it is July, August, or the weekend, arrive for your adventure early to secure a pass that entitles you to return at an appointed time. On the day we visited a 10:30 am arrival assured us of a place on the 4:30 pm return train. Remember to take warm clothing with you as it is always cold on the summit.

When you return from your mountain experience make your way to the other side of the lake to ride the **Llanberis Lake Railway** (rarely do you have to book in advance). The adorable little train that once served the slate quarries now puffs along 2 miles of track by the edge of the lake beneath the towering mountains. On fine days you have lovely views of Snowdon.

When you leave Llanberis the road climbs the pass and the scenery becomes ever more rocky and rugged: small wonder that Hillary and Hunt trained for the 1953 Everest ascent in this area. At the Pen-y-Gwryd hotel turn right on the A498 for Beddgelert. The landscape softens as you pass Lake Gwynant and, with the River Glaslyn as its guide, the road passes through a valley that is softer and more pastoral than those of Snowdonia's other lakes.

Crowding the riverbank where three valleys meet is the little village of **Beddgelert**, nestled in the foothills of Mount Snowdon. From Beddgelert, the road follows the tumbling River Glaslyn which settles into a lazy glide as it approaches **Porthmadog**, the terminus of the hard-working little **Ffestiniog Narrow-Gauge Railway**, which runs to and from nearby Ffestiniog. The train provides riders with a mobile viewpoint from which to enjoy the most spectacular scenery as it follows the coast and chugs up into rugged Snowdonia, at one point traveling almost in a circle to gain altitude, to terminate its journey at **Blaenau Ffestiniog**. Here, in summer, you can connect with a bus that takes you for a visit to the nearby slate caverns before taking you back to the station for your return journey to Porthmadog. This rugged little train for many years carried slate from the mines to the port of Porthmadog.

A short drive on the A487 brings you to Minffordd where you turn right to the extravagant fantasy village of **Portmeirion**, which looks like a little piece of Italy transported to Wales. It has a piazza, a campanile, and an eclectic mixture of cottages and buildings squeezed into a small space and surrounded by gardens full of subtropical plants and ornate pools. The village is a mass of color—the façades are terra cotta, bright pink, yellow, and cream, and the gardens full of brightly colored flowers and shrubs. Portmeirion was the realization of a dream for Sir Clough Williams-Ellis who bought this wooded hillside plot above the broad sandy river estuary and built the village to show that architecture could be fun and could enhance a beautiful site, not defile it. His architectural model was Portofino and, while there are many Italianate touches to this fantasy village, there are also lots of local recycled houses. Sir Clough rescued many old buildings and cottages from destruction (he termed Portmeirion "the home for fallen buildings"), transporting them here and erecting them on the site. Day visitors are charged an admission fee but if you really want to fully enjoy the fantasy (the setting for the BBC television series *The Prisoner*), spend the night at the hotel or in one of the rooms in the village and enjoy it after the visitors have left.

Leave the coast behind you and turn inland to Blaenau Ffestiniog where terraced houses huddle together beneath the massive, gray-slate mountain to form a village. Taking the A470 towards Betws-y-Coed, the road follows terrace upon terrace of somber gray slate up the mountainside to the **Llechwedd Slate Caverns**. Exhibits show the importance of slate mining but the most exciting part of a visit here is to travel underground into the deep mine and follow a walking tour through the caverns.

Continuing north (A470), a 15-minute drive takes you over the pass to **Dolwyddelan Castle**, a 13th-century keep built by Prince Llewyn which was captured by Edward I and subsequently restored in the 19th century.

From Betws-y-Coed take the A5 to **Llangollen**, a town that has become the famous scene of the colorful extravaganza, the international Musical Eisteddfod, the contest for folk dancers, singers, orchestras, and instrumentalists. Llangollen's 14th-century stone bridge spanning the salmon-rich River Dee is one of Wales's Seven Wonders.

Leave Llangollen on the A542 and travel over the scenic Horseshoe Pass past the ruins of the Cistercian abbey, Valle Crucis, to **Ruthin**. Nestled in the fertile valley of Clwyd and closed in by a ring of wooded hills, Ruthin is an old, once-fortified market town whose castle is now a very commercialized hotel complete with medieval banquets.

From here a fast drive on the A494 returns you to England and motorways that quickly take you to all corners of the realm. But before leaving the area, consider visiting the charming medieval city of **Chester**. The Romans settled here in 79 A.D. and made Chester a key stronghold. Much of the original Roman wall survives, although many towers and gates seen today were additions from the Middle Ages. Chester is a fascinating city with a 2-mile walk around its **battlements**—the best way to orient yourself. It's great fun to browse in **The Rows**, double-decker layers of shops—one layer of stores at street level and the other stacked on top.

London Hotel Map

Hotels

1 Dorset Square Hotel
2 Durrants Hotel
3 Charlotte Street Hotel
4 The Leonard
5 Hazlitt's
6 Covent Garden Hotel
7 22 Jermyn Street
8 The Stafford
9 Dukes Hotel
10 The Goring
11 Knightsbridge Green Hotel
12 Basil Street Hotel
13 L'Hotel
14 The Beaufort
15 Knightsbridge Hotel
16 The Cadogan
17 Durley House
18 Eleven Cadogan Gardens
19 Sloane Hotel
20 The Pelham Hotel
21 The Cranley
22 Number Sixteen

Places of Interest

A Natural History Museum
B Victoria & Albert Museum
C Buckingham Palace, The Royal
   Mews & Queen's Gallery
D Houses of Parliament, Big Ben &
   Westminster Abbey
E The London Eye
F National Gallery
G British Museum
H Covent Garden & London
   Transport Museum
I Tate Britain
J Tate Modern
K Imperial War Museum
L Tower of London
M Harrods
N Harvey Nichols
O Marks & Spencers
P Selfridges
Q John Lewis
R Liberty
S Hyde Park & Kensington Gardens
⊖ Underground station

111

If you're looking for a charming, family-owned Edwardian hotel in the heart of Knightsbridge where you can even take your (small) dog (by arrangement), head straight for The Basil Street. This hotel combines a friendly, home-away-from-home atmosphere with elegant, antique-filled surroundings. Particularly striking are the elegant front hall with its unique hanging lantern dating from 1758 and sweeping staircase; the lovely writing gallery with its impressive collection of unusual antiques and side cubby holes set with desks and chairs; and the handsome dining room with its pale-green walls, tables topped with starched linens, abundant greenery and evening piano music. Guestrooms are all different in size, shape, and decor, generally with pastel color schemes and matching drapes and bedspreads. Some have lovely moldings, some have glass-fronted wardrobes, and some have marble bathrooms, but all have a sitting area with desk, satellite TV, and 24-hour room service. Four family rooms are available. During their visit, female guests (and, by invitation only, their male guests) become honorary members of the on-site Parrot Club for women, a quiet haven for working or relaxing. Nearest Underground: Knightsbridge.

THE BASIL STREET HOTEL
Manager: Charles Lagares
Basil Street
London SW3 1AH, England
Tel: 0207 581 3311, Fax: 0207 581 3693
88 rooms
Double: £210–£227
Open: all year, Credit cards: all major
karenbrown.com/ews/thebasil.html

Nestled in a residential neighbourhood, but conveniently located just around the corner from Harrods, the Beaufort is an alluring example of a small luxury hotel that puts comfort and convenience of its guests first. Corporate travelers take advantage of the well-equipped business centre with email access and computer and fax facilities. Leisure travelers with more time on their hands can relax and enjoy the luxuries of breakfast in bed and afternoon tea with delicious homemade scones, clotted cream, and strawberry jam. Refurbished in 2002, The Beaufort has been decorated in warm pastel shades. The air-conditioned rooms are equipped with state-of-the-art interactive television, choice of film channels, and CD player. Sparkling health drinks with herbal extracts, handmade chocolates, and drinks from the bar in the sitting room are included in the price, as is Continental breakfast. The comfortable ambiance of the hotel is enhanced by an abundance of fresh flowers and soft lighting. The residents' lounge is furnished with invitingly plump sofas and chairs. Walls throughout are accented by an interesting collection of over 400 original English watercolors. Nearest Underground: Knightsbridge.

THE BEAUFORT
Owner: Ahmed Jajbhay
Manager: Anna Bambrock
33 Beaufort Gardens
London SW3 1PP, England
Tel: 0207 584 5252, Fax: 0207 589 2834
29 rooms
Double: £185–£305
Open: all year, Credit cards: all major
karenbrown.com/ews/thebeaufort.html

For over a century the Cadogan Hotel has epitomised discreet distinction. Soon after it was finished in 1888, it became inextricably linked with two of the most famous people of the age—Lillie Langtry, the beautiful actress and mistress of Edward VII, and her admirer Oscar Wilde, the famous dramatist. Lillie's drawing and dining room are still to be seen in the hotel today. From the comfortable paneled drawing room to the spacious studios and elegant suites (all soundproofed and most air-conditioned), the hotel exudes quality and the staff showers its guests with personal attention. Breakfast is served in the elegant restaurant on tables set with silver and fresh flowers. The Oscar Wilde Suite with its front corner turret, his pictures on the wall, famous plays on the bookshelves, and stylish decor—in sky blue and chocolate to reflect his character and is understandably popular for its historical interest, as this is where the great man actually resided. Guests can avail themselves of Cadogan Gardens across the road, a cool oasis of green in the summer, its tennis courts beckoning the more active. Less vigorous pursuits include enjoying afternoon cream tea with scones and strawberry jam. The Cadogan's location is handy for museums, smart shops, Hyde Park, and restaurants. Nearest Underground: Sloane Square or Knightsbridge.

THE CADOGAN
Manager: Lionel Chatard
75 Sloane Street
London SX1X 9SG, England
Tel: 0207 235 7141, Fax: 0207 245 0994
65 rooms
Double: £225–£280*
*Breakfast not included: £16.50
*VAT not included: 17.5%
Open: all year, Credit cards: all major
karenbrown.com/ews/thecadogan.html

The stunningly stylish and luxurious Charlotte Street Hotel, situated in the bustling neighborhood of North Soho, buzzes with activity, particularly in the busy brasserie, a visual feast with its open-plan kitchen and original murals depicting contemporary London life. Decor throughout has a modern, English flavor with pastel colors, gorgeous fabrics, well-placed works of art, and striking flower arrangements. The drawing room, with its beige walls and carpet, pale-blue couches, and log-burning fireplace, is irresistibly comfortable and inviting. Bedrooms, like those in the sister Covent Garden Hotel, are superbly appointed with amenities like CD players, VCRs, fax/modem points, and cellular phones, and even have color TVs in their magnificent granite-and-oak bathrooms. Particularly appealing are the four loft suites (bedrooms upstairs, sitting room with sofa bed downstairs) with their soaring ceilings and windows. For even more luxury, opt to stay in a penthouse suite. On-site facilities include a state of the art screening room (ask about the film-night/dinner package) and fully equipped gymnasium. Nearest Underground: Tottenham Court Road or Goodge Street.

CHARLOTTE STREET HOTEL
Owners: Kit & Tim Kemp
Manager: Carrie Wicks
15 Charlotte Street
London W1T 1RJ, England
Tel: 0207 806 2000, Fax: 0207 806 2002
52 rooms Double: £205–£795*
*Breakfast not included: £18.50
*Service charge: 12.5%, VAT not included: 17.5%
Open: all year, Credit cards: all major
karenbrown.com/ews/charlottest.html

In keeping with its location at the heart of London's theatre district, the Covent Garden Hotel is dramatic and exuberant in its decor, flamboyant yet tasteful, and unabashedly luxurious. The lobby welcomes you grandly with lavish flower arrangements and Oriental carpets, then the imposing stone staircase sweeps you up to the wood-paneled, red-themed drawing room which manages to look cozy despite its grand scale and quirky furniture. Bedrooms are generously sized—even single rooms have queen beds—and, while individually decorated, each has air conditioning, a hand-quilted bedspread and trademark tailor's mannequin in matching fabric, a large writing desk, a sumptuous granite and mahogany bathroom, and every modern amenity including CD player and cellular phone. Favorite rooms include 304 with its king four-poster bed, beautiful blue drapes, huge mirror, and fireplace; 205 with its coronet-draped, king-sized bed, massive oil painting, wing chairs, and lovely desk; and 417 with its high ceilings, exposed beams, and turret dining area. The hotel also features 24-hour room service, a gym, treatment room, private screening room (ask about the film-night/dinner package) and popular brasserie. Nearest Underground: Covent Garden.

COVENT GARDEN HOTEL
Owners: Kit & Tim Kemp
Manager: Helle Jensen
10 Monmouth Street
London WC2H 9HB, England
Tel: 0207 806 1000, Fax: 0207 806 1100
58 rooms Double: £255–£895*
*Breakfast not included: £18.50
*Service charge: 12.5%, VAT not included: 17.5%
Open: all year, Credit cards: all major
karenbrown.com/ews/coventgarden.html

The Cranley is a delight. A Victorian townhouse hotel on a quiet street in South Kensington, handy for museums, shopping, and exhibition areas; run by an attentive, friendly, and enthusiastic team. Its public areas and bedrooms are tastefully decorated with a superb eye for detail. The elegant drawing room is serene and inviting, with blue walls, long blue drapes, comfortable seating, antique pieces, and a lovely mirror over the fireplace. The spacious, air-conditioned guestrooms, three with four-posters, all have excellent beds with attractive white spreads, soothing decor, good lighting, working desks, ISDN lines, TV, internet access, and sparkling bathrooms stocked with plush bathrobes. Three bedrooms have views of London and the penthouse room enjoys its own terrace. Guests are spoiled with special treats such as a welcome drink, fruit basket in the bedroom, and afternoon tea, and baby-sitting service is available. Also available, but planned for renovation and/or conversion to "regular" rooms, are ten nice suites/apartments. Nearest Underground: Gloucester Road.

THE CRANLEY
Manager: Robert Wauters
10-12 Bina Gardens
London SW5 0LA, England
Tel: 0207 373 0123, Fax: 0207 373 9497
39 rooms
Double: £125–£220*
*Breakfast not included: £9.95
*VAT not included: 17.5%
Open: all year, Credit cards: all major
karenbrown.com/ews/cranley.html

Dorset Square Hotel, a beautifully restored Regency townhouse, is located in the area of London made famous by Sherlock Holmes and just down the road from Madame Tussaud's. It overlooks a tree-filled garden which was the original site of Lord's Cricket Ground. The contemporary English decor uses lots of antiques, original oils, and wonderful flower arrangements. The air-conditioned bedrooms all have marble bathrooms and the more expensive rooms are truly lovely. If you stay in one of the hotel's smallest, least expensive rooms, you find yourself enjoying the fabulous ambiance of an elegant hotel at a price that is good value for money. All are fully equipped with facilities expected by today's traveler. Below street level, The Potting Shed Restaurant, where you can hear live jazz, lives up to its name in its design, with terra cotta pots piled up against the wall, pots of flowers on the tables, and a glass ceiling over half of the room. Snuggle up in the Library with a book and a drink. There's very much a country feeling to this small hotel within easy reach of Bond Street, Regent's Park, the theaters, and the West End. Nearest Underground: Marylebone or Baker Street.

DORSET SQUARE HOTEL
Manager: Vanessa Mitchell
39-40 Dorset Square
London NW1 6QN, England
Tel: 0207 723 7874, Fax: 0207 724 3328
37 rooms
Double: £210–£315*
*Breakfast not included: £14
*Service charge: 12.5%, VAT not included: 17.5%
Open: all year, Credit cards: all major
karenbrown.com/ews/dorsetsquare.html

Completely renovated over the last few years, Dukes is a very special hotel—it remains one of our favorites. Conveniently located only steps from St. James's Street, a stone's throw from Piccadilly Circus, Dukes is tucked into its own little flower-filled, gas-lit courtyard. Just off the lobby is a snug lounge and beyond is a paneled cocktail bar famous for its dry martinis and selection of vintage cognacs. The airy conservatory is an excellent place to enjoy light meals, coffee, and afternoon tea. The air-conditioned guestrooms, decorated and furnished in country house style, vary in size from spacious rooms to splendid suites with large bedrooms and impressive lounges. All feature modern, marble bathroom facilities with sparkling glass and chrome fixtures and sumptuous towels and robes, and all are equipped with the necessities of today's business traveler. The Penthouse suite enjoys spectacular nighttime views across the rooftops to floodlit Big Ben and Westminster Abbey. All guests have access to the luxuriously appointed health club with its high-tech exercise equipment and a wide choice of personalised beauty and body treatments. Nearest Underground: Green Park.

DUKES HOTEL
Manager: Karen Marchart
35, St. James's Place
London SW1A 1NY, England
Tel: 0207 491 4840, Fax: 0207 493 1264
89 rooms
Double: £235–£700*
*Breakfast not included: £12.75–£18.50
*VAT not included: 17.5%
Open: all year, Credit cards: all major
karenbrown.com/ews/dukeshotel.html

The suites at Durley House on Sloane Street are for those who want to have their own pied-à-terre in the heart of Knightsbridge. They provide all the comfort and services of a hotel coupled with the privacy and convenience of your own apartment. No expense has been spared in outfitting the suites in an attractive, traditional country-house style. Besides a bedroom and separate living room, all have a well-equipped kitchen. Guests intending to use the self-catering facilities can call ahead and the staff will happily arrange to purchase initial grocery supplies. Alternatively there is a kitchen on-site, offering room service 24-hours a day. If requested, a waiter will bring you dinner and serve it to you in your apartment. Complete picnic catering services, right down to rugs to sit on, are available to simplify planning those occasional days out in the country. The large, luxurious suites, although expensive for two, would prove a good value for a family or couples traveling together. Energetic guests have the use of tennis courts in the private gardens across the way. A short walk brings you to Sloane Street's sophisticated shops. Nearest Underground: Sloane Square.

DURLEY HOUSE
Owner: The Stein Group
Manager: Stella Amor
115 Sloane Street
London SW1X 9PJ, England
Tel & fax: 0207 235 5537
11 rooms Double: £320–£620*
*Breakfast not included: £12.50
*VAT not included: 17.5%
Open: all year, Credit cards: all major
karenbrown.com/ews/durleyhouse.html

Built in the 1700s and owned and operated by the Miller family since the early 1920s, Durrants lays claim to being one of London's oldest privately owned hotels. Conveniently located just off busy Oxford Street, the hotel has a Georgian-style exterior which neatly conceals the four original buildings and the fascinating maze of public and private rooms that lie within. The style puts one in mind of a private club, with discreet lounges, intimate bars, dark wood paneling, comfortably inviting leather chairs, fireplaces, antiques, and artwork. Bedrooms, most of which are air-conditioned, vary greatly in size but are furnished with a similar theme and all have modern, functional bathrooms. George Street is not an overly busy thoroughfare, considering the central London location, but rooms at the rear of the building are a little quieter. Traditional English cuisine with a Continental flair is the order of the day in the formal dining room adjacent to the lobby, which is dominated by its sweeping staircase. Breakfast is served in the Spy Room, its walls adorned with caricatures of reputed spies from a past era when all Englishmen stationed abroad were eyes and ears of the Empire. Nearest Underground: Bond Street.

DURRANTS HOTEL
Manager: Ian McIntosh
George Street
London W1H 5BJ, England
Tel: 0207 935 8131, Fax: 0207 487 3510
92 rooms
Double: £165–£285*
*Breakfast not included: £15
Open: all year, Credit cards: all major
karenbrown.com/ews/durrants.html

There is no sign that this Victorian townhouse in a quiet part of Chelsea is a hotel. Having successfully overcome the mysterious house-numbering system in Cadogan Gardens, you ring the doorbell, step into the paneled hall, sign the visitors' book, and are enveloped by the refined atmosphere of days gone by. It is rather like a discreet private club with Victorian wing chairs, stern portraits, dark wood paneling and doors, guests daintily sipping afternoon tea, whispered conversations, and a chauffeured Mercedes at your bidding. Larger bedrooms are very quiet as all but one are at the back of the hotel. The suites can only be described as magnificent. Breakfast and light meals are served in the newly renovated dining room in the basement with its Portland-stone floor, cream paint, wood-paneled walls adorned with a display of ceramic plates, and original black iron range (discovered buried in the walls during recent construction activities). Other amenities include private gardens, a fully-equipped gymnasium, and aromatherapy massages. The shops and restaurants of Knightsbridge are a few minutes' walk away. Nearest Underground: Sloane Square.

ELEVEN CADOGAN GARDENS
Manager: Christopher Wallace
11 Cadogan Gardens
London SW3 2RJ, England
Tel: 0207 730 7000, Fax: 0207 730 5217
60 rooms
Double: £235–£355*
*Breakfast not included: £13, Service charge: 3%
Open: all year, Credit cards: all major
karenbrown.com/ews/elevencadogan.html

Founded in the reign of King Edward VII by the present owner's grandfather and located on a quiet side street just round the corner from Buckingham Palace, The Goring is recognized as one of London's premier hotels and takes great pride in offering guests a warm welcome and luxuriously appointed accommodations. Maintaining a personal touch, the current Mr. Goring invites guests to his Sunday cocktail party (6–7 pm). Bedrooms and suites offer the highest level of comfort with luxurious decor and furnishings and beautiful marble bathrooms. All are air-conditioned and several overlook a peaceful garden (three have private balconies). Although elegant and polished, the decor displays a humorous theme. Comic strips from Mr. Goring's personal memoirs are exhibited throughout and two large West-Country sheep sit either side of the drawing-room fireplace while the rest of the flock reside in several of the bedrooms. Relax over morning coffee and pastries in the lounge or sample English afternoon tea on the terrace. Later in the day the Garden Bar is a perfect venue to unwind, a stone's throw away from Buckingham Palace, a world away from the bustle of central London. Nearest Underground: Victoria.

THE GORING
Owner: George Goring
Manager: William Cowpe
Beeston Place, Grosvenor Gardens
London SW1W 0JW, England
Tel: 0207 396 9000, Fax: 0207 834 4393
74 rooms Double: £255–£425*
*Breakfast not included: £13-50
*VAT not included: 17.5%
Open: all year, Credit cards: all major
karenbrown.com/ews/goring.html

Named after the celebrated essayist and located a stone's throw from the theatre district in the heart of historic Soho, Hazlitt's is comprised of three Georgian townhouses. Cleverly combined over the years and recently upgraded with all modern conveniences (except an elevator), they have retained all of their original "old-world" charm. Traditional paneled rooms, brass chandeliers, comfortable old furniture, elegant wall hangings and rugs, as well as the obligatory sloping floors, give the place the feel of a working museum. Bedrooms, named after famous residents and visitors to the house, feature high ceilings, a selection of carved mahogany bedheads, and four-poster and half-tester beds. Bathrooms have retained 19th-century elements such as claw-footed freestanding tubs, enormous showerheads, and overhead toilet cisterns complete with pull chains. Thankfully, all bed linens and bath towels appear to be very much 21st-century! An ample Continental breakfast is served in your bedroom. Light refreshments are available in the residents' sitting room. Nearest Underground: Tottenham Court Road.

HAZLITT'S
Manager: Andrew Boardman
6 Frith Street
London W1D 3JA, England
Tel: 0207 434 1771, Fax: 0207 439 1524
23 rooms
Double: £205–£300*
*Breakfast not included: £8.95
*VAT not included: 17.5%
Open: all year, Credit cards: all major
karenbrown.com/ews/hazlitts.html

This little gem is the sister property of the adjacent Capital Hotel. A small brass plaque discreetly identifies its doorway and the desk in the entrance hall serves as the very informal reception. The lobby's beautifully stenciled walls are most attractive and you find lovely artwork throughout. L'Hotel is a sophisticated bed and breakfast decorated in a classically simple, French-country style. Bedrooms are delightful with pine furniture, brass beds, colorful decor, and crisp linens. No air conditioning here, but all rooms have ceiling fans, more than adequate for most days in London. Each offers some special appeal, whether it is a larger bath, more spacious bedroom, or its own fireplace. With enough notice, you may be able to reserve the two-room, top-floor suite or a fireplace room. There are no public rooms: breakfast is served either in your room or downstairs in Le Metro, the restaurant next door. Brightly contemporary with its light-wood furnishings, Le Metro also offers good-value lunches and light meals, doubling as a bar in the evening. Conveniently located close to the attractions and shopping of Knightsbridge, L'Hotel offers a less-pricey alternative to the more formal establishments in the area. Nearest Underground: Knightsbridge.

☕ ✎ 💳 ☎ 🐕 🏛 ⛲ Y P 🍴

L'HOTEL
Owner: David Levin
28 Basil Street
London SW3 1AS, England
Tel: 0207 589 6286, Fax: 0207 823 7826
12 rooms
Double: £150–£180*
*Continental breakfast included
*VAT not included: 17.5%
Open: all year, Credit cards: all major
karenbrown.com/ews/lhotel.html

Close to Harrods and Hyde Park and just a few yards from the Knightsbridge tube station, the Knightsbridge Green Hotel stands out as a hotel where the staff is wonderfully friendly, the location superb, the price reasonable, and ice always available. With an unobtrusive front door that is almost lost on the busy street front, it is located in a tall, narrow building where an old-fashioned lift takes you from the street-level lobby to the six floors of air conditioned bedrooms. Double glazing effectively eliminates any traffic noise. Rooms are spacious and suites have separate sitting rooms, some with a sofa bed. The decor is sunny, with pastel-washed walls and pretty fabrics, and bathrooms are sparkling and modern. An English, Continental, or Express breakfast is served in the rooms. Complimentary coffee and tea are available on request. Guests have the use of a nearby health club with fully-equipped gymnasium and swimming pool. This is a very popular hotel, so it is advisable to book well ahead. Nearest Underground: Knightsbridge.

KNIGHTSBRIDGE GREEN HOTEL
Owner: Marler family
Manager: Paul Fizia
159 Knightsbridge
London SW1X 7PD, England
Tel: 0207 584 6274, Fax: 0207 225 1635
28 rooms
Double: £115–£170*
*Breakfast not included: £3.50–£10.50
Open: all year, Credit cards: all major
karenbrown.com/ews/knightsbridgegreen.html

Another successful project by London hoteliers Tim and Kit Kemp, the Knightsbridge Hotel is situated in Beaufort Gardens, a quiet, tree-lined street in the heart of fashionable Knightsbridge. The hotel is just a walk away from Sloane Street's stylish international designer stores, Hyde Park, the Victoria and Albert, Natural History, and Science Museums, and sits in the shadow of Harrods. The Kemps' intent is to provide a "chic bed and breakfast hotel for discerning travelers spending their own money"—and they have succeeded quite nicely. Luxurious, individually-styled bedrooms are decorated in a modern English vein using a variety of eye-catching colors and sumptuous fabrics, and are equipped with every modern convenience for those conducting business during their stay. Spacious bathrooms feature granite and oak. Room service is available 24-hours a day and breakfast, ordered from an ample menu the evening before, is served in your room. Two spacious public areas are to be found downstairs. The drawing room is furnished with comfortable sofas and decorated with African overtones, offset by a collection of framed Scottie dogs on the wall and a stone fireplace whose mantel is adorned with carved mushrooms. The library, its comfy chairs and fireplace surrounded with floor-to-ceiling bookshelves, is a great place to settle down with a good book and a drink from the honor bar next door. Nearest Underground: Knightsbridge.

KNIGHTSBRIDGE HOTEL
Owners: Kit & Tim Kemp
Manager: Paula Place
10 Beaufort Gardens
London SW3 1PT, England
Tel: 0207 584 6300, Fax: 0207 584 6355
44 rooms Double: £180–£420*
*Breakfast not included: £14.50
*Service charge: 12.5%, VAT not included: 17.5%
Open: all year, Credit cards: all major
karenbrown.com/ews/knightsbridgehotel.html

The Leonard, occupying a historic handsome townhouse, sits on a quieter street behind Marble Arch and just steps from Portman Square. The reception area is very elegant, featuring a gorgeous flower arrangement on a lovely antique table. It extends into the comfortable drawing room with its open fireplace and an ample supply of reading matter for those quiet moments. The 21 air-conditioned suites and 23 bedrooms are beautifully decorated with a combination of traditional furniture, both contemporary and antique, elegant fabrics, and distinctive objets d'art. Each has a marble bathroom, mini-bar, satellite television, video player, telephone, and dedicated line for fax or modem. The hotel's four dramatic Grand Suites are particularly impressive. A small rooftop garden with plants and flowers, stone benches and a water feature provides extensive views over the surrounding area. The café-bar on the ground floor offers breakfast and light meals throughout the day and the professional "can-do" staff provide valet, concierge, and 24-hour room service. An exercise room and secretarial facilities are special bonuses, as is access to the private, gated-gardens of Portman Square. Nearest Underground: Marble Arch.

❄ 💳 ☎ 🛗 🏋 🚶 👥 ⅄ P 🍴 🖼

THE LEONARD
Manager: Angela Stoppani
15 Seymour Street
London W1H 5AA, England
Tel: 0207 935 2010, Fax: 0207 935 6700
44 rooms
Double: £220–£550*
*Breakfast not included: £14–£18.50
*VAT not included: 17.5%
Open: all year, Credit cards: all major
karenbrown.com/ews/theleonard.html

Number Sixteen is an elegant, upscale bed and breakfast located in the heart of fashionable South Kensington. A member of the Firmdale Hotel Group, and yet another example of the Kemps' stylish approach to London living, it forms part of a white-stucco mid-Victorian terrace. There are 42 individually decorated bedrooms each featuring hand-embroidered bedspreads and exquisite Frette bed linen, and several have terraces onto the private garden at the rear. Ornate plaster ceilings and antique furniture, modern bathrooms, and all requisite creature comforts combine to provide the feel of staying in a private house. We prefer the rooms above street level to those below stairs. Guests are encouraged to treat this deluxe pension as their home-away-from-home and two drawing rooms and a sunny conservatory are provided to entertain friends, relax, and unwind. There is no restaurant but there are a great many close by. Breakfast can be served in the garden, drawing rooms, conservatory, or in your room. Nearest Underground: South Kensington.

NUMBER SIXTEEN
Manager: Tristan McEwen
16 Sumner Place
London SW7 3EG, England
Tel: 0207 589 5232, Fax: 0207 584 8615
42 rooms
Double: £150–£250*
*Breakfast not included: £7.50–£9.50
*Service charge: 12.5%, VAT not included 17.5%
Open: all year, Credit cards: all major
karenbrown.com/ews/sixteen.html

You might well pass by The Pelham thinking this is a private club, for with its discreet exterior, only the flag and classy brass plaque signify that a hotel is within. Inside, no expense has been spared to create an inviting, traditional atmosphere—lavish bouquets of flowers, gorgeous antiques, and original oil paintings set the mood of a fetching English country house hotel. Public areas, such as the lovely wood-paneled library and drawing room, each with an open fireplace, and Kemps, the attractive lower-ground-floor restaurant and bar invite you to linger. Sedate gray-carpeted hallways lead you to the accommodations, which range from large suites to smaller rooms with twin, queen, or king beds, equipped with every amenity including mobile phones, VCRs, and high speed internet access. All have smart bathrooms fitted out in granite and mahogany. The very friendly staff really strives to make this a home-away-from-home. The restaurant's cuisine and stylish decor attract a number of celebrities. Surrounding you are the interesting boutiques, museums, antique shops, and restaurants of South Kensington and Knightsbridge. Nearest Underground: South Kensington.

THE PELHAM HOTEL
Owners: Kit & Tim Kemp
Manager: Karen Dukes
15 Cromwell Place
London SW7 2LA, England
Tel: 0207 589 8288, Fax: 0207 584 8444
50 rooms Double: £180–£690*
*Breakfast not included: £17.50
*Service charge: 12.5%, VAT not included: 17.5%
Open: all year, Credit cards: all major
karenbrown.com/ews/pelham.html

This luxurious boutique hotel is to be found a few minutes' walk from the bustling Kings Road and fashionable heart of Chelsea. One of the joys of staying at the Sloane is its avant-garde, offbeat decor, apparent from the moment you enter the lobby. The old fireplace, antique luggage piled beneath an ancestral portrait, the Napoleonic sofa covered in fake leopard skin (for those who can't resist, know that absolutely everything is for sale) are all indicators of what is to be found within. A tiny elevator whisks you up to the bedrooms, each very differently decorated, generally with heavy tapestry fabrics, and furnished with lovely antiques. I personally was taken with room 101 (a superior deluxe room) but preferred room 302, a two-level suite presided over by a grand canopied bed ornately draped in shades of lime-green and mauve. Ten newer rooms are decorated with a similar theme but are slightly larger. All are air-conditioned and have their own stylish bathroom facilities. Part of the recent expansion program has been the addition of a modernized kitchen and larger breakfast room downstairs. The Sloane takes great pride in offering guests attentive service in comfortable and eclectically decadent surroundings. Nearest Underground: Sloane Square.

SLOANE HOTEL
Owner: Xavier Colin
Manager: Richard Betin
29 Draycott Place
London SW3 2SH, England
Tel: 0207 581 5757, Fax: 0207 584 1348
22 rooms Double: £185–£280*
*Breakfast not included: £9–£12
*VAT not included: 17.5%
Open: all year, Credit cards: all major
karenbrown.com/ews/sloane.html

The bustle of London seems far away from this quiet, refined hotel in historic St. James', just a short walk from Piccadilly. Some of London's most exclusive real estate is tucked back in the privacy of this cul-de-sac. Originally built as a private residence in the mid-17th century, the Stafford maintains the air of an exclusive club. Ornate plaster ceilings grace the elegant lounge and excellent dining room. The colorful bar is worth a visit in itself. It is decorated with an eclectic collection of caps, ties, hard hats, American football helmets, and assorted pictures and memorabilia dating back to World War II when the hotel was home to (among others) the officers of the American Eagle Squadron. Outside across Blue Ball Yard, the hotel's own cobbled mews, lies the Carriage House, painstakingly converted in the 1990s and featuring the original timber beams, supposedly reclaimed from old sailing ships during the original construction. Today it houses deluxe bedrooms and the incomparable two-story Guv'nor's Suite. Like the guestrooms located within the hotel, they are all decorated in a most luxurious manner and equipped with absolutely everything your heart could desire, including the not-to-be-forgotten sailboat in every bathtub. Nearest Underground: Green Park.

❄ ⚓ ⚒ 💳 ☎ 🛗 🏋 🧍 👫 🏇 Ⓨ P 🍽 ⚓

THE STAFFORD HOTEL
Manager: Terry Holmes
16-18 St. James's Place
London SW1A 1NJ, England
Tel: 0207 493 0111, Fax: 0207 493 7121
81 rooms
Double: £255–£850*
*Breakfast not included: £18.50
*VAT not included: 17.5%
Open: all year, Credit cards: all major
karenbrown.com/ews/thestafford.html

Henry Togna's grandfather opened Twenty Two Jermyn Street in 1915 as "residential chambers," in-town accommodation for country squires. Now it's a gracious townhouse hotel on an upscale street in close proximity to West End theatres and Piccadilly. A long hallway leads you between the shopfronts of Hawkes and Curtis, bespoke gentlemen's tailors, and Bates, a wonderful old-fashioned gentlemen's hat shop. A small reception area is located at the foot of the stairs (there are no public rooms) leading to the accommodations on the floors above. Double rooms (known as studios) and suites are beautifully appointed with a mix of antique and modern funishings, bold fabrics, fresh flowers, and crisp linens. The modern granite bathrooms are all equipped with choice toiletries, hairdryers, and comfortable robes. In addition to presenting an extensive breakfast menu for delivery to your room, the kitchen provides light meals and snacks around the clock and even supplies bread for feeding the ducks in nearby St. James's Park. Guests are provided with a free membership of a local health club and swimming pool. From taking you jogging to advising you about everything London, the staff is extremely friendly and the location is perfect. Nearest Underground: Piccadilly Circus.

TWENTY TWO JERMYN STREET
Owner: Henry Togna
Manager: Laurie Smith
22 Jermyn Street
London SW1Y 6HL, England
Tel: 0207 734 2353, Fax: 0207 734 0750
18 rooms Double: £210*
*Breakfast not included: £12.65
*VAT not included: 17.5%
Open: all year, Credit cards: all major
karenbrown.com/ews/jermyn.html

England Hotels

Rothay Manor is an exceptionally enjoyable establishment in the very heart of the Lake District. It has the feel of a refined, old-fashioned British resort hotel where everything is done with kindness and without fuss. In the afternoon, an array of trim little sandwiches, decorated cakes, and biscuits tempts you to partake of tea. Children's "teas" are served so that youngsters can be tucked up in bed before parents go down to dinner. A traditional, set three- or four-course dinner is served in the dining room. Afterwards, coffee and chocolates are set out in the hall to be enjoyed in one of the comfortable sitting rooms. Premier bedrooms are those at the front with balconies. We particularly enjoyed our room 6. Room 15, a standard room in the Old Cottage and joined to the hotel by a glass-sided corridor, is an especially attractive smaller room that enjoys a small, private, garden patio. Room 15 and the adjacent 14 can be combined as a family suite. A downstairs bedroom is available for those who use a wheelchair or have difficulty with stairs. The weather report is posted in the hallway so you can be prepared for the fickle Lake District weather. The Lake District's picturesque villages and stunning scenery are easily reached by car or explored on foot. Dove Cottage, Wordsworth's home—now a museum—is nearby. *Directions:* From Ambleside, follow signs for Coniston (A593). You will find the hotel in the middle of the one-way system on the outskirts of town.

ROTHAY MANOR
Owners: Nigel & Stephen Nixon
Rothay Bridge
Ambleside
Cumbria LA22 0EH, England
Tel: (015394) 33605, Fax: (015394) 33607
19 rooms
Double: £120–£180
Closed: Jan 2 to Jan 27, Credit cards: all major
karenbrown.com/ews/rothay.html

People enjoy themselves at Amerdale House—they relax, they unwind, shed tension, and slip into unconcerned relaxation. They spend their time walking the miles of paths that beckon walkers to this part of the world, meandering along the lanes exploring the Yorkshire Dales, or just pottering round the picturebook village and popping in for a drink and a chat at the pub. Nigel and Paula Crapper set this mood of utter relaxation. While Paula concentrates on seeing that guests are well taken care of, Nigel makes sure that they are well fed, offering every evening a set menu with choices in all but the fish course. This large Victorian house lends itself beautifully to accommodating guests and while the public rooms are spacious and airy, bedrooms tend to be on the snug side. It's an utterly quiet and peaceful spot—a perfect base for touring the Dales and visiting Fountains Abbey, Skipton Castle, and Harewood House. York is just 50 miles distant and Settle (the start of the Settle to Carlisle railway) is a spectacular 14-mile drive away. *Directions:* From Grassington (on the B6265 Ripon to Skipton road) take the B6160 towards Kettlewell and just after Kilnsey Crag turn left into Littondale. Amerdale House is on your left as you enter Arncliffe.

AMERDALE HOUSE HOTEL
Owners: Paula & Nigel Crapper
Arncliffe
North Yorkshire BD23 5QE, England
Tel: (01756) 770250, Fax: (01756) 770266
11 rooms
Double: £162–£170*
*Includes dinner, bed & breakfast
Open: mid-Mar to Oct, Credit cards: MC, VS
karenbrown.com/ews/amerdale.html

Just off the main A6, between the delightful market town of Bakewell and the Victorian spa town of Buxton, is the pretty village of Ashford-in-the-Water. In the center of the village, next to the ancient Sheepwash bridge, Riverside House sits in a walled garden that borders the River Wye. The smartly appointed drawing room looks towards the river but the heart of the house is the comfortable golden-oak-paneled bar where a log fire burns brightly when needed. Here, before and after dinner, drinks are served. In the adjacent dining rooms dinner is from a set menu, which changes regularly. More casual fare is available in the conservatory. Bedrooms in the old house vary in size and are tastefully decorated, with the premier room being Kingfisher, a four-poster room with its large bay window offering lovely river views. Rooms in the "new" (albeit traditionally designed) wing are uniform in size, individually decorated, and have the advantage of immaculate modern bathrooms. Off the beaten tourist track, Derbyshire is an area of unsurpassed beauty. Long country walks in the Peak District National Park, visits to neighboring village pubs, and explorations of the stately Chatsworth estate, Haddon Hall, and Hardwick Hall are pursuits to be recommended. *Directions:* Ashford-in-the-Water is 2 miles northwest of Bakewell on the Buxton road (A6).

RIVERSIDE HOUSE
Manager: James Lamb
Ashford-in-the-Water, Bakewell
Derbyshire DE45 1QF, England
Tel: (01629) 814275, Fax: (01629) 812873
15 rooms
Double: £125–£155
Open: all year, Credit cards: all major
karenbrown.com/ews/riversidehouse.html

Blagdon Manor is a little gem of a hotel set in the gently undulating northwest Devon countryside. This is not a grand manor house but rather a farmhouse of comfortably proportioned rooms with little windows peeking out through thick stone walls. Built in the 17th century on the site of a farmhouse mentioned in the 1086 Domesday Book, the house is pleasantly rambling, with lots of interesting nooks and crannies—we particularly liked the cozy beamed bar. It stands in its own grounds well away from traffic with lawns that stretch out to a vista of fields and the distant hills. Owners Liz and Steve Morey are much in evidence, so you really feel that you are staying in the countryside with friends rather than at a hotel. Steve, formerly the chef at Gravetye Manor, offers five or six choices for each of the three courses of dinner in the low, beamed dining room. The country-cozy bedrooms are decorated in sunny colors, and each is accompanied by a very nice bathroom. I particularly liked room 5 and room 2. You can tour much of Devon and Cornwall from here. To the west lie Boscastle Harbour and the ruins of Tintagel Castle, while to the south is Llanhydrock, a not-to-be-missed stately home. *Directions:* Leave Launceston on the A388, Holsworthy road. Pass Chapman's Well and the first sign to Ashwater. Turn right at the second Ashwater sign (8 miles from Holsworthy) and first right, signposted Blagdon. The hotel is on the right.

BLAGDON MANOR HOTEL
Owners: Liz & Steve Morey
Ashwater
Devon EX21 5DF, England
Tel: (01409) 211224, Fax: (01409) 211634
7 rooms
Double: £100
Open: all year, Credit cards: all major
karenbrown.com/ews/blagdon.html

There can be no better fate for a rundown country estate than to fall into the hands of Historic House Hotels who have meticulously restored Hartwell House, which opened its doors as a luxurious country house hotel in 1989. The Great Hall with its ornate fireplace and decorative ceiling sets the scene for the grandeur of the place, yet this is no stuffy hotel—there is a comfortable air of informality. To the left is the oak-paneled bar which leads to the morning room and the library. The dining room is composed of several adjoining rooms that overlook the garden. The second-floor bedrooms, named after the court of the exiled King of France (Louis XVIII), who occupied them, are the largest and several have four-posters. Cozier, and less expensive, are the attic bedrooms, some of which open out onto a sheltered roof terrace where rabbits were reared and vegetables grown by the French émigrés. More bedrooms are found in the stable building adjacent to the conference center and Hartwell Spa with its spacious indoor swimming pool, gym, and beauty salons. A path leads into the walled garden, which houses two tennis courts. The surrounding parkland with its ruined church, pavilion, and lake is perfect for long country walks. Oxford is just 20 miles away and Heathrow airport is less than an hour's drive. *Directions:* Hartwell House is 2 miles from Aylesbury on the A418, Oxford road.

HARTWELL HOUSE
Manager: Jonathan Thompson
Aylesbury
Buckinghamshire HP17 8NL, England
Tel: (01296) 747444, Fax: (800) 260-8338
Fax: (01296) 747450
46 rooms
Double: £260–£360
Open: all year, Credit cards: all major
karenbrown.com/ews/hartwellhouse.html

The signpost to Skelwith Bridge and Hawkshead and the inn have stood at the crossroads over 400 years. The name hearkens back to Victorian times, when the landlady found her ducks lying comatose on the crossroad. She proceeded to pluck one and discovered they were not dead—but dead drunk—having imbibed beer leaking from a broached barrel. Today, the Drunken Duck offers comfortable accommodation and fine food. A range of beers, produced in their brewery on-site, are named after dogs and cats who have graced the property in recent times, Cracker, Tag Lag, Chesters and Catnap. Comfy sofas, antiques, and wall art make the sitting room a great place to escape. Indulge yourself in traditional tea and cakes served to residents every afternoon. Each of the guestrooms offers a unique blend of comfort and contemporary design with bathrooms ensuite. Our favorite is the Garden room with open-beamed ceiling, floor-length windows, views across Langdale Valley, and a private balcony above the gardens and Tarn. The restaurant features modern British cuisine and the bar is quintessentially English. Little has changed over the years; chalk-written menus, foaming pints of hand-pulled beer and open log fires offer a traditional warm welcome. *Directions:* From Ambleside take A593 (Conistone Road), turn left on the B5286 (Hawkshead Road) for 1 mile, turn right (signposted: The Duck) and the inn is on the crossroads at the top of the hill.

THE DRUNKEN DUCK   New
Owners: Steph Barton & Paul Spencer
Barngates, Ambleside
Cumbria LA22 0NG, England
Tel: 015394 36347, Fax: 015394 36781
16 rooms
Double: £90–£210
Open: all year, Credit cards: all major
karenbrown.com/ews/drunken.html

The Cavendish Hotel sits at the edge of the Chatsworth estate, which surrounds one of England's loveliest stately houses, the home of the Duke and Duchess of Devonshire. Eric Marsh, the owner, has restored and expanded what was originally an 18th-century fishing inn into a fine hotel. The Garden Room (perfect for lunch and informal dinners) frames a panoramic view of the River Derwent meandering through green fields across the estate; comfy sofas and chairs in the adjacent lounge invite you to linger and relax. The bar is a cozy gathering spot for drinks before dinner in the highly commended dining room (you can request a table in a corner of the kitchen if you are anxious to peek at what happens behind the scenes). Bedrooms in the oldest part of the hotel have a lovely feel to them: I particularly enjoyed the spaciousness and old-world ambiance of the superior rooms. An adjoining wing of bedrooms with a more contemporary style has been built to match the original building and called the Mitford Rooms after their designer, the Duchess of Devonshire, and her Mitford family. A pathway leads you on a beautiful walk through the Chatsworth estate to Chatsworth House. Explorations farther afield reveal unspoilt villages set in beautiful rolling countryside of stone-walled fields, green valleys, and spectacular dales. *Directions:* Exit the M1 motorway at junction 29 and follow signs for Chatsworth through Chesterfield to Baslow.

CAVENDISH HOTEL
Owner: Eric Marsh
Baslow
Derbyshire DE45 1SP, England
Tel: (01246) 582311, Fax: (01246) 582312
24 rooms
Double: £150–£225*
*Breakfast not included: £9–£20
Open: all year, Credit cards: all major
karenbrown.com/ews/cavendish.html

Fischer's at Baslow Hall is a dream place for a relaxed getaway, with splendid cooking, especially friendly service, and the nearby delights of the Peak District National Park. This superb house with its lead-paned windows set in stone frames, dark-oak paneling, and wide-plank wooden floors has the feeling of a Tudor manor, yet it was built only in 1907 as a home for the Reverend Jeremiah Stockdale. It continued as a home until 1989 when Susan and Max Fischer purchased it to house their successful restaurant Fischer's and also provide the most tasteful of accommodation. The house is furnished and decorated with imagination and flair, with a delightful use of soft yet quite vivid colors to create a feeling of warmth. Additional, lovely garden rooms surround an adjacent courtyard—four have views of the little walled garden while the fifth has a secluded private entry—perfect for hiding away. Max is a dedicated chef, offering traditional English dishes as well as more elaborate fare on his mouthwatering menus. The Max menu is a simpler, less expensive dining alternative to the dinner menu. The surrounding countryside offers plenty to keep you busy for a week or longer—Chatsworth House, Haddon Hall, lovely villages, and glorious scenery. *Directions:* Exit the M1 motorway at junction 29 and follow signs for Chatsworth through Chesterfield to Baslow where you follow the A623, Manchester road. Baslow Hall is on the right.

FISCHER'S AT BASLOW HALL
Owners: Susan & Max Fischer
Calver Road
Baslow
Derbyshire DE45 1RR, England
Tel: (01246) 583259, Fax: (01246) 583818
11 rooms
Double: £120–£180
Open: all year, Credit cards: all major
karenbrown.com/ews/fischersatbaslowhall.html

From the moment you enter through the rustic porchway into the long, low, whitewashed Pheasant inn, you are captivated by its charms: a front parlor all decked in chintz with an old-fashioned, open fire; a dimly lit, Dickensian bar with tobacco-stained walls and ceiling, oak settles, and clusters of tables and chairs; a long, low-beamed dining room, its tables covered with crisp damask cloths; dramatic fresh and dried flower arrangements; a blazing fire in the hearth beneath a copper hood in the large, airy sitting room, and the former farmhouse kitchen dating back over 400 years. It is reputed that the legendary John Peel used to be one of the 19th-century regulars in the bar. I can attest to the deliciousness of their traditional Cumbrian afternoon tea. Each spacious and inviting bedroom has a large, modern bathroom. Garden lodge rooms offer peace and quiet. Behind the inn, a garden with benches lining its pathways tumbles into the beechwoods, which belongs (as does the inn) to Lord Inglewood's estate. The Pheasant sits on a quiet country lane, just out of sight of Bassenthwaite Lake. This is a peaceful part of the Lake District with beautiful views round every corner. Sailing, boating, fishing, bird watching, and, of course, walking are available nearby. *Directions:* The Pheasant is signposted on the A66, at the head of Bassenthwaite Lake, between Keswick and Cockermouth.

THE PHEASANT
Manager: Matthew Wylie
Bassenthwaite Lake
Cumbria CA15 9YE, England
Tel: (017687) 76234, Fax: (017687) 76002
15 rooms
Double: £140–£180
Closed: Christmas, Credit cards: MC, VS
karenbrown.com/ews/pheasant.html

Renovated and restored to its original Georgian style, and with all the conveniences expected of a thoroughly modern townhouse hotel, Dukes enjoys a prominent position on Great Pulteney Street, one of Bath's more prestigious boulevards. As might be expected, the bedrooms and suites are named after dukes. Most are airy and spacious and have period plasterwork details and enormous sash windows looking out onto the bustle of the surrounding streets. The hotel has a chic, green-panelled bar which leads into a delightful, peaceful patio garden and provides a relaxing atmosphere to enjoy a light bite and a drink. Dukes, given adequate notice, accepts well-behaved dogs in the guestrooms. A level, five minutes' walk from the famous Pulteney Bridge, the hotel is superbly positioned to take advantage of this lovely city. *Directions:* Leave the M4 motorway at Junction 18 and head south on the A46. After approximately 9 miles, at the bottom of a long hill, follow signs onto the A4. On the outskirts of town turn left at a traffic light, signposted A36 Warminster (Bathwick Road). At the first roundabout take the second exit into Sydney Place and approximately 150 yards farther on take a half right turn into Great Pulteney Street. Dukes is on the left.

DUKES HOTEL
Manager: Christophe Bonneau
Great Pulteney Street
Bath
Somerset BA2 4DN, England
Tel: (01225) 787960, Fax: (01225) 787961
18 rooms
Double: £95–£205
Open: all year, Credit cards: all major
karenbrown.com/ews/dukesbath.html

If you want a fancy city hotel, The Queensberry Hotel is not for you. However, if you want a small, very friendly, good-value-for-money hotel in the heart of Georgian Bath on a quiet, side street, then this is the place to stay. The folks who run the front desk are very helpful and friendly and have lots of information on Bath, which you can peruse in the adjacent comfortable drawing room. After a day of sightseeing, there is no more pleasant place to relax than on the back patio with a drink. Guestrooms that were at one time enormous drawing rooms with tall and often decorative plaster ceilings command the highest tariff. I loved my attic room with its windows looking out across the rooftops, though I appreciated having the elevator as an alternative to the stairs. In fact, whether your room is below stairs or under the rafters, you will find it appealingly decorated and tastefully appointed. A Continental breakfast is served in your bedroom, while a full breakfast can be enjoyed in the stylish, contemporary "Olive Tree" basement restaurant. *Directions:* When you make your reservation, ask the hotel to send you the very specific directions on how to find The Queensberry, just a few minutes' walk from the Royal Crescent. On arrival at the hotel, double-park in front while you unload your bags and receive advice on parking.

THE QUEENSBERRY HOTEL
Owners: Helen & Laurence Beere
Russel Street
Bath
Somerset BA1 2QF, England
Tel: (01225) 447928, Fax: (01225) 446065
29 rooms
Double: £100–£285*
*Continental breakfast included, full breakfast: £9–£14
Open: all year, Credit cards: MC, VS
karenbrown.com/ews/queensberry.html

Over two hundred years ago, when the gentry came to Bath to "take the waters," the Royal Crescent was the most prestigious address. Two townhouses in the center of this famous cobbled crescent have been restored and incorporated into an elegant hotel complex with the Dower House, the Bath House, the Garden Villa, and the Pavilion buildings, reached by way of the garden. Furnished with period furniture and works of art, the hotel re-creates the atmosphere of Georgian Bath, which was the social center of England for many years. The elegant drawing room sets the quiet, refined, formal atmosphere of the hotel. An additional drawing room and the gourmet restaurant, Pimpernels, are found in the Dower House. In the main house the sweeping central staircase or the book-lined "library" lift gives access to the stylish, high-ceilinged bedrooms and sumptuous suites, many with ornate plasterwork ceilings. Two totally elegant suites are the Sir Percy Blakeney and the exquisite Duke of York. A range of grand suites and rooms is also found across the garden. To one side of the garden is a small plunge pool where you can swim against a current; to the other is the Bath House, an adult spa that takes you through a sequence of bathing and cleansing—the ultimate in relaxation and pleasure. In the evening you can take a ride in a launch along the canal. *Directions:* The Royal Crescent is prominently marked on any detailed map of Bath.

THE ROYAL CRESCENT HOTEL
Owner: Von Essen Hotels
16 Royal Crescent
Bath
Somerset BA1 2LS, England
Tel: (01225) 823333, Fax: (01225) 339401
45 rooms
Double: £240–£840
Open: all year, Credit cards: all major
karenbrown.com/ews/royalcrescent.html

Dating back in part as far as the 13th century, replete with a fascinating mix of mullioned windows, stone floors, heavy wooden beams, and large open fireplaces, The Bridge House is awash in character. Originally a clergy house, communal home to ten or twelve priests, it has been tastefully converted to a classic small country hotel and restaurant by owners Jane and Peter Pinkster. With flowers and books tucked away in various nooks and crannies, the public rooms are cozy and relaxed but on finer days guests may choose to retreat to the sunny conservatory or venture outside to the walled garden. Fourteen comfortable bedrooms of different shapes and sizes are distributed between the main house and coach house annex across the courtyard to the rear. All have fresh flowers, bright patterned bedspreads, crisp linens, fluffy pillows, and clean, well-appointed en suite bathrooms. Our favorites were the larger "superior" rooms in the main house. At the heart of the operation is the food—fresh ingredients from local farms and fishing ports are artfully transformed by the kitchen staff and served in the paneled dining room. Beaminster has some lovely Georgian houses and there are fine gardens at Forde Abbey and Clapton Court. Nearby are Sherborne (castle and abbey), Cricket St. Thomas Wildlife Park, and Cerne Abbas (abbey and giant cut in the chalk hills almost 2,000 years ago). *Directions:* Beaminster is on the A3066 between Crewkerne and Bridport.

THE BRIDGE HOUSE HOTEL
Owner: Peter Pinkster
Manager: Michelle Pursall
Prout Bridge
Beaminster
Dorset DT8 3AY, England
Tel: (01308) 862200, Fax: (01308) 863700
14 rooms
Double: £115–£145
Open: all year, Credit cards: all major
karenbrown.com/ews/bridgehouse.html

Arriving in Blanchland gives one a sense of achievement, for it is far from the beaten path, nestled in a little valley amidst moors and forests. With little cottages, a church, and the Lord Crewe Arms set round a cobbled square, it is a fascinating village which has changed little since it was bequeathed by the Crewe family, in 1721, to a trust that administers the village. Public rooms are intriguing: the abbey kitchen is now the reception-lounge with two elegant old sofas drawn round its fire; the adjacent room has a gigantic fireplace with a "priest's hole" where General Forster hid after his band of Royalist Jacobites was defeated at the Battle of Preston in 1715; the bar with its barrel-vaulted ceiling was once an abbey storeroom. Stairs twist up and around to the bedrooms: Number 17 with large windows overlooking the garden, and 19 with its four-poster bed set under the eaves, are the most spacious. Across the cobbled square an additional ten bedrooms occupy The Angel, a former rival temperance hotel. September is the biggest bedroom with a large attic window looking across the square. The Lord Crewe Arms is an ideal base for explorations of Hadrian's Wall and visiting Beamish Museum. *Directions:* From Newcastle take the A69 to Hexham and turn left in the center of town for the 10-mile drive to Blanchland.

LORD CREWE ARMS
Owners: Alex Todd, & Lindsey Sands
Blanchland
County Durham DH8 9SP, England
Tel: (01434) 675251, Fax: (01434) 675337
18 rooms
Double: £120–£150
Open: all year, Credit cards: all major
karenbrown.com/ews/lordcrewe.html

The Devonshire, previously a coaching inn, is now a traditional country house hotel resplendent with swimming pool and health spa. All the bedrooms in the Wharfdale wing are on the ground floor. If you stay there, request a room that looks out across the garden and fields to the distant hills. Rooms in the original coaching inn are especially lovely: Shepherd has lovely paintings of sheep; Crace has an elegant four-poster; and Chatsworth, with its fireplace, is especially spacious. The Duke and Duchess of Devonshire's family portraits add richness to the Long Lounge with its many groupings of comfortable chairs. Dinner in the Burlington restaurant, a beautiful conservatory, is a formal affair. For a move from country house to modern, you might want to frequent the adjacent brasserie and bar, reached by a covered flagstone passageway. Just across the garden, the barns have undergone a skillful conversion to a spa with indoor swimming pool, gym, and beauty salons. Fast roads lead to York and Harrogate. Upper Wharfedale—one of the most scenic Yorkshire Dales—begins at your back door, the ruins of Bolton Abbey are across the fields, and a short drive brings you to Haworth and the Brontë sisters' parsonage. *Directions:* The hotel is on the B6160, 250 yards north of its roundabout junction off the A59, Skipton to Harrogate Road.

THE DEVONSHIRE ARMS
Owners: Duke & Duchess of Devonshire
Manager: Eamon Elliot
Bolton Abbey
North Yorkshire BD23 6AJ, England
Tel: (01756) 710441, Fax: (01756) 710564
41 rooms
Double: £220–£380
Open: all year, Credit cards: all major
karenbrown.com/ews/devonshirearms.html

Standing high in wooded grounds just outside Borrowdale with outstanding views across the surrounding countryside, The Leathes Head is a classic, small country house hotel. This gabled Edwardian house, constructed of local Lakeland stone, has been completely renovated and refurbished by owners Janice and Roy Smith, retaining many original architectural features, stained glass, old fireplaces, and plasterwork details to combine the charm of a bygone era with modern standards of comfort and convenience. The house has been tastefully decorated and furnished in keeping with its age. All of the eleven bedrooms have en suite bathrooms. Our favorites were the two superior double rooms with magnificent views to Catbells and Maiden Moor. The restaurant uses local produce (as available), offers a wide-ranging, constantly changing menu and has established a fine reputation. The cuisine is supported by Roy's wine list, handpicked but very reasonably priced. Afternoon tea or pre-dinner drinks are served in the conservatory, furnished with comfortable wicker chairs and a thoughtful supply of games, magazines and books, and overlooks the grounds. On chillier, darker days, you might want to retreat to the snug bar. Breakfast ranges from "healthy" to "Full English" and caters to the hearty appetites of walkers who frequent the local hills. *Directions:* Leathes Hotel is 3-1/2 miles south of Keswick on B5289 Borrowdale Road. The hotel is on the left.

THE LEATHES HEAD HOTEL   **New**
Owners: Janice & Roy Smith
Borrowdale, Keswick
Cumbria CA12 5UY, England
Tel: (017687) 77247, Fax: (017687) 77363
12 rooms
Double: £146–£166*
*Includes dinner, bed & breakfast
Open: mid-Feb to mid-Nov, Credit cards: MC, VS
karenbrown.com/ews/leathes.html

Woolley Grange, a gracious, 17th-century manor just outside Bradford-on-Avon, is the only listing in this guide that actively encourages families—they have a very relaxed attitude towards children, and a resident dog completes the picture. The old coach house has been converted to a nursery (there is also a huge games room for older children) where children can spend a few hours each day. Little ones can have lunch and tea in the nursery and be tucked up in bed or watch a video in the library while parents enjoy the most excellent of dinners in the lovely dining room—the essence of a stay at Woolley Grange is eating the most delicious food. The bedrooms are scattered throughout the rambling house, the large cottage across the courtyard and newly converted pavilion. Many have old fireplaces, most have creaking old floorboards, and all have sturdy antiques and old brass or Victorian beds topped with goose-down duvets. There is a large heated swimming pool and croquet lawn on the grounds. The area is packed with interesting things to do and places to go: historic Bath and Wells, inviting Bradford-on-Avon and Lacock, Longleat House and Safari Park, and Stourhead House and Gardens. *Directions:* Woolley Grange is 8 miles from Bath at Woolley Green, off the B3109 north of Bradford-on-Avon.

WOOLLEY GRANGE
Manager: Clare Hammond
Woolley Green
Bradford-on-Avon
Wiltshire BA15 1TX, England
Tel: (01225) 864705, Fax: (01225) 864059
26 rooms
Double: £150–£340
Open: all year, Credit cards: all major
karenbrown.com/ews/woolley.html

Farlam Hall is a superb place to hide away for a relaxed holiday and be thoroughly spoiled, enjoying the pampering attentions of this family-run hotel. Mum, dad, son, daughter, and spouses make up the friendly team of one of only a handful of British hotels admitted to the French Relais & Châteaux group. You enter directly into the reception lounge, which is full of sofas and chairs — a perfect spot for afternoon tea. The quality of everything, from the abundant antique furniture to the sumptuous food, is a delight. The same quality and good taste continue in the bedrooms, which vary greatly in shape and size. My favorite larger rooms are the Garden Room, a grand, high-ceilinged room with an enormous four-poster bed, and the Guest Room, a spacious corner room whose large bathroom sports a Jacuzzi tub and separate shower. While Farlam Hall is a perfect place to break your journey if you are traveling between England and Scotland, it would be a shame to spend only one night in this charming hotel. Nearby sightseeing includes Carlisle and Hadrian's Wall. Day trips can be made to the Lake District and the Scottish border towns. *Directions:* Leave the M6 motorway at junction 43 and take the A69 towards Newcastle for 12 miles to the A689 signposted Alston. The hotel is on your left after 2 miles (not in the village of Farlam).

FARLAM HALL
Owners: Quinion & Stevenson Families
Brampton
Cumbria CA8 2NG, England
Tel: (016977) 46234, Fax: (016977) 46683
12 rooms
Double: £230–£295*
*Includes dinner, bed & breakfast
Closed: Dec 23 to 31, Credit cards: MC, VS
Relais & Châteaux
karenbrown.com/ews/farlam.html

Separated from the main road through Broadway by a grassy green, The Broadway Hotel dates back to Elizabethan times though it has had various additions over the years. The heart of the hotel is a tall, galleried sitting room whose white-plasterwork beamed walls rise to a raftered ceiling. The adjacent Jockey Bar with its horseracing memorabilia is popular with locals and full of old-world pub atmosphere. Tables in the restaurant are set in a room open to the bannistered upstairs hallway or tucked cozily under beams in a room dressed with old copper. Bedrooms stretch back in two wings with one wing accessed off an open stairway that winds up from the dining room. All the bedrooms are decorated in country-house style using modern fabrics and antiques. We enjoyed a lovely, quiet room located at the end of the hallway and overlooking the back lawn. The feeling was very traditional, with dark woods complemented by handsome plaid fabrics. Broadway is one of the most bustling Cotswold villages, along with Chipping Campden, Stow-on-the-Wold, and Moreton-in-Marsh. While in the area do not overlook the quieter villages such as nearby Snowshill where Snowshill Manor, a lovely Tudor home, is open to the public. *Directions:* Broadway is off the A44 between Evesham and Stow-on-the-Wold. The Broadway Hotel is located on the High Street with a car park to the rear.

THE BROADWAY HOTEL
Manager: Simon Foster
The Green
Broadway
Worcestershire WR12 7AA, England
Tel: (01386) 852401, Fax: (01386) 853879
20 rooms
Double: £135–£185
Open: all year, Credit cards: all major
karenbrown.com/ews/broadwayhotel.html

Set in the popular Cotswold village of Broadway, The Lygon Arms has been an inn since the 16th century. Its numerous little nooks include the "Gin Corner" with its old log fire (the original snug); the Inglenook lounge, the inn's ancient kitchen, its huge fireplace hung with blackened spits and hooks; and the domed-ceiling drawing room, all chintz and elegance. The main wing with its creaking floors, heavy beams, and charming rooms furnished with grand antique pieces has a range of different rooms from the least expensive with bathrooms down the hall to the most expensive: the Great Chamber whose ceiling soars to a thicket of beams and the Charles I suite whose oak paneling has a secret staircase. A wing of turn-of-the-century rooms leads to the 1960s Garden Wing with numerous contemporary-style rooms. Old adjoining properties have been taken over: a charming thatched cottage in the garden now houses four of the most luxurious bedrooms; the 18th-century Great Hall with its minstrels' gallery is now the Lygon's restaurant; and across the courtyard is the Lygon Arms spa where residents can enjoy a game of billiards, use the weight room, or swim in the luxurious heated pool. In an adjacent house is Oliver's brasserie. *Directions:* Broadway is off the A44 between Evesham and Stow-on-the-Wold. The Lygon Arms is located on the High Street with a car park to the rear.

THE LYGON ARMS
Manager: Andrew Buchenar
Broadway
Worcestershire WR12 7DU, England
Tel: (01386) 854405, Fax: (01386) 854470
69 rooms
Double: £240–£495*
*Service charge: 5%
Open: all year, Credit cards: all major
karenbrown.com/ews/lygonarms.html

Two miles from the hustle and bustle of Broadway is the pretty, small village of Buckland where, adjacent to the village church, sits Buckland Manor surrounded by acres of gorgeous gardens. Wisteria hugs the walls, blowzy roses fill the flowerbeds, and a rushing stream tumbles beside the woodland walk. The exterior sets the tone for an interior where everything is decorated to perfection. Add masses of flowers and enviable antiques and you have the perfect country house hotel. Relax and enjoy a drink before the huge fireplace in the richly paneled lounge, curl up with a book in the sunny morning room, and relish the sense of occasion in the refined dining room. Bedrooms are elegant and every attention has been paid to every luxurious detail—some have wood-burning fireplaces and four-poster beds. From the moment Graham, the hall porter, greets you at the door you will be enveloped in the atmosphere of hushed gentility that pervades this gracious Cotswold manor. Warm weather enables you to enjoy the swimming pool, tennis court, and croquet lawn. Surrounding Buckland are other Cotswold villages with such appealing names as Chipping Campden, Upper and Lower Slaughter, Stow-on-the-Wold, and Upper and Lower Swell. Stratford-upon-Avon, Worcester, Bath, and Oxford are all within an hour's driving distance. Garden lovers will enjoy Kiftsgate, Hidcote Manor, and Batsford. *Directions:* Buckland is 1½ miles from Broadway on the B4632.

BUCKLAND MANOR
Manager: Nigel Power
Buckland
Worcestershire WR12 7LY, England
Tel: (01386) 852626, Fax: (01386) 853557
13 rooms
Double: £235–£370
Open: all year, Credit cards: all major
Relais & Châteaux
karenbrown.com/ews/bucklandmanor.html

The clomp of hooves as horses pulled carriages down the main street of Burford has long disappeared, but the inns that provided lodging and food to weary travelers remain. If you are in search of a simple, quaint hostelry, but with modern food and service, you can do no better than to base yourself at The Lamb for the duration of your Cotswold stay. A tall, upholstered settee sits before the fireplace on the flagstone floor of the reception hall. A display of gleaming brass jelly-molds catches the eye, and an air of times long past pervades the place, particularly in winter when the air is heavy with the scent of woodsmoke and a flickering fire burns in the grate. Little staircases and corridors zigzag you up and down to the little bedrooms, all en suite and recently refurbished in modern country decor. Also recently refurbished, the restaurant offers a full à la carte menu or, if you prefer to eat less formally, a new bar menu is available. The homey, little bar with its stone-flagged floor and wooden settees has a solid mixture of character and atmosphere. Burford's main street is bordered by numerous hostelries, antique, gift, and teashops. There are mellow Cotswold villages to explore. Blenheim Palace and Oxford are less than an hour's drive away. *Directions:* Burford is midway between Oxford and Cheltenham (A40). The Lamb Inn is on Sheep Street, just off the village center.

THE LAMB INN
Owners: Rachel & Bruno Cappuccini
Manager: Caroline Knight
Sheep Street
Burford
Oxfordshire OX18 4LR, England
Tel: (01993) 823155, Fax: (01993) 822228
15 rooms
Double: £140–£200
Open: all year, Credit cards: MC, VS
karenbrown.com/ews/lambinn.html

The Fell Hotel (as it was known) has long been serving visitors to this lovely part of the Yorkshire Dales and acquired the "Devonshire" in its title in 1998 when it was purchased by the Duke and Duchess of Devonshire to be a sister hotel to the Devonshire Arms, a country house hotel just down the road. Consequently, I expected a traditional interior for this sturdy Yorkshire hotel looking over the River Wharfe to the village of Burnsall, but the interior could not be further from traditional—it is dashingly modern. With the decor offering a broad palette of vivid colors, any rainy-day gloom is instantly dispelled. Relax in the boldly decorated bar and enjoy lunch or an evening meal in the restaurant or the conservatory. Selections are made from the menu or from daily specials posted on the board. Bedrooms are found on two floors (no elevator) and range from the crisp Linton room, all decked out in black and white, to oh-so-sunny Cracoe, all in bright yellow hues. Walking is de rigueur in this part of the world and scenic footpaths are on your doorstep. Just down the road are the ruins of Bolton Abbey, while just up the road is the village of Grassington. Harrogate is close at hand while York is an hour's drive away. Ask about the very-good-value-for-money B&B plus dinner rates. *Directions:* From the A59 (Skipton to Harrogate road) take the B6160 past Bolton Abbey and north to Burnsall. As you see the village below to your right, you find the hotel on your left.

🍵 🚵 🖃 ☎ 🧍 👫 🏇 P 🍴

THE DEVONSHIRE FELL
Owners: Duke & Duchess of Devonshire
Manager: Neil Waterfield
Skipton
Burnsall
North Yorkshire ND23 6BT, England
Tel: (01756) 718111, Fax: (01756) 729009
12 rooms
Double: £115–£170
Open: all year, Credit cards: all major
karenbrown.com/ews/devonshirefell.html

The Hotel Felix, which opened in early 2003, is situated just 1 mile northwest of Cambridge city center in 4-acres of tranquil landscaped garden. Its central core, a beautifully restored and renovated brownstone Victorian mansion, houses the restaurant and café-bar as well as three large, airy bedrooms, replete with old architectural features, fine plasterwork, and moldings, tucked away on the first and second floors. All other guestrooms are located in two brand-new, custom-built wings that have been tastefully merged with the old building. All of the rooms embody an opulent simplicity complemented by state-of-the-art technology, internet and email access, and satellite movies and hi-fi system. Pastel decorations are offset with vivid splashes of color. Large wooden headboards, contemporary furniture, white Egyptian-cotton sheets and pillowcases, and comfortable duvets complete the picture. Ample modern bathrooms feature earth-tone tiles and sparkling white fixtures. The restaurant and adjacent café-bar with their clubby atmosphere are the focal point of the Felix and on pleasant days service is available on the terrace overlooking the gardens. *Directions:* Exit the A14 onto the A1307 (Huntingdon Road) and Hotel Felix is located off Whitehouse Lane half a mile down on the left.

HOTEL FELIX
Manager: Shara Ross
Whitehouse Lane, Huntingdon Road
Cambridge CB3 0LX, England
Tel: (01223) 277977, Fax: (01223) 277973
52 rooms
Double: £158–£298
Open: all year, Credit cards: all major
karenbrown.com/ews/felix.html

Castle Combe is a picture-perfect example of a Cotswold village—one hundred local residents, gold-stone buildings, slate roofs, exposed timbers, and the inevitable burbling stream. Little has changed since the 15th-century, the last house was constructed in 1647. This idyllic setting with the complete absence of street lights and television aerials has won the "Prettiest Village in England" award many times and provided the backdrop for such famous movies as Dr. Doolittle. Nestled in the market place, you'll find the Castle Inn Hotel. Inside, narrow hallways and staircases lead to the guestrooms, all named after English trees, in a wide range of shapes and sizes. The décor is quirky and eclectic: delicate pastels offset with huge splashes of intense color, brass beds or four-posters (take your choice), stuffed animals and collectables. My favorite room had a hand-painted thatch ceiling, complete with elves and pixies. All have nicely equipped en suite bathrooms, fluffy bathrobes, carafes of sherry, bottled water, candies, and fresh fruit. Breakfast is served in the conservatory with its draped ceiling or (weather permitting) outside on the patio. The old wood-beamed restaurant, walls hung with hunting scenes, is open for dinner and a reasonably priced international wine list is available. Retire to the fire in one of the lounges, or sample one of the impressive inventory of single malt whiskies. *Directions:* Castle Combe is 7 miles from junction 17 on the M4.

CASTLE INN HOTEL   **New**
Owner: Vanessa Rees
Castle Combe
Wiltshire SN14 7HN, England
Tel: 0129 783030, Fax: 0129 782315
13 rooms
Double: £100–£165
Open: all year, Credit cards: all major
karenbrown.com/ews/castleinn.html

Paul and Kay Henderson have achieved their goal of providing one of the finest small hotels and restaurants in England. Guests have come to expect the best and this is what they receive. Prices are high but so are the standards of luxury and the attention to detail. There are 15 lovely guestrooms: 14 in the beautiful, Tudor-style home and a 2-bedroom suite in a quaint, thatched cottage overlooking the croquet lawns. The largest bedrooms are on the second floor and those at the front of the house offer lovely views across the valley. The public rooms are paneled in oak with open log fires burning throughout the year. Chef Michael Caines professionally designs the evening meal, considering the fresh produce available each day from local farmers, the hotel's own garden, and the catch from local fishermen. Paul is particularly proud of his extensive wine list, one of the finest in Britain. Chagford is a delightful country town on the edge of Dartmoor. The wild beauty of Dartmoor, with its sheltered villages and towns beneath the looming moor, has a magic all its own—country rambles and cream teas are de rigueur when visiting this area. *Directions:* From Chagford Square turn right (at Lloyds Bank) into Mill Street. After 150 yards fork right and go downhill to Factory Crossroad. Go straight across into Holy Street and follow the lane for 1½ miles to the end.

GIDLEIGH PARK
Owners: Kay & Paul Henderson
Manager: Catherine Endacott
Chagford
Devon TQ13 8HH, England
Tel: (01647) 432367, Fax: (01647) 432574
15 rooms Double: £450–£575*
*Includes dinner, bed & breakfast
Open: all year, Credit cards: MC, VS
Relais & Châteaux
karenbrown.com/ews/gidleigh.html

Cheltenham was a fashionable destination during the Regency period and today the classical squares and terraces built in delightful garden settings are the town's pride. A fine Regency villa on the edge of Pittville Park has been beautifully restored and opened as a most attractive hotel by Darryl Gregory. Guests share the comfortable library-sitting room with Emily the cat and enjoy drinks and after-dinner coffee in the high-ceilinged drawing room-cum-bar. While there are several restaurants within walking distance, you can do no better than to dine in the hotel, choosing your meal from the seasonal menu or enjoying the meal of the day. The elegant, smartly decorated bedrooms are named after historic figures associated with the house. I especially enjoyed the Duke of Gloucester room, richly decorated in shades of dark red, and Mead with its sunny yellow decor. Billed as the capital of the Cotswolds, Cheltenham offers excellent shopping and lots of specialist antique shops. Horseracing takes place at Cheltenham during the autumn and winter months. A ten-minute drive finds you in the midst of the honey-colored stone Cotswold villages. *Directions:* Arriving in Cheltenham, follow signs for town center onto the one-way system, then follow signposts for Evesham. The Hotel on the Park is on the left, just as you reach Pittville Park (right) after passing a row of Regency townhouses.

HOTEL ON THE PARK
Owner: Darryl Gregory
Evesham Road
Cheltenham
Gloucestershire GL52 2AH, England
Tel: (01242) 518898, Fax: (01242) 511526
12 rooms
Double: £114–£164*
*Breakfast not included: £7.25–£9.50
Open: all year, Credit cards: all major
karenbrown.com/ews/hotelonthepark.html

Amongst the Cotswolds' picturesque villages, you'll discover the town of Chipping Campden, rich in history and exquisite architecture, where Cotswold House Hotel stands in Regency splendor in the ancient market place. Here Ian and Christa Taylor have put together an inspired mixture of the contemporary and the traditional to create a lovely hotel. You'll find sublime comfort and luxury, and cuisine of the highest quality, a hotel of charming individuality and friendly service. All 20 bedrooms, including the beamed garden cottages and suite, have recently been refurbished. Huge beds, with cashmere under-blankets, grace the delightfully decorated bedrooms. Choose the bedding or pillow style you prefer, select the contents of your mini-bar, and enjoy the high-tech entertainment system. Juliana's Restaurant and the more informal all-day Hicks' Brasserie offer dishes with plenty of flair. Cotswold House is ideally placed for visiting Shakespeare's Stratford, Regency Cheltenham, Warwick Castle, and many historic houses and gardens. Add to this the hotel's special touches—tour guides, picnics, day-membership at local golf clubs—and you have the perfect recipe for a truly memorable stay. *Directions:* From Broadway take the A44 towards Moreton-in-Marsh and turn left for Chipping Campden. Turn right at the T-junction into the High Street, and Cotswold House is on your left in the main square. (Free parking for residents behind the hotel.)

COTSWOLD HOUSE HOTEL
Owners: Christa & Ian Taylor
The Square
Chipping Campden
Gloucestershire GL55 6AN, England
Tel: (01386) 840330, Fax: (01386) 840310
20 rooms
Double: £200–£700
Open: all year, Credit cards: all major
karenbrown.com/ews/cotswoldhousehotel.html

Built in the 1930s as a re-creation of a medieval manor that once stood on the site, Bailiffscourt is today a lovely country hotel, an "authentic fake" set in spacious grounds. The snug, golden-stoned buildings really are authentic in that they are constructed from medieval stone, with woodwork and windows obtained from derelict cottages, mansions, and farmhouses. Thick stone walls, small mullioned windows, beamed ceilings, dark paneling, large open fireplaces, courtyards, peacocks, and pieces of medieval furniture all combine to give an "old-world" atmosphere. The interconnecting lounges have warm colors, tapestries, and log fires. Flagstoned halls, reminiscent of castle passageways, lead to the large bedrooms, 13 of which have four-poster beds while 8 have working fireplaces. Bathrooms are large, with wonderful 1930s fixtures, and modern plumbing is a welcome 21st-century addition. Baylies, a decadent suite, has a bathroom with side-by-side "his and hers" baths. Guestrooms are also found in several outlying buildings. The grounds contain tennis courts, an indoor and outdoor swimming pool and a spa with six treatment rooms. Just minutes from the sea, Bailiffscourt is an ideal base for exploring the south coast, being close to Arundel's magnificent castle, the Pavilion at Brighton, Chichester's celebrated theatre, and glorious Goodwood. *Directions:* Bailiffscourt is between Littlehampton and Bognor Regis just off the A259.

BAILIFFSCOURT
Manager: Chris Alger
Climping
West Sussex BN17 5RW, England
Tel: (01903) 723511, Fax: (01903) 723107
39 rooms
Double: £225–£540
Open: all year, Credit cards: all major
karenbrown.com/ews/bailiffscourt.html

In the middle of the pretty redbrick village of Cuckfield you find Ockenden Manor, in part Tudor, with Victorian and contemporary additions. Viewing the manor from the garden, you appreciate that this combination of building styles is very pleasing. The spacious sitting room overlooks the garden and the adjacent dining room, with its dark-oak paneling and low, decorative-plasterwork ceiling, is most attractive. A maze of winding corridors and stairs leads to the atmospheric rooms in the older wing with their paneled walls, uneven floors, and plethora of four-poster beds (mostly queen-sized). I particularly enjoyed the Charles room with its large stone fireplace, Elizabeth for its third-floor isolation atop a narrow staircase, and Master, a spacious, paneled twin-bedded room with an adorable little parlor overlooking the garden. Avoid the possibility of getting lost in the maze of corridors and opt for easier-to-locate rooms in the Garden Wing with its new rooms made to look old. Less than a half-hour drive finds you in Brighton where seaside honky-tonk contrasts with the vivid spectacle of the onion domes of the Royal Pavilion, the Prince Regent's extravaganza of a home. Enjoy browsing in Brighton's Lanes where old fishermen's cottages are now antique and gift shops. *Directions:* From Gatwick airport take the M23/A23 to the B2115 signposted Cuckfield. In Cuckfield village, turn right into Ockenden Lane—the manor is at the end.

OCKENDEN MANOR
Manager: Adam Smith
Ockenden Lane
Cuckfield
West Sussex RH17 5LD, England
Tel: (01444) 416111, Fax: (01444) 415549
22 rooms
Double: £160–£320
Open: all year, Credit cards: all major
karenbrown.com/ews/ockenden.html

This dignified old house was built in 1840 by a local lad, Sir Charles Hanson, who, having made a fortune in Canada, returned home to construct an impressive mansion. Fortunately, it has come into the hands of the Luxury Family Hotels group who have lovingly restored, decorated, and furnished the place. As soon as you walk in the front door you catch the spirit of the house with its spacious, airy rooms, sturdy antiques, huge windows, and comfortable, inviting settees and armchairs—all of this without one iota of hauteur. Dine al fresco in the informal Palm Court terrace or enjoy classic country-house fare in the plush, oak-paneled restaurant. A new wing of rooms was being added at the time of my visit in 2003. Suites in the older part of the house often have a small bedroom and a sitting room in addition to the bathroom. Additional bedrooms are found in the adjacent coach house. There's a lot to keep you busy: splashing in the pool and playing badminton, Nintendo, table tennis, table soccer, and pool. For the under-sevens the Bears' Den is staffed by nannies. It's a wonderful place—a perfect base for exploring Cornwall with its rugged coastline and plethora of gardens. *Directions:* One mile after Lostwithiel (going south on the A390) turn left onto the B3269 to Fowey. Follow the main road into town, bearing right on Hanson Drive. Pass the car park on the right and Fowey Hall is the next entry to the right.

FOWEY HALL
Managers: Hazel & Tim Brocklebank
Hanson Drive
Fowey
Cornwall PL23 1ET, England
Tel: (01726) 833866, Fax: (01726) 834100
25 rooms
Double: £200–£410*
*Includes dinner, bed & breakfast
Open: all year, Credit cards: all major
karenbrown.com/ews/fowey.html

Fowey is one of Cornwall's most picturesque villages. Former fishermen's cottages and narrow streets step down the steep hillside to the river estuary where boats bob in the sheltered harbor. Sitting beside the water, The Marina Hotel was built in 1815 as a handsome townhouse. It would be a shame to stay here and not have a bedroom with a view, the best views being from rooms 4, 6 and 10 with French windows opening onto private balconies. At the top of the house two lovely rooms capture the same outlook through little curved windows. Three rooms are found in Ashley house across the street. If you want to be right beside the water, opt for the Focastle Suite, a wooden cabin on the lower patio with a nautical pine interior. While the bedroom and sitting room face the patio, French windows open to a private waterside terrace. Every table in the award-winning Waterside Restaurant looks out over the harbor and the menu includes lots of fish choices. Guests often come to see the places where Fowey's most illustrious former resident, Daphne du Maurier, set her most famous novels. *Directions:* One mile after Lostwithiel (going south on the A390) turn left onto the B3269 to Fowey. Continue down into the narrow lanes of the village and turn right on the Esplanade. Park outside the hotel to unload and get parking directions.

THE MARINA HOTEL
Owner: Stephen Westwell
Manager: James Coggan
17 Esplanade
Fowey
Cornwall PL23 1HY, England
Tel: (01726) 833315, Fax: (01726) 832779
14 rooms
Double: £140–£220
Open: Mar to mid-Dec, Credit cards: all major
karenbrown.com/ews/marina.html

At the mouth of the River Helford you find the Tregildry Hotel set on a bluff high above the sea overlooking the river estuary and, in the distance, the broad reaches of Falmouth Bay—a magnificent seascape. Perhaps a former owner's desire to cram as much building as possible into this lovely spot accounts for Tregildry's higgledy-piggledy exterior. However, under the direction of Huw and Lynne Phillips Tregildry has become a harmonious whole. The spacious drawing room, decorated in soft pastels, leads to a cozy nook with low sofas drawn round the fire. Next door the dining room has an almost Caribbean flavor with high-back cane chairs. The bedrooms have been decorated with light rattan furniture contrasting with Provençal-type draperies and bedspreads, giving a crisp, airy feel to the rooms. We particularly liked room 3 with its large balcony, the view from room 2, and the spaciousness of rooms 1 and 6. Room 7, just off the dining room, is especially appreciated by folks who have difficulty with stairs. Huw is in charge of the kitchen while Lynne is the convivial hostess, making sure that guests are well taken care of. A path leads down the hillside to join the coastal walking trail. *Directions:* From Helston take the A3083 (Lizard road) for 3 miles, turn left on the B3293 signposted St. Keverne, and from here follow signposts carefully for Helford (you do not go there), then Manaccan, and finally Gillan. Tregildry is signposted from Gillan.

TREGILDRY HOTEL
Owners: Lynne & Huw Phillips
Manaccan, Helston
Gillan
Cornwall TR12 6HG, England
Tel: (01326) 231378, Fax: (01326) 231561
10 rooms
Double: £150–£190*
*Includes dinner, bed & breakfast
Open: Mar to Oct, Credit cards: MC, VS
karenbrown.com/ews/tregildry.html

The heart and soul of a successful country house hotel are its owners and at Stock Hill House Nita and Peter Hauser fill the bill perfectly, with the ebullient Nita presiding over the front of house and Peter being the chef. Prior to opening, Nita and Peter spent several years restoring and furnishing this Victorian home. The result is a pleasing, eclectic decor and the mood is that of a luxurious private residence where you can stroll through the acres of garden to work up an appetite. At dinner vegetables from the garden and local Dorset produce are the order of the day, but remember to save room for one of Austrian-born Peter's decadent desserts. Bedrooms are delightful, and while I was particularly drawn to the opportunity to repose in an elegant, extra-large, ornate wrought-iron bed, which once belonged to a Spanish princess, I settled on an equally lovely room with a non-historic bed and a large bathroom. This lovely hotel is the perfect place for you to treat yourself to an extra-special getaway. If you are tempted to leave the grounds, you'll find the location ideal for visiting Sherbourne Abbey, Stourhead Gardens, Wells Cathedral, Glastonbury with its King Arthur connections, and the Saxon town of Shaftesbury. *Directions:* Leave the M3 at junction 8 and take the A303 towards Exeter for 54 miles, turning onto the B3081 for Gillingham and Shaftesbury. Stock Hill House is on your right after 3 miles.

STOCK HILL HOUSE
Owners: Nita & Peter Hauser
Gillingham
Dorset SP8 5NR, England
Tel: (01747) 823626, Fax: (01747) 825628
9 rooms
Double: £250–£300*
*Includes dinner, bed & breakfast
Open: all year, Credit cards: MC, VS
Relais & Châteaux
karenbrown.com/ews/stockhill.html

Near the center of England lies Oakham, the proud capital of England's smallest county, Rutland. Close by is Rutland Water where you drive onto a spit of land stretching out into the middle of the lake. At its end is the quiet village of Hambleton and a jewel of a hotel, Hambleton Hall. The staff is caring, anxious above all else to please. The motto over the front door echoes the relaxed, happy atmosphere: "Fay Ce Que Voudras" or "Do As You Please". I cannot imagine anyone leaving Hambleton Hall discontented. The garden tumbles towards the vast expanse of water with rolling hills as a backdrop and behind a wall is a sheltered, heated pool. The interior is decorated with great flair and made lovely with enormous flower arrangements. The drawing room with its large inviting windows provides glorious water views. In fine weather enjoy lunch and tea on the terrace. Delicious smells will tempt you to the award-winning restaurant. The bedrooms are adorable, the decorations varying from soft English pastels to the vibrant rich colors of India. If you want total privacy, opt for the luxurious two-bedroom croquet pavilion. Sightseeing covers shopping in Oakham and Stamford, visits to the country houses of Burghley and Belton, and trips to Cambridge and Lincoln. *Directions:* From the A1 take the A606 (Oakham road) through Empingham and Whitwell and turn left for Hambleton.

HAMBLETON HALL
Owners: Stefa & Tim Hart
Hambleton
Rutland LE15 8TH, England
Tel: (01572) 756991, Fax: (01572) 724721
17 rooms
Double: £190–£600*
*Continental breakfast included, full breakfast: £12
Open: all year, Credit cards: all major
Relais & Châteaux
karenbrown.com/ews/hambleton.html

Harrogate's Hotel du Vin has its origins in eight Georgian style townhouses built facing "The Stray", a 200-acre, green parkland in the center of the city. Conjoined and a hotel since the 1930s, recently it has been completely renovated to take its rightful place as a member of the Hotel du Vin's stylish group. From the moment you step through the front door, you realize that you have arrived somewhere very special. The comfy, old leather armchairs in the entrance hall contrast with the starkly modern elegance of the oak and stainless steel staircase curving up to the guest rooms; the purple-clothed billiard table separated from the lobby by a wall of glass; and the open-plan bar with its hand-wrought, pewter-like stainless steel top and Cruvinet machine dispensing a variety of wines by the glass drawn directly from the cellar. The bustling, bistro-style restaurant features over 600 bins of wine, each one carefully chosen to accentuate the hallmark cuisine. The rooms are contemporary in décor, and even the smallest double is more than ample; all are luxuriously appointed to fulfill the needs of the most exacting traveler. The two "attic" suites approach decadence with eight-foot beds, dual side-by-side soaking tubs, and massive walk through showers. *Directions:* From A1, take A59 into Harrogate. Follow signs for "town centre" to Prince of Wales roundabout. Take the third exit (West Park). The hotel is on the right after the church.

HOTEL DU VIN   New
Manager: Stephen Watson
Prospect Place
Harrogate
Yorkshire HG1 1LB, England
Tel: 01423 856800, Fax: 01423 856801
43 rooms
Double: £95–£275
Open: all year, Credit cards: all major
karenbrown.com/ews/harrogate.html

Hathersage is a typically picturesque Derbyshire village situated in the lovely Hope Valley. It is a place that has impressed many visitors over the years, the most famous being Charlotte Brontë who was said to be so taken with it that she based parts of her novel "Jane Eyre" on it. The George sits imposingly at one end of the main street that runs through the village. Parts of the hotel date back to the 14th century when it was an alehouse, but it wasn't until the 1770s that The George became an inn. The lounge is a light and airy room, well furnished with lots of comfy sofas and decorated in blues and terra cottas, which give it warmth, while amusement is offered by the whirligig sculpture which periodically performs its antics. The bar, in the corner, makes this an ideal place to relax and enjoy a pre-dinner drink. The color schemes are carried through to the restaurant, which has an intimate, bistro-like feel. Upstairs, the bedrooms have the same light and airy feel as the lounge. I really liked room 3, which is pretty and spacious with a four-poster bed and a very unusual, round, stained-glass window depicting St. George. Hathersage is well placed for visiting the Peak District. *Directions:* Exit the M1 at junction 29 towards Baslow then take the A623 to the B6001 through Grindleford to Hathersage. At the junction with the main road The George faces you.

THE GEORGE
Owner: Eric Marsh, Manager: Philip Joseph
Hathersage
Derbyshire S32 1BB, England
Tel: (01433) 650436, Fax: (01433) 650099
19 rooms
Double: £125–£165
Open: all year, Credit cards: all major
karenbrown.com/ews/thegeorge.html

Helmsley, a collection of gray-stone houses grouped round a traditional market square, lies at the edge of the glorious North York Moors, an area of wild and magnificent scenery where webs of little roads cross vast stretches of heather-covered moorlands joining hamlets and villages nestled in snug green valleys. Bordering the market square, a traditional old Yorkshire coaching inn has served travelers for well for over 150 years in this beautiful town. Old adjoining properties have been taken over—a Georgian house and a black-and-white Tudor rectory. A large new wing of rooms has been built next to the lovely back garden where chairs are set on the lawns amongst beds of scented flowers. But The Black Swan is little changed: its higgledy-piggledy maze of little low-beamed rooms gives it a snug feeling, and its traditional furniture, lounges with old-fashioned chintz-covered chairs, and attentive staff all add to its charms. It is well worth paying the additional price for a "feature room". Eating and drinking is a great joy at The Black Swan. The chef knows how to satisfy Yorkshire tastes and appetites with traditional roasts, fillets, and chops. Fresh fish and vegetarian dishes are always on the menu. The most popular places to visit are Rievaulx Abbey, York, Castle Howard, Robin Hood's Bay, Whitby, and the folk museum at Hutton-le-Hole. *Directions:* Helmsley is on the A170 midway between Thirsk and Pickering.

THE BLACK SWAN
Manager: Simon Murphy
Helmsley
North Yorkshire Y06 5BJ, England
Tel: (01439) 770466, Fax: (01439) 770174
45 rooms
Double: £140–£160
Open: all year, Credit cards: all major
karenbrown.com/ews/blackswan.html

Langshott Manor is a beautiful Elizabethan house with 3 acres of gorgeous gardens and ponds, which, with just 22 bedrooms in the main house and adjacent mews wings, still retains the intimate feeling of a home. The interior more than exceeds the promise of the historic exterior: at every turn you admire low-ceilinged, beamed rooms, polished-oak paneling, and stained-glass windows with motifs of flowers in bloom and birds in flight. The Mulberry Restaurant is an especially spacious room overlooking a small lake and lovely gardens. Bedrooms are an absolute delight. I especially enjoyed Leeds with its four-poster bedroom and whimsical four-poster bath and Lewes, a most spacious room whose windows frame the rose garden. Two smaller bedrooms (Hever and Wakehurst) are found on the ground floor. Equally lovely rooms are found across the gardens in the former stables, now a luxurious mews offering spacious, bright rooms with king-sized beds and comfortable seating areas. The manor is just 2½ miles from Gatwick airport (not on the flight path) and offers complimentary transfer to the airport on departure. Churchill's home, Chartwell, and Brighton are amongst the most popular visitor attractions. *Directions:* From Gatwick take the A23 north (Redhill) for 2½ miles to the large roundabout with a garage in the middle and bordered by the Chequers pub. Take the Ladbroke Road exit from the roundabout and follow the lane to the hotel on the right.

LANGSHOTT MANOR
Owners: Deborah & Peter Hinchcliffe
Manager: Simon Steel
Horley
Surrey RH6 9LN, England
Tel: (01293) 786680, Fax: (01293) 783905
22 rooms
Double: £190–£330
Open: all year, Credit cards: all major
karenbrown.com/ews/langshott.html

At the Sign of the Angel is a black-and-white timbered inn at the heart of the well-preserved National Trust Village of Lacock. This 15th-century wool merchant's house is easy to spot as it contrasts strikingly with the neighboring stone buildings. The main dining room is a mixture of antique tables clustered around a large fire. A smaller, adjacent dining room is perfect for private parties. Dinner is always by candlelight and centers around a traditional English-roast main course (with a fish or vegetarian alternative) and choices of starters and desserts. Heavy old beams, low ceilings, and crooked walls add to the rustic elegance of the inn. Our favorite bedrooms are in the old house, small and cozy with low doors, uneven creaking floors, and ancient timbers. If you have difficulty with narrow stairs and uneven floors, you may prefer the ground-floor double-bedded room. Nestled on the first floor is a comfortable, inviting residents' lounge. Four additional country-style bedrooms are found in the cottage at the bottom of the garden. Be sure to leave time to visit the Fox Talbot Museum of early photographs and Lacock Abbey. Lacock is just 12 miles from Bath. *Directions:* If you are arriving from London, exit the M4 at junction 17 and take the A350 Melksham road south to Lacock.

AT THE SIGN OF THE ANGEL
Owners: Lorna & George Hardy
Church Street
Lacock
Wiltshire SN15 2LB, England
Tel: (01249) 730230, Fax: (01249) 730527
10 rooms
Double: £129–£155
Closed: last week of Dec, Credit cards: all major
karenbrown.com/ews/signoftheangel.html

The village of Lastingham is unhurried and peaceful, an oasis of green surrounded by the rugged, untamed beauty of the North York Moors National Park. Lastingham Grange preserves a 1950s style—everything is in apple-pie order, with such things as flowery wallpapers, patterned carpets, and candlewick bedspreads giving an old-fashioned air. I love the long lounge crowded with intimate groupings of sofas and chairs where in the morning the smell of furniture polish mixes with fresh-brewed coffee as you enjoy your morning coffee and homemade biscuits. The charm of the house extends outside where a broad terrace leads to the rose garden and acres of less formal gardens, which give way to fields and the distant moor. Guests of all ages and their dogs are welcome—there are listening devices for babies and a large adventure playground tucked beyond the formal garden where older children can play. The village church dates back to 1078 when a group of monks built a crypt to house the sacred remains of St. Cedd, which now remains a church beneath a church. Thirty miles distant lies medieval York and, closer at hand, narrow roads lead you to the coast with its fishing villages and long sandy beaches. *Directions:* Take the A170 from Thirsk towards Pickering. Just after Kirbymoorside turn left to Hutton-le-Hole where you turn right and cross the moor to Lastingham. The hotel is on your left in the village.

LASTINGHAM GRANGE
Owners: Jane & Dennis Wood
Lastingham
York Y062 6TH, England
Tel: (01751) 417345, Fax: (01751) 417358
12 rooms
Double: £189–£235
Closed: Dec to Feb, Credit cards: MC, VS
karenbrown.com/ews/lastingham.html

Lavenham with its lovely timbered buildings, ancient Guildhall, and spectacular church is the most attractive village in Suffolk. The Great House on the corner of the market square, a 15th-century building with an imposing 18th-century façade, houses a French restaurant-with-rooms run by Martine and Regis Crepy. Dinner is served in the oak-beamed dining room with candlelight and soft music and is particularly good value for money from Tuesday to Friday when a fixed-price menu is offered. On Saturday you dine from the à-la-carte menu. The restaurant is closed on Sunday and Monday. In summer you can dine al fresco in the flower-filled courtyard. The large bedrooms all have a lounge or a sitting area and bathroom. Architecturally the rooms are divinely old-world, with sloping plank floors, creaking floorboards, little windows, and a plethora of beams. Enjoy the village in the peace and quiet of the evening after the throng of daytime summer visitors has departed. Next door, Little Hall is furnished in early-19th-century style and is open as a museum. Farther afield are other historic villages such as Kersey and Long Melford, and Constable's Flatford Mill. *Directions:* Lavenham is on the A1141 between Bury St. Edmunds and Hadleigh.

THE GREAT HOUSE
Owners: Martine & Regis Crepy
Market Place
Lavenham
Suffolk CO10 9QZ, England
Tel: (01787) 247431, Fax: (01787) 248007
5 rooms
Double: £90–£160
Closed: Jan, Credit cards: all major
karenbrown.com/ews/greathouse.html

Lavenham is the epitome of an old-world English village with many half-timbered houses and a 16th-century cross and Guildhall, an impressive structure built in the 1520s, which now contains a museum tracing 700 years of wool trade. The Swan is now a sophisticated hotel but was once several houses—the town's ancient Wool Hall and humbler weavers' dwellings. The hotel is the flagship of the Forte Heritage group who have tastefully joined these lovely old buildings round a courtyard garden, preserving ancient beams and whitewashed plaster and timbered walls. The delightful galleried entrance leads you to quaint, beamed lounges that beckon you to partake of a traditional afternoon tea. The hub of the hotel is its snug bar whose floor is made of bricks brought to Lavenham after being used as ships' ballast and which is full of World War II memorabilia from the time it was the local for American airmen. Narrow corridors and steep staircases wind you to 51 beamed bedrooms tucked into nooks and crannies. The larger, quieter rooms with views are termed "feature rooms." The restaurant offers a set three-course dinner with lots of choices. As a dining alternative consider the Great House, a country-French restaurant on the Market Square. A few miles from here are other delightful Suffolk villages: Kersey, Long Melford, and Constable's Flatford Mill. *Directions:* Lavenham is on the A1141 between Bury St. Edmunds and Hadleigh.

THE SWAN
Manager: Martin Hucker
High Street
Lavenham
Suffolk CO10 9QA, England
Tel: (0870) 4008116, Fax: (01787) 248286
51 rooms
Double: £140–£220
Open: all year, Credit cards: all major
karenbrown.com/ews/theswan.html

As you walk directly into the oak-paneled hall, you catch the spirit of this lovely house with its enormous stone fireplace, ornate, stone mullioned windows, and plump sofas enticing you to sit and relax. The adjacent paneled dining room has the same comfortable, inviting atmosphere. The dark-oak paneling, the carvings, and the ornate plasterwork ceilings are the grand embellishments added by Lewtrenchard Manor's most famous owner, the Reverend Sabine Baring Gould, composer of many well-known hymns. Speculation has it that George Bernard Shaw based Pygmalion on the Reverend and his wife Grace. An illiterate Yorkshire mill girl when they first met, he sent her away to be educated before they married. His portrait hangs in the front hall, Grace's is in the back. Upstairs the lovely bedrooms are all different, with several named after the melodies of Gould's tunes—Melton and Prince Rupert are four-poster rooms. Within an easy drive are Castle Drogo, a fanciful Lutyens house, the Lost Gardens of Helligan, the Eden Project, Lydford Gorge, Dartington Glass, wild Dartmoor, and the north and south coasts of Devon. *Directions:* From Exeter (the M5) take the A30 for Okehampton and Bodmin and after 25 miles take the A386 slip road off the highway. Immediately turn right and then left for Bridestowe and Lewdown. After 6 miles just after The Blue Lion, on the right, turn left and Lewtrenchard Manor is on your left in ¾ mile.

LEWTRENCHARD MANOR
Owner: Von Essen Hotels
Manager: Sarah Harvey
Lewdown
Devon EX20 4PN, England
Tel: (01566) 783222, Fax: (01566) 783332
9 rooms
Double: £140–£210
Open: all year, Credit cards: all major
karenbrown.com/ews/lewtrenchardmanor.html

The Arundell Arms is a traditional fishing inn that provides its guests the opportunity to fish for salmon, trout, and sea trout in miles of river and a 3-acre lake. Owner Anne Voss-Bark, an expert fisherwoman, ably assisted by fly-fishing instructors and guides Roy Buckingham and David Pilkington, offers a variety of residential fishing courses. Fisherfolk gather in the morning in the hotel garden's 250-year-old cock pit (a long-since retired cock-fighting arena), now the rod-and-tackle room. In the evening the catch of the day is displayed on a silver platter on the hall table. The traditional fishing inn has been extended over the years to encompass the village assembly rooms—now the elegant, tall-ceilinged dining room where you enjoy the most delectable of dinners—and the courthouse and jail—now the adjacent village pub. Cozy bedrooms, all but five of which face the garden, are found in a converted stable block and the main house. Non-fisherfolk can enjoy walking, riding, golf, and, of course, traditional cream teas. Pheasant and snipe shooting are offered in the winter. Sightseers head for Dartmoor and the north Cornish coast with the ruins of Tintagel Castle and the ancient fishing villages of Boscastle and Port Isaac. *Directions:* Exit the M5 at Exeter and take the A30 (signposted Bodmin) for about 40 miles to the Lifton Village exit. Once off the dual carriageway turn right for Lifton and the hotel is on your left in less than a mile.

ARUNDELL ARMS
Owner: Anne Voss–Bark
Manager: Sally Hill
Lifton
Devon PL16 0AA, England
Tel: (01566) 784666, Fax: (01566) 784494
27 rooms
Double: £136–£180
Closed: Christmas, Credit cards: all major
karenbrown.com/ews/arundell.html

Lower Slaughter Manor sits beside the church tucked behind a high stone wall in the heart of one of England's prettiest villages. The style of the house is grand and the furnishings are elegant, but the friendly, down-to-earth hospitality saves the hotel from being too formal. One of the most attractive rooms is the blue-and-pink-paneled drawing room with its magnificent ornate-plasterwork ceiling and attractive decor. Upstairs the window seat in the galleried landing overlooks the garden and a 15th-century dovecote. The bedrooms are large and attractively decorated with quality fabrics. Splurge and request Antoinette, with its ornate 19th-century four-poster bed and views across the front lawn. I preferred the rooms in the house to the luxurious suites in the adjacent coach house. Extras include sherry, toffees, biscuits, and bathrobes. Amongst the more popular (crowded) nearby Cotswold villages are Bourton-on-the-Water, Stow-on-the-Wold, Chipping Campden, and Broadway. On the quieter side, consider the hamlets of Lower and Upper Swell, Stanton, Stanway, and Snowshill. *Directions:* From the A429 on the outskirts of Bourton-on-the-Water a small signpost indicates "The Slaughters." Follow the lane and the manor is on your right.

LOWER SLAUGHTER MANOR
Owner: Von Essen Hotels
Lower Slaughter
Gloucestershire GL54 2HP, England
Tel: (01451) 820456, Fax: (01451) 822150
16 rooms
Double: £150–£275
Open: all year, Credit cards: all major
karenbrown.com/ews/lowerslaughter.html

The gently flowing River Eye meanders past the mellow golden-stone cottages of Lower Slaughter, an idyllically pretty, much-photographed Cotswold village. With acres of lawn stretching down to the river, the Washbourne Court Hotel is made up of a row of 17th-century cottages cleverly combined and extended to form an inviting country house hotel of great charm. Flagstone floors topped with Oriental rugs, low, beamed ceilings, and huge fireplaces are the order of the day in the series of cozy lounges that lead one to the other. The spacious, more contemporary dining room is the setting for long, elegant dinners, like those served in its gracious sister hotel, Lower Slaughter Manor. Cottage suites with their own sitting rooms occupy two separate building in the grounds, but I much preferred the bedrooms in the main house. Rose is an outstandingly pretty room in the oldest party of the building while April, June, Sarah, Polly, and Amy are other very attractive bedrooms. Popular places to visit include bustling Bourton-on-the-Water and Stow-on-the-Wold. Shakespeare's Stratford-upon-Avon, Warwick Castle, Blenheim Palace, and Georgian Bath are all within an hour's drive. *Directions:* From the A429 on the outskirts of Bourton-on-the-Water a small signpost indicates "The Slaughters." Follow the lane and the Washbourne Court is on your left.

WASHBOURNE COURT HOTEL
Owner: Von Essen Hotels
Manager: Ann Hutchinson
Lower Slaughter
Gloucestershire GL54 2HJ, England
Tel: (01451) 822143, Fax: (01451) 821045
28 rooms
Double: £120–£150
Open: all year, Credit cards: all major
karenbrown.com/ews/washbourne.html

Assuredly one of the most beguiling "restaurant with rooms" that we have discovered so far, Mr Underhill's combines an idyllic setting overlooking the River Teme, hunkered down beneath the imposing walls of Ludlow castle, and cuisine that has established its reputation amongst the highest in the country. With fine cuisine, a constantly changing and innovative menu, a carefully chosen wine list, and attentive service in relaxed, comfortable surroundings, clearly dining is the focal point. The dining room offers views across the river and the opportunity to spot herons, kingfishers, assorted wildfowl, and otters in the protected freedom of their own domain. The guestrooms are all comfortably furnished and decorated to very high standards with handmade beds (two in maple, two in oak and two in cherry), crisp linens, and soft, fluffy down comforters. All have gleaming, modern bathrooms. Two small, guest sitting areas are provided. Our favorite room was, without a doubt, the suite that is found across the garden in the misleadingly named "shed" — stylishly modern, its expansive interior handcrafted from blond oak, a magnificent ensuite bathroom, and remotely operated drapes that allow you to savor the river view without leaving the enormously comfortable bed. Doze off and awaken to the sound of water in the old mill race. A special place in a very special location. *Directions:* Located in Ludow below the castle on the banks of the River Teme.

MR UNDERHILLS   New
Owners: Judy & Chris Bradley
Dinham
Ludlow
Shropshire SY8 1EH, England
Tel: 01584 8744319 rooms
Double: £95–£220
Credit cards: all major
karenbrown.com/ews/underhill.html

The Blackett family have been prominent citizens around these parts since 1673 when Sir William Blackett was knighted for his support of the king during the Civil War. The hall has grown over the years, with most of what you see having been built in the 1830s in the grand Gothic style. When Sir Hugh inherited the estate it had fallen on hard financial times, so he set about the task of keeping the ship afloat by building a golf course and converting the family seat into a country house hotel. There is also a splendid wedding and conference facility in the magnificent Great Hall with its own private entrance. For hotel guests there is an elegant drawing room with the adjacent Library and Pink room restaurant, though the heart of the place is the sunny conservatory, which also serves as the hotel's bar and gathering spot for golfers. Bedrooms range from cozy and low-ceilinged at the back of the house to enormous and high-ceilinged overlooking the golf course. Behind the hall is the picturesque estate-village of Matfen and just down the road is Hadrian's Wall, 70 miles of wall, lookout towers, and barracks built by the Romans. The beautiful Northumbrian coast with all its castles is about a 30-mile drive away. *Directions:* From the A1, take the A69 towards Carlisle and Hexham. Exit at Heddon-in-the-Wall and pick up the B6318, just before the Three Tuns pub, heading west towards Chollerford for 7 miles. The turning to Matfen Hall is on the right.

MATFEN HALL
Owners: Sir Hugh & Lady Blackett
Manager: David Hunter
Matfen
Northumberland NE20 0RH, England
Tel: (01661) 886500, Fax: (01661) 886055
53 rooms
Double: £140–£235
Open: all year, Credit cards: all major
karenbrown.com/ews/matfen.html

Perched high on a hill above Matlock with the ruins of Riber Castle as its only close neighbor, Riber Hall, which dates from the 15th century, is the most attractive of manor houses. A crackling log fire blazes in the enormous, ornate, dark-wood fireplace in the cozy lounge where guests gather for drinks before dinner. English classical and French provincial cuisine are the order of the day in the elegant dining rooms where the polished tables are set with fine china, gleaming silver, and sparkling crystal. Three bedrooms are found in the hall and the remainder across the courtyard in a converted stable block. A great attraction of the bedrooms is that many of them have antique Jacobean and Elizabethan four-poster beds—be sure to request a queen-sized bed. Room 10 is an especially spacious room with a lovely view of the garden. The tranquil setting can be appreciated in the old walled-garden and orchard while energetic guests enjoy pitting their skills against the tennis-ball machine on the tennis court. Nearby are the jewels of Derbyshire—rolling green dales and lovely stone villages, medieval Haddon Hall, and the Chatsworth estate. *Directions:* Exit the M1 at junction 28 (Chesterfield) and take the A38 and the A615 (Matlock road) to Tansley where you turn left at the Royal Oak Pub, up Alders Lane to Riber Hall.

RIBER HALL
Owners: Gill & Alex Biggin
Matlock
Derbyshire DE4 5JU, England
Tel: (01629) 582795, Fax: (01629) 580475
14 rooms
Double: £136–£182
Open: all year, Credit cards: all major
karenbrown.com/ews/riber.html

Set just off the marketplace across from the historic church, the Spread Eagle dates back to 1430 and has been welcoming guests ever since. Now completely renovated and restored, the hotel retains a wealth of period architecture. Several of the premier "feature" bedrooms located in the older parts of the building are named after prior patrons such as H. G. Wells, Hilaire Belloc, and even Queen Elizabeth I. Our favorites were Egremont, a most spacious room, with its very tall four-poster bed, and the elegantly panelled White Room, both with large, well-appointed bathrooms. Other smaller but no less comfortable rooms are in a modern wing sympathetically designed to meld with its older surroundings. Meals are served in the dining room with its Flemish stained glass windows, massive open fireplace, and Christmas puddings hanging from the beams. Enjoy a quiet pre-dinner drink by the fire in the classically English bar or indulge yourself with a special treatment in the impressive on-site health spa, exercise in the gym, or relax in the magnificent indoor pool. This very attractive hotel makes a good base for visiting Chichester, Fishbourne Roman palace, Petworth House, and the Weald and Downland open-air museum. *Directions:* From the M25 take the A3 south towards Portsmouth, exit at Milford, and take the A286 to Midhurst. The Spread Eagle sits by the market square in the old part of town.

SPREAD EAGLE HOTEL
Manager: Tim Hall
South Street
Midhurst
West Sussex GU29 9NH, England
Tel: (01730) 816911, Fax: (01730) 815669
39 rooms
Double: £99–£225
Open: all year, Credit cards: all major
karenbrown.com/ews/spreadeagle.html

This peaceful little corner of Norfolk boasts miles of flat sandy and shingle beaches backed by salt marshes lined with quaint villages of gray-flint houses trimmed with red brick. One of these villages is Morston with its pub, 13th-century church, and Morston Hall. Fortunately for visitors, Galton (Chef of the Year for 2001) and Tracy Blackiston forsook the Miller Howe in the Lake District to open Morston Hall as a small country house hotel. Being seduced by Galton's exquisite dinners is a large part of your stay here—fortunately, there are plenty of opportunities for exercise, so you can afford to repeat the divine experience. Bedrooms are extremely large, beautifully decorated, and accompanied by sparkling new bathrooms. Birdwatchers will find nearby marshes a paradise. Guests often take a boat from Morston's little quay to visit the seal sanctuary at Blakeney Point. Nearby Holkham Hall, an imposing Palladian mansion, contains grand paintings and items of bygone days. Blickling Hall is elegantly furnished. *Directions:* Morston Hall is situated on the A149 King's Lynn to Cromer road between Wells-next-the-Sea and Cley-next-the-Sea.

MORSTON HALL
Owners: Tracy & Galton Blackiston
Morston
Norfolk NR25 7AA, England
Tel: (01263) 741041, Fax: (01263) 740419
6 rooms
Double: £230–£250*
*Includes dinner, bed & breakfast
Closed: Jan, Credit cards: all major
karenbrown.com/ews/morstonhall.html

A 45-minute drive from Heathrow airport can find you dipping your toes in the River Thames and soaking up the pastoral scenery around Moulsford—the perfect place to relax after a transatlantic flight. This quiet stretch of the river was immortalized in "The Wind in The Willows", provided the setting for "The History of Mr Polly", and was home to Jerome K. Jerome who chronicled his friends' antics in "Three Men in a Boat." But here you find so much more than a pretty setting with literary connections The Beetle & Wedge hotel, with its delightfully comfortable bedrooms guarantees that you will be well fed and well taken care of by proprietors Kate and Richard Smith. For dining you can choose to eat in the elegant wall-to-wall-windowed dining room or in the lively and informal Boathouse perched on the riverbank with tables that spill out onto a riverside terrace. The latter specializes in dishes cooked on a charcoal grill. All guestrooms have large beds and an airy decor, with pastel walls highlighted with stenciling. Be sure to request a room with a river view. Take a refreshing walk by the Thames to Goring, visit nearby Henley and Marlow, or explore farther afield with excursions to Oxford, Salisbury, Bath, and Winchester. *Directions:* From junction 12 of the M4 take the A4 south. At the second roundabout head towards Wallingford, through Pangbourne and Streatley to Moulsford, where you turn right on Ferry Lane to the river.

THE BEETLE & WEDGE
Owners: Kate & Richard Smith
Ferry Lane
Moulsford-on-Thames
Oxfordshire OX10 9JF, England
Tel: (01491) 651381, Fax: (01491) 651376
10 rooms
Double: £175–£195
Open: all year, Credit cards: all major
karenbrown.com/ews/beetle.html

Chewton Glen was voted "best country house in the world" by Gourmet readers in April 2000. It's an image that Martin and Brigitte Skan have carefully nurtured and their efforts have been rewarded by considerable success—we had difficulty getting a room midweek in the summer. The secret of their success is not just the luxuriousness of the entire place—though it is indeed decadently luxurious, with lovely suites and bedrooms decked out with all the mod cons—but their understanding that luxury extends to offering absolutely outstanding, genuine service. To experience this level of service is one of the true pleasures in life. In between Nirvana-like meals you relax completely— perhaps with a little croquet on the lawn, a splash in the pool, or tea on the terrace. You can exert yourself in the spa and health club complex with its magnificent indoor pool, gym, indoor and outdoor tennis, and indulge yourself in various beauty treatments; disport yourself on the nine-hole golf course; or walk through the grounds and along the glen to the beach. If you feel the urge to go sightseeing, the New Forest, where wild deer and ponies roam is nearby. Stonehenge, Salisbury, and Winchester cathedrals are within an hour's drive. *Directions:* From the A35 follow signposts for Highcliffe (not New Milton), go through Walkford, then turn left down Chewton Farm Road—the hotel is on your right.

CHEWTON GLEN
Owners: Brigitte & Martin Skan
New Milton
Hampshire BH25 6QS, England
Tel: (01425) 275341, Fax: (01425) 272310
58 rooms
Double: £305–£780*
*Breakfast not included: £20
Open: all year, Credit cards: all major
Relais & Châteaux
karenbrown.com/ews/chewtonglen.html

The Vineyard at Stockcross takes its name and inspiration from the Peter Michael Winery in California's world-renowned Sonoma Valley. Nestled in the Berkshire countryside between Newbury and Hungerford, and conveniently located midway between Heathrow and the Cotswolds, it offers an oasis of luxury second to none. The "Fire and Water" reflecting pool sets the scene for over 1,000 pieces of original art displayed throughout this exquisite property with its origins in an 18th-century hunting lodge. Guestrooms, (named after vineyards in California, France, and Italy) with a sprinkling of four-posters, share a common opulence, all with beautiful marble bathrooms en suite. The newer Atrium Suites are decorated in a more contemporary style. Choose between those on the first floor, with their private balconies, or those the ground floor with bay windows opening to the patio. Indulge yourself with a visit to the spa with its indoor pool, steam rooms, gym, and treatment rooms. The restaurant is available for breakfast, lunch, and dinner. As might be expected, California wines feature prominently in the 23,000-bottle cellar; 800 California vineyards blend with 1,200 from around the world to accent and support the fine cuisine. *Directions:* The hotel is close to junction 13 on the M4 motorway. Take the A34 south towards Winchester, and then the A4 (3rd exit) towards Stockcross (B4000).

THE VINEYARD AT STOCKCROSS   *New*
Owner: Sir Peter Michael
Newbury
Berkshire RG20 8JU, England
Tel: 01635 528770, Fax: 01635 528398
49 rooms
Double: £245–£635*
*VAT not included
Open: all year, Credit cards: all major
Relais & Châteaux
karenbrown.com/ews/stockcross.html

As you drive by on the busy A442, it would be easy to dismiss this as "just another pub". . . but step inside the door and you realize how big a mistake you could have made! The name originates from the Middle Ages when the shires of Merry England were divided into "Hundreds." The 14th-century, half-timbered, thatched building in the parking lot was originally used as a courthouse (the stocks are on the green across the road). The main building, of Georgian origin, has been completely renovated by its current owners, the Phillips family. Entering through the public rooms is an experience in itself as you encounter a maze of bars and dining rooms decorated with baskets of local produce, tables with centerpieces of fresh herbs, and menus sophisticated enough to entrance the culinary writers of such British institutions as the Sunday Telegraph and the Observer. Heading upstairs to the bedrooms, you are struck by the brightly colored carpets and the hand-gilded walls. The rooms themselves are a sight to behold, sumptuously decorated with period-style four-poster and half-tester beds, patchwork drapes, lavender-scented sheets, and potpourri. Superior rooms at the top of the house are provided with garden swings under the eaves. If you are looking for a place to break your journey on the way north or a base from which to explore Wales, this is well worth the diversion. *Directions:* Hundred House is next to the A442 just north of Bridgenorth.

HUNDRED HOUSE HOTEL
Owners: Sylvia, Henry, Stuart & David Phillips
Bridgenorth Road
Norton, Telford
Shropshire TF11 9EE, England
Tel: (01952) 730353, Fax: (01952) 730355
10 rooms
Double: £99–£135
Open: all year, Credit cards: all major
karenbrown.com/ews/hundred.html

The Old Bank Hotel is housed within an attractive, four-story building dating from 1780, which was formerly—you guessed it—a bank. Fronting on the bustling high street, guestrooms are found on the upper levels and down the two back wings along the south-facing courtyard. Very luxurious, the two top-floor suites enable "sleeping amongst the spires" with views over the surrounding college rooftops. The guestroom interiors, the work of a French designer, are beautiful, all having the same theme of understated elegance and sumptuous well-appointed marble bathrooms. As befits a modern town hotel, the rooms are fully equipped to accommodate the needs of today's traveller with air conditioning, broadband internet connection, mini-bar, sound system, and television. Quod, the stylish bar and grill located on the ground floor, serves meals from breakfast onwards. Open to non-residents, as well as resident guests, the restaurant has a contemporary design with stone floors, wooden tables, and an oval zinc-topped bar. The cooking has an Italian influence, and in summer, weather permitting, guests can enjoy dining on the rear terrace, a secluded haven from the bustle of the city. The hotel enjoys a prestigious location in the very heart of Oxford, neighboring some of the oldest colleges and perfectly situated for exploring the city on foot. *Directions:* Located on High Street. Private parking is to the rear of the hotel off Merton Street.

❄ ⚞ ▭ ☎ ♯♯ ♈ ⚕ P ¶¶ ♿

THE OLD BANK HOTEL
Owner: Jeremy Mogford
Manager: Stephen Lewis
92–94 High Street
Oxford OX1 4BN, England
Tel: (01865) 799599, Fax: (01865) 799598
42 rooms
Double: £160–£320*
*Breakfast not included: £9–£12, Service charge: 10%
Open: all year, Credit cards: all major
karenbrown.com/ews/oldbank.html

Between Keble and Somerville colleges you find the Old Parsonage Hotel, a wisteria-draped, golden-stone building dating back to 1660. In 1989, it was purchased by Jeremy Mogford and completely remodeled as a small, upscale market hotel. Years past, the Old Parsonage grew like Topsy with a higgledy-piggledy collection of rooms and corridors added to the rear. A small, reading room is off the main lobby. The main sitting room consists of several smaller rooms combined into one, enhancing the sense of space, while the walls provide cozy seating nooks for lunches, afternoon teas, and bar suppers. The delightful bedrooms are priced by size; the less expensive are compact with just enough room for the bed, a couple of chairs, TV, and phone. All are air-conditioned and have internet connections. Marble bathrooms are small and beautifully appointed. The most attractive of the newer rooms are those overlooking the leafy, rear garden. The largest rooms, our favorites, are the four rooms in the original house. Reached through a pretty sitting room and up a narrow flight of stairs, they have slanting doors, uneven floors, and little windows peeking out through the wisteria. Drinks and meals are served beneath the parasols on the front terrace, weather permitting. Perfectly located, you can walk to everything in Oxford. Bicycles and punts are available to hotel guests. *Directions:* The Old Parsonage is just beyond St. Giles Church on the A4260, Banbury Road.

OLD PARSONAGE HOTEL
Owner: Jeremy Mogford
Manager: Marie Jackson
1 Banbury Road
Oxford OX2 6NN, England
Tel: (01865) 310210, Fax: (01865) 311262
30 rooms
Double: £140–£200*
*Breakfast not included: £12.50
Closed: Dec 24 to 28, Credit cards: all major
karenbrown.com/ews/oldparsonoxford.html

Linger too long over the dinner menu here and you'll suffer agonies of indecision over ordering—it is all so delicious you'll want everything. Come for the food, stay for the accommodation, and be delighted by the contrast between the minimalist modern decor of the restaurant and the traditional charm of the adjacent hotel. The bold red bar excites the senses, preparing you for dinner in the state-of-the-art restaurant where the food is the entire focus of your attenion. Next door is a completely different world where colors are chosen as a backdrop for old pine furniture and country antiques. On arrival you are given a key to the front door and there are no bedroom door keys. The second floor contains the three choice bedrooms. Number 1 is an especially attractive large room with comfy chairs and a huge, pine-paneled bathroom with large antique tub. Room 3 has a delightful sitting nook and a bathroom hidden behind a bookcase door. Room 4 has twin beds, inviting window seats providing views of the harbor and its dry dock, and a shower and WC tucked into a large closet. A two-bedroom apartment offers the most spacious accommodation. Penzance is a lively town and nearby are St. Michael's Mount, Mousehole, and Land's End (very commercialized). *Directions:* On entering Penzance stay on the seafront road. Just before the bridge (across the harbor) turn right and immediately left up the slipway—The Abbey Hotel is at the top of the hill.

THE ABBEY HOTEL
Managers: Kinga & Ben Tunnicliffe
Penzance
Cornwall TR18 4AR, England
Tel: (01736) 366906, Fax: (01736) 351163
7 rooms, 1 apartment (£185)
Double: £120–£190
Credit cards: all major
karenbrown.com/ews/theabbey.html

This lovely Edwardian house sits high above the pretty village of Porlock and was designed as a home where every room has views of the distant sea across the roofs and chimneys of the village. Ann and Tim have worked hard to keep the feel of a private home while adding all the amenites of a small hotel. Downstairs, guests have a snug hallway parlor with chairs drawn round a log fire and an airy sitting room with flowered sofas and pink velvet chairs arranged into conversational groupings. The dining room has been extended and picture windows added so that, no matter where you sit, you have sea views across the fields or village views across the rooftops. Upstairs, the bedrooms enjoy identical interesting views. Though some are a bit larger than others, all rooms are priced alike and offer the same high standards, and each retains its own individual character. Stroll around the village with its attractive houses and shops and drive the short distance to the harbor of Porlock Weir. Just inland is Lorna Doone Country—the church at Oare was the scene of her wedding. *Directions:* From Dunster, as you enter Porlock down the hill on the one-way system, turn left into the hotel just as the road becomes two-way.

THE OAKS HOTEL
Owners: Anne & Tim Riley
Porlock
Somerset TA24 8ES, England
Tel: (01643) 862265, Fax: (01643) 863131
9 rooms
Double: £120–£130
Open: mid-Mar to Oct, Credit cards: all major
karenbrown.com/ews/theoaks.html

The Yorke Arms nestles beside the village green in Ramsgill, a handful of houses and farms and a tiny church. This hotel is a "foodie haven" in Nidderdale, one of Yorkshire's quietest and most attractive dales. Frances Atkins and her brigade perform culinary magic, offering food that enjoys modern flourishes but is firmly focused on fine local produce. Husband Bill calmly runs the front of the house. There's plenty of old-world charm: flagstone floors, traditional bars, and a comfortable dining room with high-backed Windsor chairs, an old dresser gleaming with pewter, and a blazing log fire. Bedrooms are very comfortable but by no means grand. Several rooms have received a complete update, so ask for one of these when making a reservation. I particularly liked Grouse and Pheasant, both spacious accommodations in the oldest part of the inn. For the roomiest quarters, opt for Gouthwaite, Ramsgill, or Longside with its grand four-poster bed. You can take beautiful walks from the hotel, which vary in length from strolls by the local reservoir to daylong hikes over the moorlands. The ruins of nearby Fountains Abbey are an awesome sight and medieval York and the 18th-century spa town of Harrogate are popular day trips. *Directions:* From Ripon take the B6285 to Pateley Bridge where you cross the river and turn right for Ramsgill. The Yorke Arms is beside the village green.

THE YORKE ARMS
Owners: Frances & Bill Atkins
Ramsgill
North Yorkshire HG3 5RL, England
Tel: (01423) 755243, Fax: (01423) 755330
13 rooms
Double: £100–£170*
*Includes dinner, bed & breakfast
Open: all year, Credit cards: all major
karenbrown.com/ews/yorkearms.html

The Burgoyne family were people of substance hereabouts for they secured the premier building site in this picturesque Swaledale village and built an impressive home that dwarfs the surrounding buildings, now a welcoming hotel run by Derek Hickson and Peter Carwardine. Derek makes guests feel thoroughly at home while Peter makes certain that they live up to their motto, "Tis substantial happiness to eat." Peter prepares a fixed-price, four-course meal every evening with plenty of choices for each course. The handsome lounge is warmed by a log fire in winter and full of inviting books on the area. There's abundant scope for walking and driving in this rugged area using Reeth as your base, though you'll be hard-pressed to find a lovelier dales view than the one from your bedroom window of stone-walled fields rising to vast moorlands (one bedroom faces the back of the house). Redmire, being more spacious, is the premier room, while Marrick is a most luxurious four-poster suite. Robes and slippers are provided for the occupants of Keld, Grinton, and Thwaite who have to slip across the hall to their bathrooms. Richmond with its medieval castle and the Bowes Museum, near Barnard Castle, with its fine collection of French furniture and porcelain, are added attractions. *Directions:* From Richmond take the A6108 towards Leyburn for 5 miles to the B6270 for the 5-mile drive to Reeth. The Burgoyne Hotel is on the village green.

THE BURGOYNE HOTEL
Owners: Derek Hickson & Peter Carwardine
Reeth
Yorkshire DL11 6SN, England
Tel & fax: (01748) 884292
8 rooms
Double: £110–£160
Closed: Jan 2 to Feb 13, Credit cards: MC, VS
karenbrown.com/ews/burgoyne.html

Ripley is an estate village remodeled in 1827 like a French village with cobbled square, stocks, and a cross. The Ingilby family, who have lived here for 26 generations, reside in the castle where Cromwell stayed after winning the Battle of Marston Moor. Today's visitors stay at The Boar's Head Hotel, an inviting mixture of country house hotel, traditional restaurant, bistro, and pub. Prior to the hotel's opening, the village had been "dry" for 71 years and so immense was everyone's relief on opening night that the vicar came to bless the beer taps. There are 25 very attractive bedrooms found in the main house, the courtyard, and across the quiet village street in Birchwood House. Guests can enjoy elegant food in the restaurant or more casual fare in the courtyard bar where traditional ales are served straight from the wood. You can tour the castle (even get married there) and guests at The Boar's Head have complimentary access to the walled gardens and grounds, which include lakes and a deer park. Just up the road is Harrogate, a town of flowers, Turkish baths, elegant shopping, and the famous Betty's tearooms. Brontë lovers head for Haworth where Charlotte, Emily, and Anne lived in the parsonage, which is now a museum. Less than an hour's drive will find you at the well-organized park-and-ride for visiting York. *Directions:* From Harrogate take the A61 towards Ripon for 3 miles. Turn left into Ripley village and the hotel is on your right.

THE BOAR'S HEAD HOTEL
Owners: Sir Thomas & Lady Ingilby
Manager: Steve Chestnut
Ripley, Harrogate
North Yorkshire HG3 3AY, England
Tel: (01423) 771888, Fax: (01423) 771509
25 rooms
Double: £125–£150
Open: all year, Credit cards: all major
karenbrown.com/ews/boars.html

The St. Enodoc Hotel occupies an exquisite location on one of England's most scenic coastlines overlooking the broad Camel estuary. Combine this with a refreshing, stylishly chic, Mediterranean interior and you have a real winner. Enjoy the peace and quiet of the comfortable sitting room or take advantage of the well-stocked library featuring books on Cornwall and books by Cornish authors. Soak in the panoramic water view from the smart, split-level bar and restaurant specializing in New World cuisine, or stroll down the lane and take the little ferry across to the ancient fishing port of Padstow with its array of shops and restaurants. Bedrooms are very nicely decorated. There is a choice of king- or twin-bedded rooms, several with a large window seat that can be converted to a small child's bed, though families often opt for having bunk beds set up in the living room or using the sofa bed. With its heated outdoor pool (May through September), billiard room, gym, and adjacent golf course, the St. Enodoc is an ideal holiday hotel. The nearby little fishing village of Port Isaac with its craft and antique shops is charming, but also drive to Carbis Bay and take the little train to St. Ives for a visit to the Tate Gallery, or meander up the coast to Tintagel of King Arthur fame. *Directions:* At the Wadebridge roundabout follow signs for Wadebridge, then at the next roundabout turn right for the 4-mile drive to Rock.

ST. ENODOC HOTEL
Manager: Victoria Rowe
Rock
Cornwall PL27 6LA, England
Tel: (01208) 863394, Fax: (01208) 863970
20 rooms
Double: £110–£230
Closed: mid-Dec to mid-Feb (except New Year)
Credit cards: all major
karenbrown.com/ews/stenodoc.html

Romaldkirk epitomizes a traditional north-of-England village with honey-colored stone cottages set spaciously round the large village green where the old pump and even older stocks (for punishing wrongdoers) still stand. The surprisingly sophisticated Rose and Crown pub bordering the village green has a pretty sitting room (where guests can escape the hubbub of the bar) and a paneled dining room serving four-course dinners. However, like all great pubs, The Rose and Crown also has an excellent traditional bar where beams are decorated with horse brasses and locals gather for a pint in the evenings. Delectable bar meals are served here or in the adjacent Crown Room. Up the narrow stairs you find five attractive bedrooms (room 10 is a lovely large double-bedded room overlooking the village green) and two suites, which are especially suitable for families as the sofas in the sitting rooms make into beds for children. Five additional, more modern bedrooms are in the courtyard behind the hotel. Walking is a popular pastime hereabouts and a few minutes' drive brings you into quiet Pennine countryside. Barnard Castle is a lively local market town where the Bowes Museum merits an all-day visit. A 40-minute drive finds you at Beamish Museum, a turn-of-the-century mining town hosted by costumed staff. *Directions:* Romaldkirk is 6 miles northwest of Barnard Castle on the B6277 in the direction of Middleton in Teesdale.

THE ROSE & CROWN
Owners: Alison & Christopher Davy
Barnard Castle
Romaldkirk
County Durham DL12 9EB, England
Tel: (01833) 650213, Fax: (01833) 650828
12 rooms
Double: £110–£124
Closed: Christmas, Credit cards: MC, VS
karenbrown.com/ews/roseandcrown.html

Stone House, the manor house for Rushlake Green, has belonged to the Dunn family for over 500 years. Built in 1495 with an addition in 1778, this glorious house, set on a 1,000-acre estate, is filled with wonderful antique furniture and old English china, which is complemented by chintzes and family memorabilia. There is a croquet lawn and a billiard table. Bedrooms vary in size from small and cozy to large and spacious. Almost all have old beams and are furnished with care and provided with practically everything you might need from TV to hot-water bottles, sewing kits, books, and tempting biscuits. Two rooms are gorgeous, with four-poster beds and equally lovely bathrooms—one of the bathrooms is decorated with antique samplers. A sumptuous dinner and breakfast are served in the oak-paneled dining room, and Continental breakfast is available in your bedroom. The 18th-century walled garden, old-fashioned rose garden, and lime walk are yours to enjoy. Other glorious gardens include Sissinghurst, Great Dixter, Scotney Castle, and Sheffield Park. Close by is the Glyndebourne Opera House (May to September). Nearby, Churchill's home, Chartwell, and Rudyard Kipling's home, Batemans, are very popular. *Directions:* From Heathfield take the B2096 towards Battle and then the fourth turn on the right to Rushlake Green. Turn left in the village (with the green on your right) and Stone House is on the far left-hand corner of the crossroads.

STONE HOUSE
Owners: Jane & Peter Dunn
Rushlake Green
East Sussex TN21 9QJ, England
Tel: (01435) 830553, Fax: (01435) 830726
6 rooms
Double: £145–£235
Closed: Dec 23 to Jan 6, Credit cards: MC, VS
karenbrown.com/ews/stonehouse.html

The delightfully pretty little fishing village of St. Mawes, with its narrow, steep streets and boat-filled harbor strung along the River Fal, sports quite a Mediterranean look. The town's sheltered position makes it a warm hideaway even in winter and there is no more splendid place to hide away than in the elegant Hotel Tresanton. Terracing up steep steps, this spectacularly located, scrumptious hotel is dashingly modern, with a nautical, Mediterranean flair. Its minimalist decor—mainly in white and soft, neutral tones with royal-blue accents—is a perfect balance between classic and modern. Bedrooms all have magnificent sea views and two are spacious family suites for up to five people. Naturally, the restaurant specializes in seafood. Enjoy the hotel's extensive library or choose a film to watch in the hotel's cinema. Follow the coastal path past the castle to the 14th-century church at St. Just in Roseland. You can hire many different boats including the hotel's 48-foot classic yacht. Sightseers have lots of scope, from St. Michael's Mount to the Tate Gallery at St. Ives, while garden lovers are spoilt for choice: Trelissick, Glendurgan, Trebah, the Lost Gardens of Heligan, and The Eden Project. *Directions:* From St. Austell take the B3287 for 16 miles to St. Mawes where you follow the road along the front of the harbor, coming to the Tresanton on your right. Park in front, go up to reception, and the staff will unload your bags and park your car.

HOTEL TRESANTON
Manager: Federica Bertolini
St. Mawes
Cornwall TR2 5DR, England
Tel: (01326) 270055, Fax: (01326) 270053
29 rooms
Double: £220–£265
Credit cards: all major
karenbrown.com/ews/tresanton.html

The gallows sign outside The George stood as a warning to highwaymen not to rob coaches departing from the Stamford inn. The waiting room for London coaches is now an oak-paneled private dining room, while the adjacent York waiting room serves as a friendly bar. History positively oozes from this place and the staff is always happy to enliven your stay with tales of resident ghosts and secret passages. Do not be put off by the hotel's austere façade directly on the main road because most bedrooms face a peaceful inner courtyard and you are not aware of the road once you are inside the hotel. Horses once clip-clopped across the cobbled courtyard where overflowing tubs of flowers paint a pretty picture and tables and chairs are set beneath umbrellas for traditional afternoon tea. Most bedrooms face this pretty courtyard and I particularly enjoyed the historic ambiance of room 29 (a standard double) with its dark-oak paneling (apparently Princess Anne has slept here) and room 49 decked out in maroon and blue and overlooking a quiet garden. Traditional roast dinners are the hallmark of the dining room—be sure to save room for an old-fashioned pud—while lighter, more casual fare is served in the indoor Garden Lounge. Stamford has lots of antique shops. *Directions:* From Peterborough take the A1 north for 14 miles to the first roundabout where you take the B1081 to Stamford. The George is on the left by the traffic lights.

THE GEORGE OF STAMFORD
Manager: Chris Pitman
71 St. Martins
Stamford
Lincolnshire PE9 2LB, England
Tel: (01780) 750750, Fax: (01780) 750701
47 rooms
Double: £110–£225
Open: all year, Credit cards: all major
karenbrown.com/ews/georgestamford.html

The Royalist's boldly simple claim to be "the oldest inn in England" (circa 947 A.D.) has been verified by carbon dating and accepted by the Guinness Book of Records. Evidence suggests that the building actually began its life as part of a Saxon community as early as 514 A.D. Its history is wreathed in myths and truths supported by leper holes, sealed tunnels, dry wells, bear pits, and the inevitable ghosts. All in all, it's a fascinating destination in its own right, but the number of reasons to visit The Royalist has grown as a result of changes wrought by its current owners, former schoolteachers Peter and Amanda Rowan. Eight luxuriously appointed bedrooms, all with modern en suite bathrooms, have been artfully engineered into the irregular spaces of the old structure. Meals are served in the appropriately named 947 A.D. restaurant, with pre-dinner drinks and post-dinner coffee in the comfortable residents' lounge in front of the log fire. For a less formal atmosphere you can meet the locals in the adjoining Eagle and Child pub, which shares not only a common wall but also the kitchen, providing typical bar meals of the same high standard. Here you can dine al fresco in the garden or in the conservatory. This is a perfect location for exploring the Cotswolds. *Directions:* From the A429 at Stow-on-the-Wold turn left into Sheep Street (Unicorn Pub on the corner) and drive 200 yards into the center of the village. The Royalist is set back on the left-hand side.

THE ROYALIST
Owners: Peter & Amanda Rowan
Manager: Tracey Davies
Digbeth Street
Stow-on-the-Wold
Gloucestershire GL54 1BN, England
Tel: (01451) 830670, Fax: (01451) 870048
8 rooms
Double: £140–£180
Open: all year, Credit cards: MC, VS
karenbrown.com/ews/royalist.html

Plumber Manor has been a country home of the Prideaux Brune family since the early 17th century. Portraits hanging in the upstairs gallery hint at the grandeur of the family's past. (There is also a portrait of Charles I, which he personally presented to his mistress, a member of the family.) Billed as a restaurant with bedrooms, Plumber Manor is under the personal supervision of the family. Richard and Alison Prideaux Brune look after guests; Brian Prideaux Brune, the chef, conscientiously provides a high standard of cuisine and wine. Six comfortable, spacious bedrooms are in the main house and, just across the garden, ten rooms surround a courtyard. Our favorites are 14, 15, 16, and 17 — spacious, two-level rooms with luxurious modern bathrooms. Ten miles away lies Milton Abbas, a picture-perfect village of thatched cottages built in 1770 by the Earl of Dorchester who had the old village razed because it interfered with his view. Another pretty village is Cerne Abbas with thatched and Tudor cottages, 7 miles north of Dorchester (Hardy's Casterbridge). Within reach are Salisbury, Longleat, and the many attractions in and around Bath. *Directions:* In Sturminster Newton turn left from the A352 onto the road leading to the village of Hazelbury Bryan. Plumber Manor is 1¼ miles beyond on the left.

PLUMBER MANOR
Owner: Prideaux Brune family
Hazelbury Bryan
Sturminster Newtown
Dorset DT10 2AF, England
Tel: (01258) 472507, Fax: (01258) 473370
16 rooms
Double: £110–£170
Closed: Feb, Credit cards: all major
karenbrown.com/ews/plumber.html

Midway between the outstandingly pretty Cornish fishing villages of Looe and Polperro, Talland Bay Hotel sits in a quiet cove offering beautiful gardens with unobstructed views of headlands and the sea. Parts of this lovely Cornish manor date back to the 16th century. The bar-lounge and fine paneled dining room are comfortably informal and overlook the gardens. All the bedrooms are very different. I especially enjoyed room 9 with terrific views—even from the loo, and rooms 12 (set under the eaves up lots of stairs), 28, and 29 with their spectacular sea views. However, all of these are completely eclipsed by the hotel's most luxurious room 30 with its private garden, sitting area (suitable as a room for children), decadent bathroom, and sensational view. If you want total privacy, consider one of the three little cottages in the grounds (without sea view). The swimming pool on the back patio is heated during the summer months and a putting course is set up on the lawn. Gardens terrace down towards the headland where the coastal path takes you to either Polperro or Looe. The idyllically pretty seaside villages of Fowey, Looe, and Polperro are great attractions as are The Eden Project and National Maritime Museum. *Directions:* From Plymouth take the A38 towards Truro then turn left on the A387 towards Looe and Polperro. At the T-junction turn towards Polperro and turn first left for Talland.

TALLAND BAY HOTEL
Owners: Mary & George Granville
Talland-by-Looe
Cornwall PL132JB, England
Tel: (01503) 272667, Fax: (01503) 272940
23 rooms
Double: £140–£220*
*Includes dinner, bed & breakfast
Closed: Jan, Credit cards: all major
karenbrown.com/ews/talland.html

You cannot find any more picturesque countryside than this—it is hard to believe that you are only a twenty-minute drive from Salisbury and Stonehenge. The honey-colored stone cottages of Teffont Evias are strung along a quiet country lane beside the tumbling baby River Teff. Just down the road from the grand manor house hidden behind a tall wall, Howard's House, built in 1623, was for many years the estate's dower house. Its bedrooms, decorated in quiet, restful colors and all but one (a twin) with king-sized beds, are most attractive. I especially liked rooms 1 and 2 with their views down the long expanse of garden. Room 3 is a romantic four-poster. The sitting room offers a large stone fireplace and French windows opening to acres of garden with lots of places to sit and enjoy a drink on a warm summer evening before going in to dinner. The Chilmark stone used to build this village also built Salisbury Cathedral. Salisbury with its cathedral and close is a great draw for visitors as are Stonehenge, Stourhead Gardens, and Longleat House. An hour's drive will bring you to the hustle and bustle of Georgian Bath or the Dorset coast. *Directions:* From Salisbury take the A36 to Wilton and the A30 (Shaftesbury). After 3 miles turn right (B3089) towards Mere and Teffont, then after 4½ miles at Teffont turn left, following the sign to the hotel, 400 yards down the lane.

HOWARD'S HOUSE HOTEL
Owner: Noele Thompson
Teffont Evias, near Salisbury
Wiltshire SP3 5RJ, England
Tel: (01722) 716392, Fax: (01722) 716820
9 rooms
Double: £145–£165
Open: all year, Credit cards: all major
karenbrown.com/ews/howardshouse.html

Dale Head Hall occupies a stunning, isolated position on the shores of Thirlmere, one of Cumbria's quietest, most pastoral lakes, and provides the perfect base for exploring the entire Lake District. Front bedrooms offer gorgeous lake views while the delightful rooms at the back in the old part of the house are low-ceilinged with old latch doors and beams. One of the back bedrooms has a small cradle room snug above the inglenook fireplace. Two lake-view rooms on the ground floor are handy for those who have a problem with stairs. I particularly like the ground-floor twin with its private lake-facing patio and own entrance patio with chairs. Superior rooms are rented only on a dinner, bed, and breakfast basis. Much of the lovely oak furniture found throughout the hotel is the handiwork of personable Alan Lowe who joins his wife Shirley, daughter Caroline, and son-in-law Hans in making certain that guests are well taken care of and well-fed. Walks from the hotel range from a stroll around the lake to challenging hikes up the nearby fells. For a week's stay, Dale Head Hall has several delightful apartments in the adjacent stables. *Directions:* Leave the M6 at junction 40 and take the A66 towards Keswick then the B5322 signposted Windermere to join the A591, which you take in the direction of Windermere for ½ mile. The entrance to Dale Head Hall is on your right.

DALE HEAD HALL
Owners: Shirley & Alan Lowe
Thirlmere, Keswick
Cumbria CA12 4TN, England
Tel: (017687) 72478, Fax: (017687) 71070
12 rooms, 7 apartments (£195–£450 weekly)
Double: £95–£115
Open: Feb to Dec, Credit cards: all major
karenbrown.com/ews/daleheadhall.html

Tucked away at the edge of the small town of Thornbury is Thornbury Castle and from the moment you see it you will be enchanted. Construction began in 1510 at the order of the 3rd Duke of Buckingham, but ceased when he was beheaded in 1521 at the Tower of London. The current owners continue the upkeep of this partially restored castle, leaving other areas as a romantic ruin. Dinner in the baronial dining rooms is a leisurely affair. Softly carpeted hallways lead to the bedrooms—this is no longer a castle of drafty stone passages. The guestrooms are elegantly decorated as befits their castle surroundings, several with four-poster beds, all with lovely bathrooms. The large octagonal tower room has a four-poster bed and its own turret staircase. Nearby Slimbridge Wildfowl and Wetlands Centre was founded by Sir Peter Scott (son of the explorer) in 1946. Just south of Slimbridge you find Berkeley and Berkeley Castle where Edward II was murdered in the dungeon in 1327. Also in the grounds is the Jenner museum, a tribute to Edward Jenner, discoverer of the smallpox vaccination. *Directions:* At the junction of the M4 and M5 motorways take the A38 north to Thornbury. At the bottom of the hill in the High Street fork left down Castle Street and the entrance to the castle is on the left of the parish church. Follow brown historic signs.

THORNBURY CASTLE
Owner: Von Essen Hotels
Manager: Brian Jarvis
Thornbury
Gloucestershire BS35 1HH, England
Tel: (01454) 281182, Fax: (01454) 416188
26 rooms
Double: £140–£370
Credit cards: all major
karenbrown.com/ews/thornbury.html

Victorians flocked to Tunbridge Wells—in fact, the young Princess Victoria always stayed here when she came to town. The Hotel du Vin's interior has changed considerably since those days, now presenting a light, airy, and uncluttered look. Like its sister hotel in Winchester, the hotel's theme is wine—the wine list is extensive and very well priced as is the accompanying bistro menu with its tempting selections of top-quality food. Bedrooms are stylishly simple in their decor yet equipped with all the modern conveniences. They are generally high-ceilinged rooms, very smartly decorated in a tailored style with superb beds made up with Egyptian cotton linens. Each bedroom is accompanied by a sleek modern bathroom with oversized tub, power shower, and fluffy towels. Splurge and request a larger room with a view of the park. A short walk finds you in the heart of the town with its elegant Regency parades and houses designed by Decimus Burton. The Regency meeting place, The Pantiles, a terraced walk with shops behind a colonnade, is especially memorable. You can also use Tunbridge Wells as your base for visiting the gardens at Scotney Castle and Sissinghurst and exploring Hever and Bodian castles, and the lovely town of Cranbrook with its white-board houses. *Directions:* From the railway station in Tunbridge Wells go up the hill and at the first set of traffic lights turn right onto Crescent Road. The hotel is on your right in 150 yards.

HOTEL DU VIN
Manager: Matthew Callard
Crescent Road
Tunbridge Wells
Kent TN1 2LY, England
Tel: (01892) 526455, Fax: (01892) 512044
35 rooms
Double: £95–£200*
*Breakfast not included: £9.50–£13.50
Open: all year, Credit cards: all major
karenbrown.com/ews/vintunbridge.html

Touching the water's edge, the Sharrow Bay Hotel has one of the most glorious views in England—a panorama of Ullswater mirroring the surrounding mountains. Now a member of the Von Essen group of hotels, it continues to be run in its world-renowned "country house-style" by a dedicated, staff team, many of whom have been at Sharrow for over thirty years. The main event is the superb, evening long dinner enjoyed in the Lakeside restaurant with its views across Ullswater. Bedrooms are furnished with antiques and come with absolutely everything. Seven are in the main house. The premier Garden rooms are just steps from the house with luxury suites on two levels, panoramic views of the lake and fells, and two lovely, double rooms. Just down the road is Bank House, where guests enjoy a chauffeur-driven car to and from dinner, breakfast in the beamed refectory dining room, large bedrooms, and stunning views of the lake from this hillside location. Idyllic Lake District scenery is on your doorstep, tempting you to go no farther than the terrace patio. Close by are plenty of good walks, fishing, and boating. *Directions:* Exit the M6 at junction 40 onto the A66 towards Keswick. At the roundabout, take the A592 towards Lake Ullswater. Turn left at the lake, then go through Pooley Bridge and turn right at the church, following signs for Howtown to Sharrow Bay.

SHARROW BAY HOTEL
Owner: Von Essen Hotels
Manager: Andrew Pratt
Ullswater
Cumbria CA10 2LZ, England
Tel: (017684) 86301, Fax: (017684) 86349
24 rooms Double: £320–£470*
*Includes dinner, bed & breakfast
Open: all year, Credit cards: MC, VS
Relais & Châteaux
karenbrown.com/ews/sharrowbay.html

Upper Slaughter, just up the hill from its sister village, Lower Slaughter, is a quiet, tranquil collection of idyllic cottages surrounded by bucolic Cotswold countryside. In the center of the village lies the former home of the Witts family, "lords of the manor" hereabouts for over 200 years. A massive portrait of the Reverend Witts, sitting regally on his stallion, graces the drawing room. Facing lush, rolling countryside, the main house, with its well-proportioned, high-ceilinged rooms, exudes country-house charm and peacefulness—three of the five largest bedrooms have four-posters. Cleverly blended into this large home is a curving wing of rooms built to appear like other farm buildings that overlook the narrow lane. Smaller than the grander rooms of the main house, these rooms are smartly outfitted and have well-equipped bathrooms. A path leads through the fields to the old mill at Lower Slaughter. It is a perfect location for forays through the Cotswolds; nearby Lower and Upper Swell are very picturesque. Broadway and Bourton-on-the-Water are best visited early in the morning to avoid the crowds. The Cotswold Farm Park with its rare farm animals is nearby. *Directions:* From the A429 on the outskirts of Bourton-on-the-Water, a small signpost indicates "The Slaughters." Follow the lane through Lower to Upper Slaughter.

LORDS OF THE MANOR HOTEL
Manager: Colin Heaney
Upper Slaughter, Cheltenham
Gloucestershire GL54 2JD, England
Tel: (01451) 820243, Fax: (01451) 820696
27 rooms
Double: £160–£310*
*Service charge: 12.5%
Open: all year, Credit cards: all major
karenbrown.com/ews/lordsofthemanor.html

Standing on the River Frome on the edge of the lovely town of Wareham, this 16th-century building was once the priory of Lady St. Mary, a Benedictine monastery, and is now a particularly lovely hotel. The entrance, through a little walled courtyard, sets the tone for this most delightful hotel. Decorated in soft colors, the dining room is most inviting. Lovely furniture and a grand piano highlight the beamed living room whose French windows lead under the wisteria-laden trellis to a broad expanse of lawn, which slopes down to the lazily flowing river—a perfect place to enjoy lunch on a warm summer day. A narrow maze of corridors and stairs winds amongst the rooms, which are on the small side but very smartly outfitted. If you are looking for the most deluxe of quarters, request one of the suites in the riverside boathouse. The gardens are a delight, full of roses in the summer, with a series of small, sheltered walled gardens. Wareham is an interesting mix of architectural styles encircled by earth banks built by the Saxons. Lawrence of Arabia's home is open to the public at nearby Clouds Hill. There are many wonderful places to visit, such as Lulworth Cove, Corfe Castle, Poole Harbor, Wool, Bindon Abbey, and Durlston Head. *Directions:* Wareham is on the A351 between Poole and Swanage.

THE PRIORY
Manager: Jeremy Merchant
Church Green
Wareham
Dorset BH20 4ND, England
Tel: (01929) 551666, Fax: (01929) 554519
18 rooms
Double: £170–£295
Open: all year, Credit cards: all major
karenbrown.com/ews/theprioryuk.html

I was very pleased to find a hotel in this lovely part of Northumberland. The Waren House Hotel was more or less derelict when Anita and Peter Laverack bought it in 1988, but over the years they have undertaken a complete renovation and refurbishment program, taking care to retain all the lovely old architectural features of this traditional, Georgian country house. The chandelier-lit entrance hall is home to a grand piano and many dolls from Anita's extensive collection. The ornately decorated drawing room is furnished with deep sofas and the library with traditional leather. By contrast, the large dining room, decorated in soft peach, is much more restful on the eye, with family portraits and pictures adorning the walls. Bedrooms are decorated in different styles: Maria is very French while the Gray suite is all gray silk. Edwardian is a most spacious suite with a large bedroom and sitting room divided by a bathroom with curved tub. This is a particularly attractive part of Northumberland: Bamburgh Castle commands a rocky outcrop high above the dunes with the stone cottages of the village in its shadow. A short drive brings you to Holy Island, historically known as Lindisfarne. The island is surrounded by water only at high tide, so careful attention must be paid to tide tables. *Directions:* Forty-five miles north of Newcastle on the A1, turn right to Waren Mill and the hotel is on your right at the far end of the village.

WAREN HOUSE HOTEL
Owners: Anita & Peter Laverack
Belford
Waren Mill
Northumberland NE70 7EE, England
Tel: (01668) 214581, Fax: (01668) 214484
12 rooms
Double: £130–£205
Open: all year, Credit cards: all major
karenbrown.com/ews/waren.html

Tucked behind a rambling, timbered façade with mullioned windows and steeply pitched roof, Wesley House is a delightful "restaurant with rooms" offering fabulous fare to appreciative travelers and faithful locals. From the entry with its comfortable seating, you can look through to the staggered levels of the attractive restaurant whose enticing menu makes for difficult choices. Ask to be seated in the atrium with its countryside views. Climb the stairs of this inn, whose oldest part dates to 1435, to five snug guestrooms, each named for a local meadow. The smallest, charmingly named Mumble Meadow, has a double bed and is attractively decorated in fabrics of cream and reds. Embury, the oldest room and housed in what was once the fireplace, has twin beds and a sloping floor. At the back, Sandy Hollow has a twin or double bed; while Almsbury, like the restaurant below, enjoys a private terrace and views across to Sudeley Castle. Setchley is also identified as the emergency fire escape, so residents of this room would be the first ones out! On weekends, a full English breakfast and a three-course dinner are included in the rates. Prices for bed & breakfast-only are available. *Directions:* Winchcombe is on the B4632 between Cheltenham and Broadway. Wesley House is easy to find on the main street at the corner of Castle Street.

WESLEY HOUSE
Owner: Matthew Brown
High Street
Winchcombe
Gloucestershire GL54 5LJ, England
Tel: (01242) 602366, Fax: (01242) 609046
5 rooms
Double: £150–£180*
*Includes dinner, bed & breakfast
Open: all year, Credit cards: all major
karenbrown.com/ews/wesley.html

Centrally located in the historic city of Winchester sits the most attractive Hotel du Vin and Bistro in an elegant townhouse designed by Christopher Wren (of St. Paul's fame). The hotel's theme is wine, with each bedroom named for its sponsoring winery that provided the photos and memorabilia decorating the walls. The rooms' overall decor is very similar—smart striped curtains, a duvet-topped queen- or king-sized bed (there is one king four-poster), television, and bathroom with oversized tub and Victorian shower with power head. I particularly enjoyed the most expensive and very large Courvoisier room with its ornate plasterwork ceiling, large window framing the garden, and two-part bathroom. Beringer's view of the car park was more than compensated for by its spaciousness and attractive photos of the famous winery. Trompe l'oeil plasterwork is an interesting feature of the spacious drawing room. Continental breakfast is available in the privacy of your room. The bistro is central to the operation and its menu is fun and varied. *Directions:* Turn off the M3 at Junction 11 to Winchester and follow signposts for the city center. The Hotel du Vin is on the left with lots of parking to the rear.

HOTEL DU VIN
Manager: Mark Huntley
14 Southgate Street
Winchester
Hampshire SO23 9EF, England
Tel: (01962) 841414, Fax: (01962) 842458
23 rooms
Double: £109–£225*
*Breakfast not included: £9.50–£13.50
Open: all year, Credit cards: all major
karenbrown.com/ews/hotelduvin.html

Family holidays for John Cunliffe meant coming to stay with grandma at Gilpin Lodge. When he saw the former family home for sale in the '80s, he and his wife forsook their restaurant with rooms in Bath and purchased the property, moving to the Lake District and bringing their longtime manager, Richard Marriott. Wings of bedrooms have been added and a brigade runs the kitchen, but John and Christine, joined by son, Barney, and his wife, Zoë, still keep the integrity of a luxurious, family home. Enjoy spacious lounges and sitting nooks, and dine in one of four lovely rooms that make up the restaurant. Bedrooms range in all shapes and sizes, from traditional to contemporary décor. All are beautifully decorated and appointed, as one would expect from a top-of-the-line country house hotel. It's a peaceful spot overlooking rolling, sheep-dotted hills. A stone's throw away is Windermere golf course and just down the road is the bustle of Windermere. A ferry takes you across the lake to Near Sawrey and Beatrix Potter's home, Hill Top Farm. Wordsworth fans head for Rydal House and Dove Cottage, while walkers head for the hills. Gilpin Lodge can arrange for a private car and driver to escort you on your sightseeing. *Directions:* Exit the M6 at junction 36, taking the A591 around Kendal towards Windermere. At the large roundabout, turn onto the B5284 through Crook Village to Gilpin Lodge on the right.

GILPIN LODGE
Owners: Christine & John Cunliffe
Manager: Richard Marriott
Crook Road
Windermere
Cumbria LA23 3NE, England
Tel: (015394) 88818, Fax: (015394) 88058
14 rooms Double: £220–£290*
*Includes dinner, bed & breakfast
Open: all year, Credit cards: all major
karenbrown.com/ews/gilpin.html

Windermere is one of the most popular and most crowded Lake District towns, but Holbeck Ghyll is set far from the traffic-clogged streets high above Lake Windermere in a rhododendron-filled garden overlooking the lake and the peaks of the Langdale fells—idyllic scenery that has made the Lake District such a magnet for visitors. Mellow, golden-oak paneling in the entrance hall extends up the staircase of Holbeck Ghyll and heavy beams create a nook large enough for chairs round a cozy winter fire. In summer guests prefer the sitting rooms whose window seats offer a magnificent view of the lake and the distant mountains. Dinner is delicious: there are lots of choices for each course and vegetarian dishes are available. Bedrooms come in all shapes and sizes, the premier rooms, of course, being those that offer lake views. Room 7, in the tower, has its own private, narrow staircase and is worth the climb for its view from the four-poster bed. Room 11, tucked under the eaves, has a sitting alcove that enjoys the same spectacular view. However the most breathtaking views are those offered by the six deluxe, luxuriously appointed Lodge rooms. Pamper yourself with a beauty treatment in the health spa. Within a 20-minute drive are Dove Cottage, Rydal Mount, and the villages of Hawkshead and Grasmere. *Directions:* From Windermere take the A591 (Ambleside road) for 3 miles, turn right on Holbeck Lane, and the hotel is on your left.

HOLBECK GHYLL
Owners: Patricia & David Nicholson
Holbeck Lane
Windermere
Cumbria LA23 1LU, England
Tel: (015394) 32375, Fax: (015394) 34743
20 rooms
Double: £230–£340*
*Includes dinner, bed & breakfast
Open: all year, Credit cards: all major
karenbrown.com/ews/holbeckghyll.html

The Samling is set high in the seclusion of its own sixty-seven acre estate with sweeping views down to Lake Windermere. Built in the late 1700s, the property consists of the main house and cottage-style outbuildings, all of which have been extensively, but aesthetically, renovated and converted into ten luxury suites, nine directly overlooking the lake. Tyan, reputedly the favorite of Tom Cruise and Nicole Kidman, has a rich, blue décor. Manmire is a duplex cottage suite. Its large sitting room has a private terrace and large bathroom with rustic wood walls. Pym is a large junior suite set into an attic space with large roof windows. Our favorite was The Bothy, a cottage with split-level living accommodation, separate living room, and private south-facing terrace. Its bathroom features an antique shower reputedly owned by Winston Churchill. Wander the estate, woodlands, fields and gardens dotted with contemporary works by well-known artists including iron work by William Pym, a wooden man by Walter Bailey, a spire of slate and glass by Charles Bailey. Relax with your chosen drink in the drawing room. Full English breakfast is delivered to your room. The dining room specializes in local produce supported by a reasonably priced international wine list. *Directions:* From Windermere, take A59 towards Ambleside for 3 miles. Turn right up the hotels steep driveway.

THE SAMLING   New
Owner: Tom Maxfield
Manager: Nigel Parkin
Ambleside Road
Windermere
Cumbria LA23 1LR, England
Tel: 015394 31922, Fax: 015394 30400
11 rooms
Double: £205–£405
Open: all year, Credit cards: all major
karenbrown.com/ews/samling.html

Seven 17th-century townhouses at the very heart of this delightful Cotswold town have been cleverly interwoven to create this charming hotel. This accounts for the maze of little staircases seemingly going every-which-way up and around to the bedrooms. Several with high ceilings, all are different and are decorated in soft, muted colors in a most appealing, country-house style. Nightingale, Jay, Swan, and Robin are particularly attractive rooms. Equally delightful rooms (Barn Owl, Osprey, Skylark and Partridge) are found in an adjacent cottage, as is the expansive Peacock suite. The recently refurbished dining room is enhanced by dramatic, large flower arrangements. There is a large drawing room upstairs. A central, log fireplace burns a cheery blaze in the bar with its wood-paneled floor. The Bistro bar is available for informal lunch and dinner. French windows open up to a small garden where tables, benches, and colorful hanging baskets are encircled by a high, stone wall—a lovely spot to enjoy lunch in the summer. The small town of Woodstock is at its best after the crowds have left. Walk through the grounds to visit Blenheim Palace. Oxford is 8 miles away and Stratford-upon-Avon is 32 miles. Cotswold villages are at your doorstep. *Directions:* Market Street is off Oxford Street, the A44 Oxford to Stratford Road.

THE FEATHERS
Manager: Gavin Thomson
Market Street
Woodstock
Oxfordshire OX20 1SX, England
Tel: (01993) 812291, Fax: (01993) 813158
20 rooms
Double: £145–£195*
*Service charge: 12.5% on meals
Open: all year, Credit cards: all major
karenbrown.com/ews/thefeathers.html

York, where Romans walked, Vikings ruled, and Normans conquered, is a fascinating city, its historical center encircled by a massive stone wall. The Grange, a lovely townhouse hotel, lies just beyond the city walls and ten minutes' walk from the Minster (cathedral), making it an ideal spot for exploring this wonderful city. The morning room, which leads directly off the stone-flagged lobby, has a rich, traditional feel with its Turkish carpet and Victorian portrait hung over the fireplace. The Ivy Restaurant's decor was chosen to enhance the gilt-framed oil paintings of St. Ledger winners on loan from the York Racehorse Museum. A seafood dinner, which is very good value for money, is available in the adjacent Seafood Bar, while the basement brasserie offers simpler, lighter fare. Each of the bedrooms—some with canopied four-poster or half-tester beds— has different decor: several are very dramatic. I was impressed by the amount of space in the standard double rooms. Though the standard king-bedded rooms had bigger beds, I found them tight on room space. York takes several days to explore: attractions include the Minster, the Jorvik Viking museum, the Treasurer's House, the medieval streets of The Shambles, the castle and its adjacent museum, walks along the walls, and a boat ride on the River Ouse. *Directions:* The Grange is located along Bootham, which is the A19, York to Thirsk road.

THE GRANGE
Manager: Graham Usher
1 Clifton
York YO30 6AA, England
Tel: (01904) 644744, Fax: (01904) 612453
30 rooms
Double: £130–£250
Open: all year, Credit cards: all major
karenbrown.com/ews/thegrange.html

Middlethorpe Hall is an imposing, red-brick William-and-Mary country house built in 1699 for Thomas Barlow, a successful cutler who wished to distance himself from his industrial success and establish himself as a country gentleman. It has been skillfully restored by Historic House Hotels and is now a very grand hotel, but without one iota of stuffiness. The two refined dining rooms have large windows overlooking the grounds. After enjoying elegant, country-house fare you retire to the enormous, graceful drawing room for coffee, chocolates, and liqueurs round the fire watched over by the massive portraits of long-departed gentry. Up the magnificent carved-oak staircase, bedrooms enjoy high ceilings, tall windows (those at the back with views across the grounds), and Edwardian-style bathrooms. Additional, very attractively decorated bedrooms are in the stable block across the courtyard. The spa contains a pool, steam room, sauna, fitness room, and three beauty-treatment rooms. York (a ten-minute drive away) will keep you busy for at least two days—add Castle Howard, explorations of the dales, moorlands, and the coast, and you can justify staying for a week. *Directions:* The hotel is situated just outside the village of Bishopthorpe, next to York racecourse. Leave the A64 (which forms the southern part of the York Outer Ring Road) at the A1036, in the direction of York city center (signposted York West) and follow the hotel's map.

MIDDLETHORPE HALL
Manager: Lionel A.Cnatard
Bishopthorpe Road
York YO23 2GB, England
Tel: (01904) 641241, Fax: (01904) 620176
29 rooms
Double: £165–£370*
*Breakfast not included: £14.95
Open: all year, Credit cards: MC, VS
karenbrown.com/ews/middlethorpe.html

Scotland Hotels

Fifteen miles of winding, single-track road lead you through land and sea lochs in some of Scotland's wildest scenery to Achiltibuie, a few cottages straggling along the road overlooking a broad expanse of bay and the Summer Isles, grassy little islands whose name extends to include the five tiny communities on the peninsula of which Achiltibuie is one. Just beyond the post office you find the Summer Isles Hotel run by Mark and Geraldine Irvine. It has been in their family since the '60s. Guests come to enjoy solitude and wild scenery in the daytime and in the evening experience the cooking of Michelin-starred chef Chris Firth-Bernard, Scottish Chef of the Year 1998. Bar meals are also available. Accommodation is in four distinct categories: rooms in the main house (ask for one facing the sea); the turf-roofed log cabins (lots of country charm but no view and priced accordingly); cottage rooms (very attractively decorated with two rooms offering views of the sea across the fields); the boathouse suite (fireplace in the sitting room and spectacular view from the bedroom atop a spiral staircase); and cottage suites (with view, sitting areas, and amazing bathrooms with high-pressure showers). You can take a local boat round the islands to see seals and birds. *Directions:* Achiltibuie is 85 miles from Inverness. Take the A835 for 10 miles beyond Ullapool and turn left for Achiltibuie.

SUMMER ISLES HOTEL
Owners: Gerry & Mark Irvine
Achiltibuie
Wester Ross IV26 2YG, Scotland
Tel: (01854) 622282, Fax: (01854) 622251
13 rooms
Double: £122–£188
Open: Easter to mid-Oct, Credit cards: MC, VS
karenbrown.com/ews/achiltibuie.html

Ardsheal House has a fabulous location on a bluff overlooking Loch Linnhe and the Morvern Mountains. A 1½-mile driveway and an 800-acre estate give an off-the-beaten-track feel to a house that is excellently situated for sightseeing. The Sutherlands are extremely enthusiastic about their lovely home, which dates back to the 1760s. When Neil inherited the estate the house had been sold to pay the inheritance tax but he and Philippa bought it back in 1994. It had been a hotel for many years and was rather large as a home for two people, so they decided to open it up to guests. The heart of the house is the oak-paneled entry hall with its cheery open fire and sitting nook overlooking the garden. Breakfast is served under the watchful eye of Neil's ancestors, though often it is served in the conservatory. Interesting furniture abounds as Neil's grandfather was a trader in Java, and Phillippa and Neil have lived in Hong Kong. Discuss your sleeping requirements when booking since there are bedrooms to suit all tastes, from a Javanese four-poster to a family room with a double and two single beds. Ardsheal House is a splendid base for exploring the Western Highlands, visiting Glencoe and Glenfinnan, and making day trips to the islands of Mull, Staffa, and Iona. *Directions:* Ardsheal House is 17 miles south of Fort William and 30 miles north of Oban, located on the A828, 5 miles south of Ballachulish Bridge between Glencoe and Appin.

ARDSHEAL HOUSE
Owners: Philippa & Neil Sutherland
Appin, Kentallen of Appin
Argyll PA38 4BX, Scotland
Tel: (01631) 740227, Fax: (01631) 740342
3 rooms
Double: £90–£130
Open: Feb to Nov, Credit cards: all major
karenbrown.com/ews/ardsheal.html

Five years of hard work by owners Wendy and Don Matheson have seen Boath House transformed from a "house beyond economic repair" to a magnificent example of a fully restored, grade-A-listed Georgian mansion set in 20 acres of grounds with its own Victorian walled garden and trout-stocked lake. The spectacular bedrooms are just the beginning. My favorite has a view of the lake and a bathroom with a free-standing, centrally located tub that begs you to soak in it. Guest facilities include a comfortable sitting room with fireplace, an award-winning dining room (the five-course dinner menu changes daily), and, conveniently located in the basement, a gymnasium, sauna, and aromatherapy spa. Contemporary art from local artists is displayed throughout the house and the Mathesons encourage guests to move selected items to their room on a "try before you buy" basis. A separate double-bedded guest cottage in the grounds provides a secluded hideaway. Golfers head to the championship courses at Nairn and Dunbar but Don urges them not to overlook the local good-value-for-money courses. Just outside Nairn you can visit the massive sand dunes that swallowed the village of Culbin. Loch Ness and Cawdor Castle are great attractions. *Directions:* From Inverness take the A96 towards Aberdeen. Go through Nairn and Boath House is on your left after 2 miles.

BOATH HOUSE
Owners: Wendy & Don Matheson
Auldearn, Nairn
Inverness-shire IV12 STE, Scotland
Tel: (01667) 454896, Fax: (01667) 455469
6 rooms, 1 cottage (£220)
Double: £170–£220
Open: all year, Credit cards: all major
karenbrown.com/ews/boath.html

If your vacation plans take you anywhere near southwest Ayrshire (maybe while traveling between Scotland and the Lake District or Ireland), treat yourself to a stay—house party-style—at luxurious Glenapp Castle, an elegant 1870 mansion in 30 acres of delightful grounds overlooking the Irish Sea. Fay and Graham Cowan devoted six years to bringing the castle from dilapidation to perfection—walls glow with attractive tiger-stripe oak paneling, tall windows are beautifully dressed with rich fabrics, chandeliers sparkle, lovely antiques and original oil paintings are expertly placed, and comfortable, plump-cushioned sofas and chairs are grouped invitingly around open fires. There are two dining rooms, both overlooking the sea: one, in a golden-yellow decor, for breakfast and lunch, and the other, dramatically decorated in burgundy and with spectacular sunset views, for outstanding six-course dinners. Guestrooms offer every amenity and the two master bedrooms are particularly lavish and spacious. Nine rooms have gas fires, lit for guests' arrival, and many bathrooms have beautifully renovated original marble walls and floors. This is the Cowan family's home and they bring a very warm and personal touch to this absolutely irresistible hotel. Advance reservations are a must. *Directions:* Going south on the A77, pass through Ballantrae and turn right just after the bridge at the edge of the village. Drive 1 mile to the hotel gates on the left.

GLENAPP CASTLE
Owners: Fay & Graham Cowan
Ballantrae
Ayrshire KA26 0NZ, Scotland
Tel: (01465) 831212, Fax: (01465) 831000
17 rooms
Double: £385–£515*
*Includes dinner, bed & breakfast
Open: Apr to Oct ("exclusive use" rest of year)
Credit cards: all major, Relais & Châteaux
karenbrown.com/ews/glenapp.html

Royal Deeside is an area of outstanding beauty and it is "royal" because the Royal Family have their summer home, Balmoral, here. Sitting at the end of a quiet lane with its gardens looking over Ballater golf course to the distant hills of Glen Muick, this sturdy Edwardian-style house was skillfully converted to a hotel by Priscilla and John Finnie. Guests have a small sitting room with lots of magazines and interesting books on local castles, which adjoins a convivial, cozy bar. Little tables are spaciously arranged in the large dining room where a four-course dinner is served—there are no hidden extras and canapés, coffee, and petits fours are included. The first-floor (second in America) bedrooms are spacious and furnished in traditional style while the four that nestle under the eaves are more contemporary in their decor and snugger in size. Ballater is a perfect location for exploring castles such as Drum, Crathes, Dunnottar, Fraser, Corgarff, Balmoral, and Craigievar. Golf, gardens, and art galleries round out the list of local attractions. *Directions:* From Aberdeen take the A93 for 40 miles to Ballater. Continue on A93 through the village towards Braemar, and Braemar Place is the last street on the left before you begin to climb the hill to leave the village.

BALGONIE HOUSE
Owners: Priscilla & John Finnie
Braemar Place
Ballater
Grampian AB35 5NQ, Scotland
Tel: (013397) 55482, Fax: (013397) 55497
9 rooms
Double: £1235–£135
Closed: mid-Jan to mid-Feb, Credit cards: all major
karenbrown.com/ews/balgonie.html

With lush lawns stretching beside the confluence of the Dee and Feugh rivers, Banchory Lodge has a magnificent setting. There has been a hostelry here since the 16th century when the mail coach halted at Banchory to change horses. Over the years it has evolved into a pleasing, rather rambling country house hotel. The first thing I always notice at Banchory House is the abundance of flower arrangements, from little posies on coffee tables to grand floral arrangements alongside splendid oil paintings. Log fires and oversized chairs set the relaxed, comfortable atmosphere of the place. Dinner is served in the grand dining room, which has a comfortable formality, with guests both in jacket and tie and casual attire. Country-house fare is the order of the day here, but if you wish to dine more simply, just choose one or two courses from the menu. Bedrooms are delightfully old-fashioned: room 9 with its semi-circular window was a particular favorite—though I would settle for any of the rooms that face the tumbling river. Fishing (the hotel has four beats), golfing, and walking are popular pastimes. Nearby Crathes Castle (an L-shaped tower house) has an early-18th-century formal garden, while Drum Castle has a magnificent rose garden. Farther away lie Fyvie and Craigievar. *Directions:* From Aberdeen take the A93 for 17 miles to Banchory. Turn left at the traffic lights and left just before you cross the river.

BANCHORY LODGE
Owner: Margaret Jaffray
Banchory
Grampian AB31 5HS, Scotland
Tel: (01330) 822625, Fax: (01330) 825019
22 rooms
Double: £130–£160
Open: all year, Credit cards: all major
karenbrown.com/ews/banchory.html

The Sutherland family made a fortune in jute manufacturing and in 1840 built Kinloch House, an impressive baronial-style mansion, as their country home. Kinloch has emerged as a luxurious country house hotel while maintaining all the atmosphere of a grand Scottish country home. The golden-oak-paneled entry hall rises to a first-floor gallery lit by an intricate leaded-light ceiling. Here the hall fire blazes a welcome to this lovely hotel, which marries all the style and elegance of days gone by with the amenities of a first-class hotel. Bedrooms off the gallery are generally large and spacious (one is smaller). Rooms at the front of the house offer lovely views across a field of highland cattle to the rolling Sidlaw Hills and glimpses of nearby lochs. All the spacious bedrooms with their large bathrooms in the east wing capture the same lovely countryside view. Enjoy the pool and fitness center and choose from over 40 golf courses within an hour's drive. Blair Castle and Scone Palace are popular with visitors. *Directions:* From Perth take the A9 (Inverness road) for 10 miles to Dunkeld and the A923 (Blaigowrie road) for 7 miles.

KINLOCH HOUSE
Owners: Betty & Eric Allen, Anne & Graeme Allen
Blairgowrie
Tayside PH10 6SG, Scotland
Tel: (01250) 884237, Fax: (01250) 884333
18 rooms
Double: £240–£300*
*Includes dinner, bed & breakfast
Closed: Dec 18 to Dec 29, Credit cards: all major
Relais & Châteaux
karenbrown.com/ews/kinloch.html

Originally the house of the local laird, Hobsburn dates back to the 17th century. Set in its 75-acre estate and connected to the village by a long driveway, it has now become home to Christopher and Jacqui McLean May, their two dogs, Moscow and Findlay, and their award-winning herd of pedigree Highland cattle. Guests have the run of the home, including the formal drawing room complete with paintings of family forbears and an extremely comfortable sitting room with log-burning stove. Breakfast is served in the expansive country kitchen or, weather permitting, outside on the patio. A four-course dinner with complimentary drinks is available with advanced reservations, though guests often walk down the drive to the Horse and Hounds pub. Two spacious, tastefully decorated bedrooms each have a twin and a double bed and their own private bathroom across the hall. An additional small double-bedded room is available to rent with either of these rooms. Situated just north of the border with England, with easy access (one and a half hours by car) to both Newcastle and Edinburgh, Hobsburn is surrounded by historic sights. Shoppers head for the nearby wool and cashmere factory shops. *Directions:* Cross the border on the A68. Turn left on the A6088 towards Hawick for the 8-mile drive to Bonchester Bridge where you find the entrance to Hobsburn on your left almost opposite the Horse and Hounds pub.

HOBSBURN
Owners: Jacqui & Christopher McLean May
Bonchester Bridge
Roxburghshire TD9 8JW, Scotland
Tel: (01450) 860720, Fax: (01450) 860330
3 rooms
Double: £80
Open: all year, Credit cards: MC, VS
karenbrown.com/ews/hobsburn.html

There has been a fortified tower house beside the sea on the Beauly Firth since the 16th century. Simon Frazer, the eighth lord of Lovat, incorporated the tower into his home when he married Jean Stewart in 1621—you can see their stone marriage lintel above the drawing-room fireplace and see the tower walls with their arrow slits behind the paneling. Terry Mckay now offers guests a warm Scottish welcome here. Bunchrew's position on the banks of the Beauly Firth is magnificent—even if you do not secure a room with a water view, you are assured of enjoying the view at dinner. Bedrooms and bathrooms are comfortable rather than luxurious and improvements are constantly being made. Three new rooms were added in 2001, one being the old nursery in a tower room. Some guestrooms have charming old furniture, while others have reproduction furniture, and all is spotlessly clean and well cared for. Hot-water pipes running through rooms and along corridors are an unusual feature of the older part of the house. Inverness and Loch Ness with its famous resident are just down the road. *Directions:* Arriving in Inverness, follow signposts for the city center and the A82 Fort William road for a short distance to the A862 Beauly road, which takes you along the Beauly Firth for 3 miles to the little village of Bunchrew. Bunchrew House is on your right.

BUNCHREW HOUSE
Owner: Terry Mackay
Bunchrew
Inverness-shire IV3 8TA, Scotland
Tel: (01463) 234917, Fax: (01463) 710620
14 rooms
Double: £130–£215
Open: all year, Credit cards: all major
karenbrown.com/ews/bunchrew.html

Callander is such an attractive, bustling little town. I selected Brook Linn for its lovely location and outstanding warmth of welcome. Built as a private home for a wealthy wool merchant, this solid Victorian home is set high on the hill well away from the bustle of the town but close enough for a ten-minute walk to find you at its heart. A hearty Scottish breakfast is the only meal served, and Fiona and Derek are happy to recommend restaurants nearby. Brook Linn is furnished in a clean and tidy manner appropriate to the house. The principal bedrooms have particularly nice bathrooms. With two twin, two double, and two single rooms, Derek and Fiona can accommodate most combinations of travelers. The Trossachs with their rolling pasture and heather moors, mountains, and glens are on your doorstep. The Wallace Monument Museum and Stirling Castle are just a short drive away. *Directions:* Take the A84 into Callander going north through the town and turn right just beyond Pinewood Nursing Home into Leny Feus. Follow the road up the hill and right into Brook Linn's driveway.

BROOK LINN
Owners: Fiona & Derek House
Leny Feus
Callander
Perthshire FK17 8AU, Scotland
Tel & fax: (01877) 330103
6 rooms
Double: £50–£66
Open: Easter to Oct, Credit cards: MC, VS
karenbrown.com/ews/brooklinn.html

We defy you not to wax lyrical over the Three Chimneys and The House Over-By, an outstanding restaurant with rooms. The Three Chimneys restaurant, which serves some of the finest food in Scotland, is housed in an historic croft packed with all the old-world charm of thick walls, low beams, and cozy dining nooks, while the six exquisite bedrooms are found in The House Over-By, a contemporary building built to echo the historic restaurant. The Spears have run the restaurant for almost two decades and in this time Shirley has gained a worldwide following for her food. Incorporating as much fresh local produce as possible from Skye and the Highlands, many of her dishes are based on traditional ideas but given a modern slant. Accommodation in the adjacent House Over-By is stylishly chic. The large luxurious bedrooms are decorated in soft, earthy Highland colors, and each has a sparkling, state-of-the-art shower room and views across Loch Dunvegan to the Outer Hebrides. In the mornings a generous buffet is served in the breakfast room. For sightseeing, you are just 5 miles from Dunvegan Castle. Narrow lanes wind you round the north of Skye, with its bays, beaches, and spectacular views then, continue up the peninsula to the most westerly point of Skye. *Directions:* From the outskirts of Dunvegan take the B884 towards Glendale for 4 miles to Colbost where you find Three Chimneys and The House Over-By on the left beside the Croft Museum.

THREE CHIMNEYS & THE HOUSE OVER-BY
Owners: Shirley & Eddie Spear
Colbost
Isle of Skye IV55 8ZT, Scotland
Tel: (01470) 511258, Fax: (01470) 511358
6 rooms
Double: £225
Closed: 6 Jan to 25 Jan, Credit cards: all major
karenbrown.com/ews/threechimneys.html

Beyond a vast expanse of immaculately mown lawn stands Culloden House, a beautiful Georgian mansion built to incorporate the ruins of Culloden Castle, Bonnie Prince Charlie's headquarters before the fateful battle of 1746. Culloden House has always had a reputation for hospitality, a tradition that is continued today by Stephen Davies and his staff, who offer the warmest of welcomes. After canapés in the clubby bar, dine in the gracious dining room with its lofty ceiling, faux-marble columns, and original plaster medallions, enjoying dinner served by staff uniformed in the Culloden tartan. Finish the evening with coffee and homemade chocolates in the grand drawing room. Bedrooms and suites in the main house vary in size from vast to snug, with bathrooms that run the gamut from small and rather ordinary to large and luxurious. Several of the most elegant rooms have smaller bathrooms, so be sure to discuss your choice of room when you make reservations. Parties of friends traveling together may wish to stay in the luxurious Adam-style pavilion. Culloden battlefield, just down the road, is a "must visit" as are nearby Cawdor Castle and Loch Ness. *Directions:* Take the A9 south from Inverness to the A96 Aberdeen and Nairn turnoff. Go straight over the first roundabout and take the next right to Culloden. Go through two sets of traffic lights and take the next road left to the hotel.

CULLODEN HOUSE
Manager: Stephen Davies
Culloden, Inverness
Inverness-shire IV2 7BZ, Scotland
Tel: (01463) 790461, Fax: (01463) 792181
28 rooms
Double: £209–£289
Open: all year, Credit cards: all major
karenbrown.com/ews/culloden.html

The tree-lined drive winds through a vast estate to the parklike lawns surrounding Cromlix House. Little rabbits hop gaily around—they're so tame that you can approach within a few yards of them before they disappear into the surrounding woodlands. The heavy Victorian exterior of the building hides an absolute jewel of an interior. Cromlix House, converted in 1981 from the Eden family home, was named as Andrew Harper's Hideaway Hotel of the Year for 1999/2000. It retains much of the original furniture designed for the house, along with family paintings and porcelain and all the old fittings dating back to when this grand house teemed with servants. The tone of an elegant Victorian home is set by the stately front hall with its wooden ceiling and richly paneled walls and is carried through into the inviting morning room, peaceful, well-stocked library, and garden conservatory. There is a private chapel with its organ pipes along one of the staircases. Upstairs are six luxurious rooms and eight very spacious, beautifully decorated and furnished suites. Serene countryside walks to little lochs or a visit to the family and pet cemeteries offer the chance for utter peace and quiet. Stirling Castle and the Trossachs with their lovely lakes are close by. Golf at Gleneagles is a 20-minute drive away. *Directions:* Take the A9 out of Dunblane, turn left onto B8033, go through Kinbuck village, and take the second left turn after a small bridge.

CROMLIX HOUSE
Owners: Ailsa & David Assenti
Kinbuck
Dunblane, Stirling
Perthshire FK15 9JT, Scotland
Tel: (01786) 822125, Fax: (01786) 825450
14 rooms
Double: £295–£410
Open: all year, Credit cards: all major
karenbrown.com/ews/cromlixhouse.html

Kinlochfollart, with its spectacular views straight up Loch Dunvegan, was built as a manse, a vast home for the former minister, which dwarfs the tiny country church across the loch. However, the upkeep of the place overwhelmed the parish, so the clergy was moved to snugger quarters and now Kinlochfollart is the lovely home of Rosemary and Donald MacLeod. Guests enjoy the kind of luxury that was totally unknown to earlier occupants and the MacLeods really go the extra mile to treat their guests as visiting friends. All guests arrive on a Monday and stay till Friday so a sojurn here really is a traditional house party. You are welcomed with a reviving cup of tea on arrival, enjoy pre-dinner drinks together, then eat your evening meal with fellow guests round the dining-room table. Visitors have the run of the house with the library, sitting room, and conservatory being open for their use. This is MacLeod country and the home of the MacLeod chief, Dunvegan Castle, the oldest inhabited castle in Scotland, is just up the road and well worth a visit. The island abounds in spectacular drives and you can take local boat excursions to view the nearby seal colonies. *Directions:* Arriving on Skye, take the A85 to Sligachan then the A863 to Dunvegan. Enter the village and take a small road to the left signposted Glendale (ignore the first Glendale turning). After half a mile Kinlochfollart is the white house to your right set in the trees beside the loch.

KINLOCHFOLLART
Owners: Rosemary & Donald MacLeod
Dunvegan
Isle of Skye IV55 8WQ, Scotland
Tel: (01470) 521470, Fax: (01470) 521740
3 rooms
Double: £500*
*4 nights, includes dinner, packed lunch, laundry,
bed & breakfast
Closed: Christmas & New Year, Credit cards: all major
karenbrown.com/ews/kinlochfollart.html

Drumsheugh Gardens is a quiet square of Victorian townhouses grouped round a leafy garden just three minutes' walk from Princes Street. Three of these spacious townhouses have been beautifully restored as The Bonham hotel, which offers the elegance of an old exterior, a spacious interior, a tongue-in-cheek modern decor, and the most up-to-date of everything. You feel like Alice standing before the enormous looking glasses in the dining room, while in the sitting room there's the Cheshire cat sculpture sitting beside the fire, inviting you to sit on the circular cherry-red couch that swirls upward to an enormous light fixture. Bedrooms range in size from petite to grand suites and range in their decor from sedate to vibrant. Several enjoy lovely views over the Firth of Forth. A great many have whimsical touches such as a mural of a parrot in a porthole in a room with a nautical theme and an ornate chimney pot painted on the bedhead in a spacious room overlooking the rooftops. Bedrooms are in the forefront of technology, with an integrated system that turns the TV into a computer screen and provides CD audio, DVD, and full Internet access. Beds are large, bathrooms gleamingly modern. *Directions:* Take George Street (parallel to Princes Street) through Charlotte Square (Hope Street) and onto Queensferry Road. Just as the road goes downhill, turn left into Chester Street and first right into Drumsheugh Gardens. Double-park on arrival.

THE BONHAM
Owner: Peter Taylor
Manager: Hans Riosmann
35 Drumsheugh Gardens
Edinburgh EH3 7RN, Scotland
Tel: (0131) 623 9301, Fax: (0131) 226 6080
48 rooms
Double: £127–£245
Credit cards: all major
karenbrown.com/ews/bonham.html

A brisk, fifteen-minute walk from Princes Street brings you to Channings, a delightful country house-style hotel encompassing five large Edwardian townhouses whose front parlors are now quiet sitting rooms. Its public areas are decorated with the greatest taste. Bedrooms are smart and individually decorated with lovely fabrics and provide every amenity such as satellite TV, direct-dial phones with voice mail, modem point, and trouser press, and one of the garden-level Club Rooms even has its own private garden. Some bathrooms have Jacuzzis or slipper roll-top baths. Our "superior" bedroom was a beautifully decorated twin with comfortable armchairs, an alcove with desk and chair, and an enormous, gleaming bathroom with bidet, slipper bath, and separate shower. Rooms tucked under the eaves have pine furniture and sloping ceilings, which give them a pleasant cottage-cozy ambiance. Channings' warm and traditional restaurant, which serves first-class food, contrasts strikingly with the light and contemporary wine bar and conservatory. *Directions:* Take George Street (parallel to Princes Street) through Charlotte Square (Hope Street) and onto Queensferry Road. Cross the river, take the second right (beside Learmonth Hotel) and follow South Learmonth Gardens to Channings. Double-park on arrival.

CHANNINGS
Owner: Peter Taylor
Manager: Duncan Johnston
15 South Learmonth Gardens
Edinburgh EH4 1EZ, Scotland
Tel: (0131) 623 9302, Fax: (0131) 332 9631
46 rooms
Double: £131–£185
Closed: Christmas, Credit cards: all major
karenbrown.com/ews/channings.html

The location is absolutely perfect—just a ten-minute stroll from Princes Street in the heart of Georgian Edinburgh. Three townhouses have been combined to form this luxury hotel, which has the air of a private club. No expense has been spared to create the look and feel of a sumptuous home. Beautiful fabrics, antiques, gorgeous furniture, and lots of flowers set an elegant mood. The drawing room centers on an elaborate crystal chandelier. There is no bar: guests order from the butler. Each bedroom has a different decor and color scheme. A great many of the bathrooms are especially grand, several with claw-foot tubs, others with a bath and separate shower, and the suites have luxurious steam showers. Three terrace suites have their own private terrace and entrance to Great King Street. The Howard has its own fine restaurant, The Atholl, specializing in traditional Scottish fare, and there are many more, from formal to funky, within easy walking distance. *Directions:* From the west end of Princes Street (with the castle on your right) turn left into Charlotte Square then turn right into Queen Street. Turn third left into Queen Street Gardens East, which becomes Dundas Street, then take the third right onto Great King Street. The Howard is on the right with a car park to the rear.

THE HOWARD
Owner: Peter Taylor
Manager: Johanne Falconer
34 Great King Street
Edinburgh EH3 6QH, Scotland
Tel: (0131) 557 3500, Fax: (0131) 557 6515
18 rooms
Double: £220–£475
Closed: Christmas, Credit cards: all major
karenbrown.com/ews/howard.html

A long, tree-lined drive leads to 17th-century Prestonfield, located in 13 acres of gardens and parkland just ten minutes' drive from the city center. Peacocks strut gracefully on a circular lawn in front of this grand, white stone manor, setting the scene for this exquisitely revamped hotel. Under the watchful eye of renowned local restaurateur James Thomson, the two oval Regency dining rooms built in 1816 have been transformed into the Rhubarb restaurant. (Prestonfield was the first place that rhubarb was grown in Scotland after its introduction from China.) These glamorous rooms are decorated with rich rhubarb red, gold, and black silk fabrics and massive portraits, and furnished with heavily fringed tub chairs and banquettes. A most indulgent dining experience is enhanced by choice wines from the hand-picked contents of the over 1,000-bin wine cellar. The clubby malt whisky bar with leather armchairs at the fireside has a huge selection of fine malts to whet your appetite. Opulence abounds in the air-conditioned bedrooms with their velvet-upholstered walls and all modern conveniences required by today's discerning traveler, from internet access to plasma television. Splendid bathrooms are lined with Carerra marble accented with Venetian glass mosaic tile. *Directions:* From the city center take the A68 (A7). Turn left at the lights after passing the Commonwealth swimming pool.

PRESTONFIELD
Owner: James Thomson
Priestfield Road
Edinburgh EH16 5UT, Scotland
Tel: (0131) 668 3346, Fax: (0131) 668 3976
31 rooms
Double: £120–£275
Open: all year, Credit cards: all major
karenbrown.com/ews/prestonfield.html

Danube Street was built in 1826 as one of the most fashionable streets in Stockbridge, an area of Edinburgh that lies a ten-minute walk from Princes Street and the heart of the city. Towards the middle of this lovely terrace is number 7, home to friendly Fiona and Colin Mitchell-Rose, who have the most delicious sense of humor. It's very much a comfortable family home, with dogs Doris and George (the official greeters) in their basket in the hall. Breakfast comes complete with homemade jam and scones, fruit salad, and traditional cooked breakfast served at the long dining table. Guestrooms, all beautifully decorated and with pretty bedlinens, are below stairs: a spacious four-poster room overlooks the garden and has its tea- and coffee-making tray set atop the old kitchen range (this was once the home's kitchen), while a large twin-bedded room and snug single room face the street. Guests have their own private entry and can come and go as they please. Just round the corner Fiona and Colin offer a lovely two-bedroom apartment with a well-equipped kitchen, a queen-sized four-poster room, a twin-bedded room, and a living room with pull-out sofa. This provides excellent and luxurious accommodation for longer stays. *Directions:* From Princes Street take Frederick Street north across George Street, through Circus Place to the bottom of the hill. Cross the bridge and turn left into Leslie Place. Danube Street is the second turning to the left.

⊥ ◨ ⚡ 🖩 ☎ 🕴 P

SEVEN DANUBE STREET
Owners: Fiona & Colin Mitchell-Rose
7 Danube Street
Edinburgh EH4 1NN, Scotland
Tel: (0131) 332 2755, Fax: (0131) 343 3648
3 rooms, 1 2–bedroom apartment (£140)
Double: £100–£130
Closed: Christmas, Credit cards: MC, VS
karenbrown.com/ews/danube.html

Susie and Andrew Hamilton are only the fourth family to call 16 Lynedoch Place home since it was built almost 180 years ago. This classical Georgian townhouse is packed with architectural features (cantilevered staircase, roof cupola, bow-walled dining room), but one of the beauties of the place is that it has both a front and back garden—a most unusual feature for an Edinburgh townhouse. Guests have their own front-door key and come and go as they please, often seeking out Susie in the kitchen (and along the way saying hello to Gerty and Holly, the resident pets) to discuss their sightseeing or dining plans. A breakfast that will set you up for the entire day is served in the elegant dining room. Below stairs you find three absolutely delightfully decorated guestrooms (a double, a twin, and a single), each equipped to the highest of standards. On this level guests also have a cozy sitting room supplied with reference books, a pay phone, and decanter of whisky for a nightcap. For planning explorations of the Highlands and islands, Andrew has a "Highland" itinerary that he is happy to share. *Directions:* Take Queens Street (parallel to Princes Street) onto Randolph Crescent then turn right onto Queensferry Road. As the road goes downhill, bear left into Lynedoch Place (if you go across the river you have gone too far). Park to unload and Susie will direct you to street parking (a five-minute walk) where you can leave your car for the duration of your stay.

SIXTEEN LYNEDOCH PLACE
Owners: Susie & Andrew Hamilton
16 Lynedoch Place
Edinburgh EH3 7PY, Scotland
Tel: (0131) 225 5507, Fax: (0131) 226 4185
3 rooms
Double: £70–£110
Closed: Christmas, Credit cards: MC, VS
karenbrown.com/ews/lynedoch.html

Windmill House has the feel of a country estate with a city address. There's a family of resident badgers by the tree stump, an ancient windmill, and acres of grounds stretching down to the Water of Leith—all just a mile as the crow flies from the center of Edinburgh. A remarkable setting with a remarkable home that looks hundreds of years old, though it was actually built just a few years ago—Michael is a builder and Georgian home restorer. It's a home so lovely that you are thrilled to stay there—or is it just that the Scotts put you in a euphoric mood? Judge for yourself. Pinch yourself as you sip tea in the drawing room or put your feet up and watch the television in the sitting room. Climb the elegant staircase to the spacious bedrooms, each beautifully decorated in sunny Georgian colors and accompanied by a top-of-the-line bathroom. One bedroom has an adjacent room for a child. Go through the garden gate and you are in the grounds of the Museum of Modern Art whence a path leads you along the river and into the heart of the city. Those who prefer to ride will find the bus stop an eight-minute walk away. There are plenty of local restaurants for dinner. *Directions:* Going down Princes Street (castle on left) follow signs for Glasgow (go straight at the end of Princes Street). Follow the road for a mile until just before the BMW showroom (on left)—turn right and immediately right into Coltbridge Avenue, leading to Coltbridge Gardens.

WINDMILL HOUSE
Owners: Vivien & Michael Scott
Coltbridge Gardens
Edinburgh EH12 6AQ, Scotland
Tel & fax: (0131) 346 0024
3 rooms
Double: £100–£120
Closed: Christmas & New Year
karenbrown.com/ews/windmill.html

Ettrickshaws, a former hunting lodge, is my idea of a blissful county house hotel: tucked away in a peaceful valley far enough from the beaten path to ensure quiet repose but close enough for interesting sightseeing forays; five bedrooms—the perfect size to ensure lots of attention; and owners who cook and take care of you. A log fire warms the hallway sitting room and the clubby bar is manned in the evening by the amiable Graham, who is also your sommelier. Jenny does the cooking and changes her set menu every day, offering four choices of starters and desserts with a set main course (a vegetarian alternative can be provided). Ask about the dinner, bed, and breakfast rates when making a reservation—these offer very good value for money. Of the five bedrooms I particularly enjoyed room 1, decorated in sunny shades of yellow, and room 2, the premier room with a large sleigh bed and bay window sitting nook with views across Ettrick Water to the countryside. Fishing for salmon and brown trout is available on the hotel's beats. Horse riders head for the Buccleuch Country Ride. Selkirk, Galashiels, and Hawick produce tweed, wool, and cashmere and all have their own mill shops. Locally there are a great many abbeys, castles, and historic houses. *Directions:* From Selkirk town square follow the A708 Moffat road for ½ mile and turn left on the B7009 to Ettrickbridge. Go through the village and Ettrickshaws is on your left in 1 mile.

ETTRICKSHAWS
Owners: Jenny & Graham Oldfield
Ettrickbridge, Selkirk
Selkirkshire TD7 5HW, Scotland
Tel & fax: (01750) 52229
5 rooms
Double: £100–£130
Open: all year, Credit cards: MC, VS
karenbrown.com/ews/ettrickshaws.html

Set on a quiet road high above Loch Linnhe with its gardens terracing down to a terrific view across the loch to distant mountains, The Grange has a countryside feel to it, yet you are just a few minutes' walk from the center of Fort William. Built for a wealthy lady in 1884, The Grange, with its gracefully sloping roofs, has a decidedly feminine feel to it, a feeling that is continued indoors where Joan and John Campbell have decorated their home throughout in a light, airy decor. A very comfortable sitting room is there for you to enjoy and breakfast, the only meal offered, is served in the dining room. The lovely bedrooms are decorated to the highest of standards and have the advantage of all having loch views. If I had to choose a favorite, it would be the delicious ground-floor room with its patio and luxurious bathroom with both a claw-foot tub and a shower. Guests often walk down to the pier to enjoy a seafood dinner at the Cranogg Restaurant. Countless possibilities exist for touring by car, while a favorite non-car excursion is to take the steam train from Fort William to Mallaig through some of Scotland's most fabulous scenery (summer only). *Directions:* Arriving in Fort William from the south with the loch on your left, turn second right into Ashburn Lane and left into Grange Road. The Grange is on the corner of Ashburn Lane and Grange road.

THE GRANGE
Owners: Joan & John Campbell
Grange Road
Fort William
Highland PH33 6JF, Scotland
Tel: (01397) 705516, Fax: (01397) 701595
4 rooms
Double: £90–£110
Open: Mar to mid-Nov, Credit cards: MC, VS
karenbrown.com/ews/grange.html

Nestling in the foothills of the mighty Ben Nevis, Inverlochy Castle sits amongst some of Scotland's finest scenery. Its magnificence does not appear to have altered since Queen Victoria visited in 1873. In her diaries she wrote, "I never saw a lovelier nor more romantic spot." Surrounded by landscaped gardens overlooking its own private loch, the turreted and gabled house was built to resemble a castle. Central heating and modern plumbing appear to be the only 21st-century additions. The two-storied Grand Hall with its frescoed ceiling sets the tone of this memorable hotel and the furnishings and decor throughout are luxurious. Dinner is an experience to savor in any of the three dining rooms, each decorated with period and elaborate furniture given as gifts by the King of Norway. The staff outnumbers the guests and attention to detail ensures that things are done properly. Inverlochy Castle is a very grand, very expensive, and most outstanding hotel. The small number of rooms and the hotel's popularity mean that early reservations are necessary. There are various outdoor activities available to guests including fly fishing for brown trout in the private loch, clay-pigeon shooting, guided walks, and grouse stalking. You can take the Road to the Isles, a lovely drive that brings you to Mallaig where you can take ferries to the isles of Skye, Rhum, Eigg, Canna, and Muck. *Directions:* The castle is on the A82, Inverness road, 3 miles north of Fort William.

INVERLOCHY CASTLE
Manager: Norbert Lieder
Torlundy
Fort William
Highland PH33 6SN, Scotland
Tel: (01397) 702177, Fax: (01397) 702953
17 rooms
Double: £290–£550
Closed: Jan 6 to Feb 4, Credit cards: all major
Relais & Châteaux
karenbrown.com/ews/inverlochy.html

In a fashionable Glasgow suburb three adjoining grand Victorian mansions, once the homes of wealthy industrialists, now form a small luxury hotel. The houses are interconnected. The dining room, bar, and one drawing room are in number 5, The Boardroom meeting room is in 3, and the reception and second drawing room are in 3. Spectacular features of 2 are the enormous, two-story stained-glass windows in the stairwells. The well-equipped bedrooms, generally very spacious and high-ceilinged, all have comfortable seating areas and some have large dressing areas. All but twin rooms have king-sized beds. Many rooms have four-posters swathed in yards of striking, dark-colored fabric—one room is dramatically done entirely in black. State your preference for bold or traditonal decor when booking. Public areas are delightful: number 3's comfortable drawing room reflects its Victorian heritage, with beautiful moldings, coal fire, overstuffed furniture, and lots of paintings, while number 1's is tailored and soothingly elegant in creams and browns. The dining room, serving very fine cuisine, looks light and fresh, papered in cream, and the bar is dark and cozy. *Directions:* Leave the M8 at junction 17 onto the Great Western Road (A82), which you follow to Hyndland Road. Turn left, then first right, right at the mini-roundabout, and right again at the end of the road.

ONE DEVONSHIRE GARDENS
Manager: Stephen McCorkell
Devonshire Gardens
Glasgow G12 0UX, Scotland
Tel: (0141) 339 2001, Fax: (0141) 337 1663
35 rooms
Double: £145–£485*
*Breakfast not included: £12–£17
Open: all year, Credit cards: all major
karenbrown.com/ews/onedevonshire.html

Golf players will be enchanted with Greywalls because it is on the very edge of the Great Muirfield golf course founded in 1744. Even if you have no interest in the game, you will love this most beautiful of houses built in 1901 by Sir Edwin Lutyens and you will adore the gardens laid out like a series of rooms by Gertrude Jekyll. It was the Weaver family home until 1948 when they turned it into a hotel—family photos and letters decorate the ladies' loo (perhaps they also adorn the gents' too—I did not visit) and photos of famous guests, particularly golfers, are grouped around the reception area. The dining room overlooks the tenth tee. The lounges are especially attractive, particularly the paneled library with its interesting pictures, shelves of books, and open fireplace. The bar is most convivial. Edward VII used to stay here and, because he admired the view, a special outside loo-with-a-view was built for him near the garden wall: now it's a suite called King's Loo. Guests can choose it or from an array of bedrooms which overlook either the flower-filled gardens or the golf course. Golfers have Muirfield as well as ten other courses nearby. Eighteen miles to the west lies Edinburgh. *Directions:* From Edinburgh take the city bypass to the A198, go through Gullane, and the hotel is on your left.

GREYWALLS
Owners: Ros & Giles Weaver
Manager: Sue Prime
Muirfield
Gullane
East Lothian EH31 2EG, Scotland
Tel: (01620) 842144, Fax: (01620) 842241
23 rooms
Double: £220–£260
Open: Apr to Oct, Credit cards: all major
karenbrown.com/ews/greywalls.html

Dunain Park Hotel is a lovely country home overlooking the famous Caledonian Canal, which joins Loch Ness to the Moray Firth. The large sitting room all decorated in shades of green with its crackling, open fire provides a snug retreat on stormy days. Ann Nicoll loves to cook, using vegetables from the garden and lamb, beef, venison, and salmon fresh from local suppliers, mixing traditional Scottish cooking with modern Continental. The bedrooms are all very attractive. Room 1 overlooks the back garden and has an elegant, four-poster canopy bed and a delicate writing desk tucked into one corner. Room 11 is a particularly pretty upstairs corner suite with lovely views across the garden. A suite consists of a very large bedroom, a small adjacent sitting room where the sofa can be made into a child's bed, and an immaculate, modern bathroom. You find a small heated swimming pool in a log cabin almost hidden by tall bushes in the extensive grounds. A very pleasant drive leads around Loch Ness to Fort Augustus and back on the other bank. The Monster Research Centre is on the north bank near Drumnadrochit. *Directions:* Dunain Park Hotel is just off the A82, 2 miles southwest of Inverness.

DUNAIN PARK HOTEL
Owners: Ann & Edward Nicoll
Inverness
Inverness-shire IV3 8JN, Scotland
Tel: (01463) 230512, Fax: (01463) 224532
11 rooms, 2 cottages (£178)
Double: £158–£178
Closed: two weeks Jan, Credit cards: all major
karenbrown.com/ews/dunainpark.html

The Isle of Eriska is a 300-acre private island off the west coast of Scotland linked to the mainland by a decorative wrought-iron bridge. In 1884 the splendidly named Hippolyte Blanc designed a grand baronial mansion, now a hotel and home to the welcoming Buchanan-Smith family, with son Beppo in charge of the day-to-day running of the hotel. A grand paneled hall, complete with blazing log fire, sits at the center of the house and it is here that morning coffee and a traditional afternoon tea are served, which you can enjoy in the comfortable drawing room overlooking the grounds. Wild badgers come to the library steps at night to be fed, oblivious to guests enjoying a drink—perhaps one of the hotel's excellent assortment of malt whiskies. Bedrooms come in all shapes and sizes, with Kerrera, Lismore, Skye, and Glensanda providing the most spacious quarters. Eriska is a splendid base for exploring the Western Highlands, visiting Glencoe, and making day trips to the islands of Mull, Staffa, and Iona. However, there are also many attractions on the island, including a magnificent indoor swimming pool, a six-hole golf course, a tennis court, clay-pigeon shooting, or tramping round the island to find the donkeys. *Directions:* From Crianlarich take the A85 towards Oban. At Connel take the bridge towards Fort William (A825) for 4 miles to the village of Benderloch. Turn left and left again following signposts to the Isle of Eriska for the 4-mile drive to the hotel.

ISLE OF ERISKA
Owner: Buchanan-Smith family
Manager: Beppo Buchanan-Smith
Isle of Eriska, Ledaig, Oban
Argyll PA37 1SD, Scotland
Tel: (01631) 720371, Fax: (01631) 720531
17 rooms
Double: £260–£375
Closed: Jan, Credit cards: all major
karenbrown.com/ews/eriska.html

Overlooking the romantic ruins of Kildrummy Castle and surrounded by acres of lovely gardens and woodlands, Kildrummy Castle Hotel is a grand mansion house. The richly paneled and tapestried walls and ornately carved staircase give a baronial feel to this grand house, a feel that is echoed in the lounge and bar whose large windows overlook the romantic castle ruins and the gardens. Yet this is not a stuffy, formal hotel: the smiling, friendly staff does a splendid job, offering people a really warm welcome. Dinner in the richly furnished dining room is a delight. The bedrooms (named after various pools in the hotel's trout stream) are tastefully decorated and traditionally furnished. Their size ranges from a snug attic bedroom with a private balcony to a grand corner room with enormous windows framing the countryside. Guests are given a card which gives them complimentary access to the adjacent Kildrummy Castle Gardens which present an idyllic picture at all times of the year. From Kildrummy you can join the Speyside Whisky Trail and enjoy a wee dram. At Alford lies Craigiever, a fairy-tale castle unchanged since it was built in 1626. Between Kildrummy and Braemar, home of the September Royal Highland Gathering, lies Balmoral Castle whose grounds are open in June and July when the Royal Family is not in residence. *Directions:* From Aberdeen take the A944 through Alford to the A97 where you turn right for Kildrummy Castle.

KILDRUMMY CASTLE HOTEL
Owners: Mary & Thomas Hanna
Kildrummy, Alford
Aberdeenshire AB33 8RA, Scotland
Tel: (019755) 71288, Fax: (019755) 71345
16 rooms
Double: £155–£180
Closed: Jan, Credit cards: all major
karenbrown.com/ews/kildrummycastlehotel.html

Ballathie House is a large turreted, Victorian, Scottish country estate home on the banks of the River Tay, surrounded by lawns, fields, and woodlands. While the house is imposing, it has a wonderfully warm atmosphere and a homey feel as well as glorious views over the river. A grand sweep of staircase leads up from the enormous hallway where sofas and chairs are grouped around a blazing fire. The drawing room, with its tall windows framing views across the lawn to the river, is made more intimate by cozy groupings of tables and chairs. My favorite accommodations are the spacious bedrooms with turret bathrooms and the smaller bedrooms with river views. Beyond the kitchen there is a ground-floor suite equipped for the handicapped. For complete peace and quiet request a riverside room in the adjacent building—upstairs rooms have balconies. The bar is a lively place, and dinner is delicious. Red squirrels are found on the Ballathie estate, and you may be fortunate and catch a glimpse of one of these rarely-seen animals. Nearby is Dunkeld, a delightful town with a ruined cathedral set in expansive lawns. Scone Palace, where Scottish kings were once crowned, has fine furniture, clocks, porcelain, and needlework. *Directions:* From Perth take the A9 towards Inverness for about five minutes to the B9099, Stanley road. Go through Stanley and take a right-hand fork towards Blairgowrie, following signs for Ballathie House.

BALLATHIE HOUSE
Manager: Christopher Longden
Kinclaven
Perthshire PH1 4QN, Scotland
Tel: (01250) 883268, Fax: (01250) 883396
43 rooms
Double: £158–£220
Open: all year, Credit cards: all major
karenbrown.com/ews/ballathie.html

Set at the foot of the Black Isle (a sheltered spit of land just north of Inverness), The Dower House was built as the retirement home for the owners of baronial Highfield House. While Highfield fell into disrepair, The Dower House flourished and was remodeled into a cottage orné, an adorable, single-story doll's house. The cute exterior belies a more spacious interior. The dining room and sitting room open up from the entrance hall. Mena has played on the interesting architecture and decorated the house in a most appealing, flowery, feminine way, adding attractive Victorian furniture and all the special touches that make you feel you are staying with friends. Robyn's delectable food has earned him a two AA Rosettes. As an alternative to rooms in the house, consider staying in the lovely, three-bedroom gate lodge. An enjoyable day trip is to explore the villages of the Black Isle of which the historic port of Cromarty is a highlight. You can enjoy magnificent Highland scenery on the train journey from nearby Dingwall to Kyle of Lochalsh. The local distillery at Glen Ord offers tours and samples. Traditional Scottish tweeds and woolens are available in nearby Beauly. *Directions:* Take the A862 from Inverness through Beauly to Muir of Ord. The Dower House is on the left, 1 mile beyond the town on the Dingwall road.

THE DOWER HOUSE
Owners: Mena & Robyn Aitchison
Highfield
Muir of Ord
Ross-shire IV6 7XN, Scotland
Tel & fax: (01463) 870090
5 rooms, 1 cottage (£150)
Double: £120–£150
Open: all year, Credit cards: MC, VS
karenbrown.com/ews/dowerhouse.html

This 1780s former manse sits surrounded by acres of lawns and trees in the heart of the picturesque seaside town of North Berwick, just a half-hour train ride from Edinburgh. The Scotts' furniture complements their lovely home perfectly. Gwen has a real eye for design and color and has done the most stylish job of decorating. From the front hallway a door opens to the downstairs wing, a suite of rooms with two bedrooms, one bathroom, and a cozy sitting room—absolutely perfect for families or friends traveling together. Upstairs are two more lovely bedrooms and bathrooms. Breakfast is the only meal served round the long dining-room table but there is no shortage of restaurants and pubs to walk to for dinner. Golfers are in heaven staying here for there are 18 courses within a 20-minute drive, including those at Gullane and Muirfield. A half-hour train ride finds you at the bottom of Edinburgh Castle, which makes for hassle-free day trips to all the shopping and historic sights. North Berwick's beach is a two-minute walk away as is the High Street with its shops and restaurants. Bass Rock, an important nesting site for sea birds can be visited. There are castles, museums, and a whisky distillery nearby. *Directions:* From Edinburgh take the A1 towards Berwick-upon-Tweed for 10 miles. Exit onto the A198 for North Berwick, keeping to the A198 through the town. Turn left on Law Road and The Glebe House is on your left after 100 yards.

THE GLEBE HOUSE
Owners: Gwen & Jake Scott
Law Road
North Berwick
East Lothian EH39 4PL, Scotland
Tel: (01620) 892608, Fax: (01620) 893588
4 rooms
Double: £70–£80
Closed: Christmas & New Year
karenbrown.com/ews/glebe.html

Oban, with its broad sweep of sheltered harbor, is the gateway to the islands—from here ferries ply their way to the isles of Mull, Iona, Coll, Staffa, Tiree, Colonsay, and Lismore. On a quiet street right on the bay, just beyond the bustling ferry terminal, sits The Manor House, built in 1780 as the principal home of the Duke of Argyll's Oban estate. Today this stylish hotel is the perfect place to stay to enjoy various day trips to the Western Isles. Bedrooms are not large but each is accompanied by a snug bath or shower room, and all are most attractively decorated. It is well worth the few extra pounds to secure a room with a sweeping water view across to Mull, Lismore, and the hills of Morvern. The most popular day trips are to Mull, Staffa, and Iona. Walk to the nearby ferry terminal for the 10 am boat to Mull and pick up a scenic bus tour of the island in Craignure. Alternatively, venture onwards to Iona, the historic cradle of Christianity and burial place of many Scottish kings, including the infamous Macbeth, or to Staffa to explore Fingal's Cave, immortalized by Mendelssohn. Remember to wear sensible footwear and waterproof clothing for trips to Iona and Staffa. On the mainland Glencoe is a popular destination. *Directions:* Arriving in Oban, enter the one-way system following signposts for the ferry and Gallanach. Do not turn for the ferry but continue towards Gallanach—The Manor House is on the right after 300 yards.

THE MANOR HOUSE
Manager: Gabriella Wijker
Gallanach Road
Oban
Argyll PA34 4LS, Scotland
Tel: (01631) 562087, Fax: (01631) 563053
11 rooms
Double: £140–£180
Closed: Christmas, Credit cards: all major
karenbrown.com/ews/themanor.html

Pitlochry developed in the latter half of the 19th century as a Highland health resort and remains today an attractive town of sturdy Victorian houses standing back from the wooded shores of Loch Faskally. Knockendarroch House sits above the rooftops of the town, isolated by its own little hill and surrounding garden. Tony and Jane Ross run their hotel with great enthusiasm and warmth. Dinner guests are treated to a glass of sherry as they peruse the four-course menu. Intertwining flowers decorate the stained-glass windows which filter sunlight onto the staircase leading up to the simply furnished, spacious, high-ceilinged bedrooms—two of the snug attic bedrooms have little balconies overlooking the town's rooftops. All the crisply decorated rooms have shower rooms and are equipped with telephones, TVs, and coffee- and tea-makings. If you have difficulty with stairs, request the ground-floor bedroom. Pitlochry and the surrounding countryside have much to keep visitors occupied for several days. During the summer season the Pitlochry Festival Theatre has a repertoire of plays, which makes it possible for you to see as many as four plays in a three-night stay. *Directions:* Enter Pitlochry from the south (A9). Pass under the railway bridge, turn right on East Moulin Road and take the second turning left onto Higher Oakfield (the hotel is on your left).

KNOCKENDARROCH HOUSE
Owners: Jane & Tony Ross
Higher Oakfield
Pitlochry
Perthshire PH16 5HT, Scotland
Tel: (01796) 473473, Fax: (01796) 474068
12 rooms
Double: £112–£146*
*Includes dinner, bed & breakfast
Open: Feb to Nov, Credit cards: all major
karenbrown.com/ews/knockendarroch.html

If you are looking to unwind completely, book a room at Knockinaam Lodge, a gray-stone Victorian country house set beside the Irish Sea amidst 30 acres of sheltering wooded hills and pretty gardens. The private beach is perfect for contemplative strolls—such as Churchill and Eisenhower might have taken when they stayed here during World War II. Inside, furnishings and decor respect the house's heritage while white-painted woodwork and pastel-colored walls create a light and cheerful atmosphere. Guests relax in the attractive sitting room or drawing room with their comfortable armchairs, tall windows, and decorative moldings. Delicious, innovative dinners, an important feature of the Knockinaam Lodge experience, are accompanied by wines from a 30-page list. After dinner, guests often repair to the cozy wood-paneled bar with its log fire, mounted stags' heads, and extensive collection of single-malt whiskies. There are nine individually decorated bedrooms of various sizes, all with en suite bathrooms, TVs, VCRs, and direct-dial phones. The most luxurious room (original master bedroom) has a king bed, a huge bathroom, and partial sea views. One of the three rooms with unobstructed sea views has a canopied queen-sized bed. *Directions:* From the A77 follow signs to Portpatrick, then 2 miles west of Lochans, turn left for the Colfin smokehouse and drive about 3 miles. (Best to arrive in daylight.)

KNOCKINAAM LODGE
Owners: Sian and David Ibbotson
Portpatrick
Wigtownshire DG9 9AD, Scotland
Tel: (01776) 810471, Fax: (01776) 810435
10 rooms
Double: £260–£350*
*Includes dinner, bed & breakfast
Open: all year, Credit cards: all major
karenbrown.com/ews/knockinaam.html

Viewfield House has always been home to the Macdonald family and there have always been Macdonalds on Skye. At the end of the 19th century this prosperous family remodeled Viewfield House adding a huge extension of large, grand rooms and completing the refurbishment with a baronial tower. Continuing a tradition begun by his grandfather, Hugh and Linda welcome guests to their home. Trophies of hunts and safaris (along with a smattering of British wildlife specimens) decorate the vast entrance hall and guests enjoy the large living room and the grand dining room hung with Macdonald family portraits. In the evenings guests enjoy four-course dinners at their own separate dining table. Bedrooms come in all sizes from spacious to cozy depending on whether you are in the Victorian or Georgian wing of the house or tucked under the eaves in the old nursery. There are washers and dryers for the use of guests. Portree is the only town on the island, built round a natural harbor where colorful cottages line the port and houses rise steeply up to the main streets of the town. It is a bustling, lively town, which hosts Skye week in June, a folk festival in mid-August, Highland Games in August, and a fiddlers' rally in September. *Directions:* From Kyle of Lochalsh take the bridge to Skye, then the A87 to Portree. Just as you enter the town, Viewfield House is on your left-hand side.

VIEWFIELD HOUSE
Owners: Linda & Hugh Macdonald
Portree
Isle of Skye IV51 9EU, Scotland
Tel: (01478) 612217, Fax: (01478) 613517
12 rooms
Double: £130–£150*
*Includes dinner, bed & breakfast
Open: Easter to mid-Oct, Credit cards: MC, VS
karenbrown.com/ews/viewfield.html

Originally built as a hunting lodge in 1820 and subsequently expanded in 1880, Finnart Lodge, the home of Annie and Archie Boyd, offers an idyllic lochside retreat. The folly and the conservatory are lovely spots for enjoying the stunning views across the water to the surrounding hills. Blue, a king size double, offers an en suite bathroom with its own private view down the loch. Green, a twin, offers an en suite bath and shower. Trellis and Wing, both twins, have a private bath and shower. Advance reservations must be made for dinner, which features local produce and homegrown vegetables in season. Tastefully and comfortably furnished throughout and with a liberal sprinkling of antiques and curios, the house provides a great base for walking and fishing. Archie will happily provide the use of a boat and fishing gear. If you fancy a day out on the train, consider visiting Oban or Mallaig from Rannoch station. *Directions:* Eleven miles north of Pitlochry on the A9 (Perth to Inverness), exit for Calvine. Drive through Calvine then turn right to Kinloch Rannoch via Trinafour (13 miles from the A9). In Kinloch Rannoch, turn left over the little stone bridge, then take the first right on South Loch Road. After 10 miles, the gates to Finnart Lodge are on the loch side of the road.

FINNART LODGE
Owners: Annie & Archie Boyd
Rannoch
Perthshire PH17 2QF, Scotland
Tel: (01882) 633366, Fax: (01882) 633232
3 rooms
Double: £80
Closed: Christmas & New Year
karenbrown.com/ews/finnart.html

Shieldaig has an overwhelmingly beautiful location facing a small, tree-covered island on the shores of Loch Torridon. Here single-track roads wind you through spectacular, rugged scenery of mountains rising straight from the sea and sea lochs penetrating far inland. A wonderful place to stay in Shieldaig is Tigh an Eilean, an 18th-century house converted to a hotel and personally run by Cathryn and Christopher Field. The decor is quiet and soothing with soft beiges and warm pastels. Dinner is taken in the airy dining room overlooking the loch and there are snug little lounges and an honesty bar. Bedrooms are cozy and very comfortable—be sure to request a loch view. The hotel will pack you a picnic lunch or you can obtain supplies from the Fields' little shop next door. Walking, birdwatching, and fishing are popular pastimes with the Beinne Eighe Nature Reserve and the 15,000-acre National Trust estate nearby. Guests often drive around the Applecross Peninsula with its awesome, twisting pass of Bealach-na-Bo and its views of Skye and the Outer Hebrides. Tigh An Eilean is an excellent place to stop if you are traveling between Skye (Kyle of Lochalsh) and Ullapool and do not want to rush through all this magnificent scenery in one day. *Directions:* Shieldaig is 68 miles from Inverness. Take the A832 (Ullapool road) to Garve and then on to Kinlochewe where you turn left on the A896 (single-track road) to Shieldaig. The hotel is on the waterfront.

TIGH AN EILEAN (HOUSE BY THE ISLAND)
Owners: Cathryn & Christopher Field
Shieldaig, on Loch Torridon
Wester Ross IV54 8XN, Scotland
Tel: (01520) 755251, Fax: (01520) 755321
11 rooms
Double: £130
Open: Apr to Nov, Credit cards: MC, VS
karenbrown.com/ews/tighaneilean.html

On a rocky spit of land almost surrounded by water, the whitewashed Eilean Iarmain hotel, a Harris Tweed shop and a huddle of cottages face Isle Ornsay, a tiny island whose lighthouse was built by Robert Louis Stephenson's grandfather. Across the sound mountains tumble directly into the sea, adding a wild, end-of-the-earth feel. The Eilean Iarmain (pronounced "Ellen Earman") is a hotel with a lot of style. Chintz chairs add a homey touch to the cozy parlor and in the dining room you find that the menu is in Gaelic, thankfully with an English translation (the staff speak Gaelic and English). A tartan-patterned carpet leads up the pine stairs to six bedrooms. They have varied tariffs to match the great variety of size and decor: room 2 has a canopied half-tester bed that once resided in Armadale Castle; the turret room is paneled in mellow pine and has a seating area in the turret. More rooms are found in the cottage across the road. In addition there are four luxurious suites with sitting room and bathroom downstairs and bedroom upstairs. Step out of the front door of the hotel and round the side and you find yourself in the old-fashioned pub (bar meals are served) where locals gather—on Thursday evenings they often bring their instruments. Be sure to visit Armadale Castle. *Directions:* From Kyle of Lochalsh take the bridge to Skye, then the A850 to the A851 towards Armadale: turn left to Eilean Iarmain.

EILEAN IARMAIN (ISLE ORNSAY HOTEL)
Owners: Sir Iain & Lady Noble
Sleat
Isle of Skye IV43 8QR, Scotland
Tel: (01471) 833332, Fax: (01471) 833275
16 rooms
Double: £125–£235*
*Service charge: 10%
Open: all year, Credit cards: all major
karenbrown.com/ews/eileaniarmain.html

The Creggans Inn stands next to the shore of Loch Fyne on the doorstep of some of the most remote and unspoiled countryside in Scotland. Previously owned by Sir Fitzroy McLean (thought to have been the role model for Ian Fleming's James Bond, otherwise known as "007"), the property is now in the hands of the Robertson family who brought years of experience in hotel ownership on the Isle of Mull to its renovation and upgrading. The work was well in hand when we visited and the rooms that we inspected had been finished to a very high level of comfort. Guest facilities include a private second-floor sitting room, lounge areas, and restaurant, all with expansive views across the loch to the low, rolling hills beyond. A small but lively public bar at the end of the inn also serves as headquarters to the local shinty (hockey) team whose photographs adorn the walls. Here you have the opportunity to take a "wee dram" or sample some fine Scottish ale in the company of the locals. Strachur is easily accessible and well located as a base for touring and walking on the west coast. Nearby sights include castles (Inverary is home to the Duke of Argyll) and gardens (Younger botanical gardens benefit from the milder climate). *Directions:* From Glasgow take the M8 to Gourock, cross the Clyde by ferry to Dunoon, and take the A815 to Strachur where you find The Creggans Inn across the road from the loch.

THE CREGGANS INN
Owners: Onny, Alex & Thomas Robertson
Strachur
Argyll PA27 8BX, Scotland
Tel: (01369) 860279, Fax: (01369) 860637
14 rooms
Double: £120–£160
Open: all year, Credit cards: all major
karenbrown.com/ews/creggans.html

Kilcamb Lodge Hotel occupies a picture-perfect remote location on the shores of Loch Sunart. The house itself, a former hunting lodge, has been meticulously converted to a country house hotel and its interior is as delightful as the surrounding scenery. Try to secure one of the loch-facing rooms. Rooms 6, 7, and 8, with either a king or twin beds, offer spectacular loch views in rooms large enough to accommodate spacious sitting areas. Room 5 also shares the same lovely view but is smaller, with a double bed. The dining room with its fine cuisine and the sitting room also overlook the loch. Apart from the utter peace and quiet of the place, the surrounding scenery is a tremendous attraction—a paradise for lovers of wildflowers, animals, and birds. To the south are the Morvern Hills and Mull is an enjoyable day trip from the hotel. To the west is the Ardnamurchan Peninsula, the most westerly point in the British mainland. The scenery here varies from stark glens and soaring hills to lush valleys, and the little inlets with their white-sand beaches overlooking the distant islands of Rum, Muck, Eigg, and Skye are unforgettable. *Directions:* From Glasgow take the A82 north to the Corran ferry (7 miles before Fort William)—the ferry runs every half-hour and reservations are not necessary. Leaving the ferry, turn left and follow the A861, a narrow two-lane road, for 12 miles to Strontian where you find the hotel on your left beside the loch.

KILCAMB LODGE HOTEL
Owners: Sally & David Fox
Strontian, Ardnamurchan
Highland PH36 4HY, Scotland
Tel: (01967) 402257, Fax: (01967) 402041
11 rooms
Double: £104–£145
Open: all year, Credit cards: MC, VS
karenbrown.com/ews/kilcamb.html

Quite the most impressive building that you see for many a mile along the breathtakingly beautiful, rugged coast of Wester Ross is the Loch Torridon Hotel, a grand shooting lodge built by the Earl of Lovelace in 1887. The Earl picked an isolated spot where the mountains descend almost to the lochside, leaving just enough room for this imposing building and its sweep of lawn to the water's edge. The public rooms are huge: an enormous bay window frames the idyllic view of loch and mountains and the pretty pink-and-navy damask sofas and chairs seem almost lost in the vastness of the sitting room. The large pine-paneled entry and the dining room have a tribute to the 50th anniversary of Queen Victoria's reign painted just below the ceiling as a border encircling the rooms. The principal bedrooms are very large and enjoy magnificent bathrooms—I particularly admired the turret bathroom in room 2 and the grand tub sitting center stage in room 1. Smaller bedrooms are tucked cozily under the eaves. Be sure to request a room with a view. The area is renowned for its beautiful Highland scenery and you can take a spectacular drive by following the southern shore of Loch Torridon to Applecross, over the hair-raising Pass of the Cattle, and returning to Torridon via the A896. *Directions:* Torridon is 64 miles from Inverness. Take the A832 (Ullapool road) to Kinlochewe where you turn left on the A896 (single-track road) to Torridon.

LOCH TORRIDON HOTEL
Owners: David & Geraldine Gregory
Rohaise & Daniel Rose-Bristow
Torridon
Wester Ross IV22 2EY, Scotland
Tel: (01445) 791242, Fax: (01445) 791296
21 rooms
Double: £148–£323
Closed: Jan, Credit cards: all major
karenbrown.com/ews/torridon.html

Ullapool is a fishing port, ferry terminal, and popular holiday resort set on the shores of Loch Broom, a broad sea loch. The Ceilidh Place has the façade of a whitewashed row of fishermen's cottages but the interior is anything but traditional: this is a somewhat Bohemian, very eclectic establishment and the nicest place in town. Ceilidh (pronounced "kaylee") is Gaelic for meeting socially—add a song and some impromptu music and that would make it a grand ceilidh. Jean Urquhart and her late husband opened a coffee shop, which grew to include music and the sale of pictures, then along came accommodation, a bookstore, an exhibition hall, a restaurant, and a snug pub. Accommodation is in the hotel with its modern extension to the rear or dormitory accommodation in the clubhouse across the road. The rooms are contemporary in their decor, often with a built-in desk and fitted furniture (but no TV). Guests tend to gravitate towards the upstairs sitting room with its homey mix of furniture arranged in cozy seating areas, tea- and coffee-makings, and honor bar. The coffee bar is a great place to enjoy a cappuccino or a meal or you might prefer the more up-market restaurant. Possible day trips include Inchnadamph Caves, Ardvreck Castle, and Lochinver with its heart-stopping views. *Directions:* Ullapool is 60 miles northwest of Inverness on the A835. West Argyll Street parallels the harbor one street back from the water.

🛳 ☕ 🧹 CREDIT ☎ 🐕 🚶 🚶‍♀️ P 🍽 🐾

THE CEILIDH PLACE
Owner: Jean Urquhart
14 West Argyll Street
Ullapool
Wester Ross IV26 2TY, Scotland
Tel: (01854) 612103, Fax: (01854) 612886
13 rooms
Double: £90–£140
Open: all year, Credit cards: all major
karenbrown.com/ews/ceilidh.html

Wales Hotels

The Olde Bull's Head has a long and interesting history. The walls of its traditional beamed bar are decorated with antique weaponry and the town's ancient ducking chair provides a most unusual curio. Guests have the use of a large comfortable sitting room. Dine in the stylish new brasserie or à-la-carte restaurant situated upstairs in the former hayloft. David Robertson, one of the owners, takes care of the front of the house. Charles Dickens stayed here, hence most bedrooms are named after Dickens characters. Each room is decorated differently, with matching drapes and bedspread and coordinating wallpaper and armchair. All have modern bathrooms, television, and phone and either a lovely antique brass or iron bed. Castle Street leads to Beaumaris Castle, a squat, concentric fortification commissioned by Edward I. Nearby, the Marquis of Anglesey's house and gardens are open to the public. Past Bangor, on the mainland, is Caernarfon Castle where Prince Charles was invested as Prince of Wales. *Directions:* From Chester take the A55, coast road, to Anglesey and cross on the Britannia Road Bridge, then follow the A545 to Beaumaris.

THE OLDE BULL'S HEAD
Owners: David Robertson & Keith Rothwell
Castle Street
Beaumaris
Isle of Anglesey LL58 8AP, Wales
Tel: (01248) 810329, Fax: (01248) 811294
13 rooms
Double: £98–£150
Closed: Christmas & New Year
Credit cards: all major
karenbrown.com/ews/oldebullshead.html

Tan-y-Foel, "the house under the hillside," sits high above the Conwy Valley, just outside Betws-y-Coed, within 8 acres of rugged woodland and pasture on the edge of the Snowdonia National Park. This small country house, owned and run by Janet and Peter Pitman and their daughter Kelly, has a contemporary rather than a traditional style. The interior decor, featuring bold and vibrant modern designs, completely belies the building's conventional exterior. Rooms 4, 5, and 6 enjoy spectacular countryside views. Rooms 1 and 9 (a converted hayloft) are external annex rooms providing extra privacy. All rooms are furnished with thoughtful touches such as toiletries, bathrobes, even ironing equipment. Janet, a Master Chef of Great Britain, uses organic and fine local produce and takes pride in her menu, which changes daily. Dinner is served in a delightful refurbished dining room that in past years was the dairy. The rugged grandeur of the Snowdonia mountain passes is in complete contrast to the pretty countryside around Tan-y-Foel. Castle lovers head for Conwy and Caernarfon. *Directions:* From the Llandudno roundabout on the A55 take the A470 towards Betws-y-Coed through Llanrwst and continue for 2 miles. Turn left at the signpost for Capel Garmon and Nebo (do not take the single-track road) and Tan-y-Foel is on your left after 1½ miles. Manchester airport is about an hour and a half's drive away.

TAN-Y-FOEL
Owners: Peter, Janet & Kelly Pitman
near Betws-y-Coed
Capel Garmon
Conwy LL26 0RE, Wales
Tel: (01690) 710507, Fax: (01690) 710681
6 rooms
Double: £143–£157
Closed: Dec, Credit cards: MC, VS
karenbrown.com/ews/tanyfoel.html

Sitting high above the River Conwy, with glorious views of Snowdonia and overlooking Conwy Castle across the broad river estuary, The Old Rectory Country House offers guests friendly hospitality and the chance to learn a little about the Welsh and their culture. In summer a harpist often plays for guests before they go in to dinner. The dining tables are elegantly set with crystal and silver, the polished wood floors are covered with lovely patterned carpets, and fine watercolors hang on the walls. Dinner here is a highlight as Wendy is a Master Chef of Great Britain. After dinner, coffee is served in the pine-paneled drawing room. Michael will help to plan sightseeing routes. Bedrooms, though not large, are well equipped with an iron and small ironing board, television, telephone, mineral water, fruit, and flowers. Walnut, Mahogany, and the coach-house rooms have splendid garden, river, and mountain views. Mahogany has a half-tester bed and a mahogany-paneled bathroom with a large corner tub. Glorious Bodnant Gardens, best know for its azaleas and rhododendrons, is just down the road while also nearby is the medieval town of Conwy with its dramatic castle. Beyond lie all the rugged delights of Snowdonia. *Directions:* The Old Rectory is half a mile south of Conwy on the A470, just a one-and-a-half-hour drive from Manchester airport.

⚓ ☕ 💳 ☎ 🐕 👤 👥 🏇 P 🍴 🚭 🖼

THE OLD RECTORY COUNTRY HOUSE
Owners: Wendy & Michael Vaughan
Llanrwst Road, Llansanffraid Glan Conwy
Conwy
Clwyd LL28 5LF, Wales
Tel: (01492) 580611, Fax: (01492) 584555
6 rooms
Double: £119–£169
Open: Jan 15 to Dec 15
Credit cards: MC, VS
karenbrown.com/ews/theoldrectory.html

Ynyshir Hall shares its location on the Dovey river estuary with a 1,000-acre bird reserve, home to herons, oystercatchers, curlews, and cormorants. Nestled in acres of gardens full of azaleas and rhododendrons, the hall was built in the 16th century, its most illustrious owner being Queen Victoria. Now it is home to professional artist Rob Reen and his wife Joan who have done the most wonderful job of decorating their country house hotel in rich colors, with each room accented by Rob's oils, acrylics, and watercolors. Relax round the fire in the elegant blue drawing room, enjoy a drink in the richly decorated bar, and dine on country-house fare in the turquoise-blue dining room. Bedrooms are named after famous artists. Monet, a ground-floor suite has a conservatory sitting room. A frieze of wispy clouds adds whimsy to the bathroom in the Renoir suite, which has particularly lovely views of the garden. Ynyshir Hall's central location makes it an ideal base for exploring the rugged Snowdonia National Park to the north and coastal paths to the south. Outstanding castles in the vicinity include Harlech, Powys, and Chirk. In nearby Machynlleth a traditional Welsh street market is held every Wednesday. *Directions:* From Aberystwyth take the A487 for 11 miles (towards Machynlleth) to Eglwysfach. Turn left in the village and Ynyshir Hall is on your right after half a mile.

YNYSHIR HALL
Owners: Joan & Rob Reen
Eglwysfach, Machynlleth
Powys SY20 8TA, Wales
Tel: (01654) 781209, Fax: (01654) 781366
10 rooms
Double: £180–£350
Closed: Jan 5 to 25, Credit cards: all major
Relais & Châteaux
karenbrown.com/ews/ynyshir.html

The Griffin's bright terra cotta exterior contrasts with the lush green Welsh countryside and immediately sparks your curiosity. Step inside and experience the refreshing simplicity and comfort of this country inn, completely renovated and opened for business in 2001. Bedrooms are decorated on a minimalist theme, with soft-pastel-painted walls, white ceilings, and stripped wooden floors accented by an eclectic collection of antique furnishings and beds, including some four-posters, goosedown pillows, Irish linens, and Welsh blankets. Modern bathrooms feature deep tubs to soak your bones after walking in the surrounding hills. Downstairs, as befits the local pub, the public rooms are truly public. Flagstone floors, painted-stone and blue-paneled walls, exposed wood beams, natural-slate-topped bars, open fires, and an upright piano all contribute to a very relaxed atmosphere. Food and drink and the enjoyment thereof are a major part of the "Griffin experience." Local ales and fine wines are available. Breakfast is served on large tables in the Old Back Kitchen. Make your own toast on the cream-colored Aga, which is also used to cook informal breakfasts every Sunday. 2003/2004 Wales Restaurant of the Year. *Directions:* The Griffin is located beside the A470 a little over 4 miles north of Brecon.

THE GRIFFIN
Owner: Charles Inkin
Felin Fach, Brecon
Powys LD3 0UB, Wales
Tel: (01874) 620111, Fax: (01874) 620120
7 rooms
Double: £92.50–£115
Open: all year
Credit cards: MC, VS
karenbrown.com/ews/griffin.html

From taking bed-and-breakfast guests to helping to get the farm on its feet, through expanding the traditional slate-hung farmhouse, to leasing the land and hiring a chef, Ty'n Rhos is Nigel and Lynda Kettle's Welsh success story. Over the years guests have become friends, returning year after year for a countryside holiday in this exceptionally beautiful part of Wales. I was particularly impressed by the very good-value-for-money prices and the genuine warmth of welcome that Lynda, Nigel, and now, son Andrew extend to new and old friends. Dinner is either a set, four-course meal or à-la-carte, except on Sunday evenings when the set menu, the only one available, offers two choices for each course. All the bedrooms are beautifully appointed—request a room with a view of wonderful open countryside across the Menai Straits to the island of Anglesey. I particularly liked the ground-floor rooms whose patio doors open onto the garden. Ty'n Rhos is located between the sea and the wild mountains of Snowdonia National Park. Caernarfon Castle is close at hand as is the Snowdon mountain railway, the little steam train that ascends Mount Snowdon. *Directions:* From Chester take the A55. Just before Bangor (Junction 11) turn left on the A5 (signposted Betws-y-Coed) and immediately right on the B4366 (signposted Llanberis). After 4 miles cross the roundabout and take the first right towards Seion. Ty'n Rhos is on your left after half a mile.

TY'N RHOS
Owners: Lynda & Nigel Kettle
Llanddeiniolen, Caernarfon
Gwynedd LL55 3AE, Wales
Tel: (01248) 670489, Fax: (01248) 670079
11 rooms
Double: £86–£120
Open: all year
Credit cards: all major
karenbrown.com/ews/tynrhos.html

Tyddyn Llan is a delightful gray-stone country house set in the peaceful Vale of Edeyrnion. It was once a shooting lodge for the Dukes of Westminster. Bedrooms are lovely, decked out in country-house style—rooms on the first floor (second in America) are more spacious than those tucked under the eaves. You can hike the old drovers' roads and tramp into the nearby Berwyn Mountains. (Llandrillo was an important point on the drovers' route, which was used for hundreds of years for driving livestock from Welsh farms to the markets in England.) Steam trains run on a narrow track down one side of the lake. A more scenic train ride is from Blaenau Ffestiniog, a slate town where slate crags overhang the houses, to Porthmadog on the coast. On the way to the train visit Llechwedd slate caverns. Many visitors head into the walled city of Chester with its half-timbered shops. *Directions:* Tyddyn Llan is near Llandrillo, on the B4401 between Corwen (A5) and Bala.

TYDDYN LLAN
Owners: Susan & Bryan Webb
Llandrillo
Clwyd LL21 0ST, Wales
Tel: (01490) 440264, Fax: (01490) 440414
13 rooms
Double: £130–£180
Open: all year
Credit cards: all major
karenbrown.com/ews/tyddynllan.html

I always hope that a beautiful region and a beautiful hotel will coincide and such is the case here. Snowdonia provides the most beautiful of Welsh scenery and Bodysgallen Hall provides the most beautiful of Welsh hotels. Built around a 13th-century watchtower and overlooking Conwy Castle, this large, rambling hotel looks surprisingly uniform, considering six centuries of additions, alterations, and restorations. The mellow elegance and character of the house are preserved throughout. The spacious, dark-oak-paneled Jacobean entrance hall and the drawing room on the first floor have large fireplaces, mullioned windows, and comfortable furniture that create a warm, relaxed atmosphere. Nineteen beautiful bedrooms are found in the main house: none of the rooms are large, neither are their bathrooms, but they are all delightful—I particularly enjoyed my stay in room 8, which has a sitting nook and the loveliest of views of the gardens. Sixteen suites are located in adjoining little cottages. There is an award-winning spa with a spacious indoor swimming pool, gym, and beauty salons. The grounds are an absolute delight and include a 17th-century knot garden, an 18th-century walled rose garden, and a woodland walk that offers spectacular views. *Directions:* Take the A55 from Chester to Junction 19 on the outskirts of Conwy where you turn right on the A470. The hotel entrance is on your right after 2 miles.

BODYSGALLEN HALL AND SPA
Manager: Matthew Johnson
Llandudno
Clwyd LL30 1RS, Wales
Tel: (01492) 584466, Fax: (01492) 582519
35 rooms
Double: £170–£310
Open: all year, Credit cards: all major
karenbrown.com/ews/bodysgallen.html

The Lake Country House Hotel can best be described as a lavishly appointed country retreat in the heart of Wales. A destination in its own right, with 50 acres of manicured gardens and grounds, fishing in the lake or river, a par-three golf course, clay-pigeon shooting, archery, tennis, and horse riding. But let's not forget the house itself—built as a hunting and fishing lodge in the mid-1800s, it has been transformed into a luxury country house hotel under the watchful eyes of owners Jan and Pierre Mifsud. Comfortable elegance is the theme, expressed in richly furnished public rooms, fine fabrics, antiques, and artwork, and invitingly comfortable chairs and sofas. Sumptuously appointed bedrooms, all with modern bathrooms, and suites with their own stylish sitting rooms all have views across the property. Hearty breakfasts are the order of the day. Gaelic cuisine features prominently on the lunch and dinner menus, ably supported by a comprehensive wine list. For those who simply cannot restrain themselves, afternoon tea, a specialty of the house, is served between 3 and 6 pm daily. Sample the delights of Welsh cakes, scones, and traditional teas, on balmy summer days beneath the chestnut tree in the garden or, in less pleasant weather, next to the fire. *Directions:* Leave Builth Wells west on the A483 towards Llanwrtyd Wells and turn off south to Llangammarch Wells immediately past the village of Garth.

THE LAKE COUNTRY HOUSE HOTEL
Owners: Jan & Pierre Mifsud
Llangammarch Wells
Powys LD4 4BS, Wales
Tel: (01591) 620202, Fax: (01591) 620457
18 rooms
Double: £150–£300
Open: all year
Credit cards: all major
karenbrown.com/ews/lakecountry.html

This grand and dignified house was designed by Sir Clough Williams-Ellis (of fanciful Portmeirion) and rescued from ruin by Sir Bernard Ashley (of Laura Ashley fame). The lounging rooms are a delight: a great hall with an open fire, antiques, huge sofas, and interesting pictures, a flowery sitting room, and a book-filled library with leather chairs and a snooker table. Each bedroom or suite is individually planned and quite different from the next—some are very flowery, others very masculine. The suites are up two long flights of stairs under the eaves. The smaller rooms of the north wing are most attractive—several have small four-poster beds and Welsh mineral water, sherry, and fluffy robes are provided. The hall has collected a plethora of awards including a Michelin star for its cuisine. The Wye river valley offers several places of interest and nearby are the ruins of Tintern Abbey, celebrated by Wordsworth. You can visit Hereford, a lovely, sleepy, medieval city astride the River Wye, its cathedral built in several styles from the 11th century, and Hay-on-Wye with its many bookstores. There is an abundance of pretty countryside, from the stark beauty of the Brecon Beacons to the soft prettiness of the Wye valley. *Directions:* Llangoed Hall is on the A470, midway between Builth Wells and Brecon.

LLANGOED HALL
Owner: Sir Bernard Ashley
Brecon
Llyswen
Powys LD3 0YP, Wales
Tel: (01874) 754525, Fax: (01874) 754545
23 rooms
Double: £200–£360
Open: all year, Credit cards: all major
karenbrown.com/ews/llangoed.html

A soft pink colorwash brightens the exterior of this spacious home in the village of Newport. Cnapan House is very much a family-run affair, with John and Eluned Lloyd, their daughter Judith, and her husband Michael Cooper extending a warm welcome. John and Michael are your genial hosts while Eluned and Judith work together in the kitchen. Lunchtime fare emphasizes whole-food cooking with old-fashioned, hearty soups and puddings (vegetarian dishes available). Tables are covered with lace cloths for dinner, adding a romantic touch to a special meal where the main course is always served with five or six vegetables. Guests can enjoy before-dinner drinks in either the sitting room or the bar, both snug rooms filled with country antiques and overflowing with charm. The bedrooms are artfully decorated in a light, airy style and immaculately furnished, with every nook and cranny filled with old family treasures. One guestroom is a family room with a small adjoining bunk-bedroom for the children. (Nursery teas are served in the early evening so that parents can put the children in bed before coming down to dinner.) You will love the welcoming, free-and-easy atmosphere that pervades this home. Just down the lane you find Newport's pretty beach and a particularly lovely section of the Welsh coastal path. *Directions:* Newport is on the A487 11 miles west of Cardigan and 7 miles east of Fishguard (not to be confused with the other Newport near Cardiff).

CNAPAN HOUSE
Owners: Lloyd & Cooper families
East Street
Newport
Dyfed SA42 0WF, Wales
Tel: (01239) 820575, Fax: (01239) 820878
5 rooms
Double: £74
Closed: Jan & Feb, Credit cards: MC, VS
karenbrown.com/ews/cnapan.html

Penmaenuchaf Hall is a lovely country house hotel with a quite unpronounceable name. According to owners Lorraine Fielding and Mark Watson, "pen mine ich av" is a somewhat accurate pronunciation. Lorraine, Mark, and daughter Lara moved here in 1989 and spent two years converting this beautiful old home into a hotel. Lorraine says the most enjoyable part was deciding upon the color schemes and choosing the fabrics—you'll be pleased with her choices: the decor throughout is absolutely delightful. From the log fire that warms the hallway sitting room through the comfortable lounge to the cozy dining room, the house exudes a welcoming ambiance. The principal bedroom, Leigh Taylor, is named after the wealthy Lancashire cotton magnate who built Penmaenuchaf as a grand holiday home. Today it can be your holiday home in northern Wales. Venture to explore Snowdonia National Park and the central Welsh coast and return in the evening to enjoy an excellent dinner. Of particular interest are the rugged scenery of Snowdonia, Portmeirion village with its Italianate houses, the narrow-gauge Ffestiniog railway, 13th-century Harlech Castle, Llechwedd Slate Caverns, and Bodnant, one of the world's finest gardens. *Directions:* From the Dollgellau bypass (A470) take the A493 towards Tywyn and Fairbourne. The entrance to Penmaenuchaf Hall is on the left after ¾ mile.

PENMAENUCHAF HALL
Owners: Lorraine Fielding & Mark Watson
Dolgellau
Penmaenpool
Gwynedd LL40 1YB, Wales
Tel: (01341) 422129, Fax: (01341) 422787
14 rooms
Double: £124–£184
Open: all year, Credit cards: all major
karenbrown.com/ews/penmaenuchaf.html

Maes-y-Neuadd, a 14th-century manor nestled into the hillside 3 miles from Harlech Castle, translates as "the hall in the field" an apt description for this sturdy home. With its 16th-, 18th-, and 20th-century additions, this rambling country house hotel has lots of character. Four hospitable owners, Doreen, Lynn and the two Peters, are on hand to make you feel thoroughly at home in this relaxed, unstuffy, friendly hotel. Enjoy a drink in the convivial bar before dinner looking out over rolling countryside to the distant mountains of Snowdonia National Park. The set-price dinner offers choices for all courses and always has a tempting Welsh lamb dish on the menu. Bedrooms come in all shapes and sizes, with most containing queen or king/twin beds. I particularly enjoyed Wynne, decorated in soft pinks, and Moelwyn, a deluxe room in the coach house (just a few steps from the main building) with its roof rising to the rafters and a wood-burning stove. Apart from exploring castles and Snowdonia, one of the delights of staying here is to ride on the nearby Ffestiniog Railway with its steam train that takes you through spectacular countryside. On Friday evenings in summer you can enjoy "steam cuisine" (a delicious Maes-y-Neuadd dinner) as you ride the rails. *Directions:* Maes-y-Neuadd is off the B4573, 3 miles north of Harlech.

MAES-Y-NEUADD
Owners: Lynn & Peter Jackson, Doreen & Peter Payne
Talsarnau
Gwynedd LL47 6YA, Wales
Tel: (01766) 780200, Fax: (01766) 780211
16 rooms
Double: £141–£235
Open: all year
Credit cards: all major
karenbrown.com/ews/maesyneuadd.html

Index

Fountains Abbey, 75
Fowey
    Fowey Hall, 167
    Marina Hotel (The), 168
Framlingham, 50
    Castle, 50

G

Gairloch, 96
George (The), Hathersage, 173
George of Stamford (The), Stamford, 204
Gidleigh Park, Chagford, 161
Gillan
    Tregildry Hotel, 169
Gillingham
    Stock Hill House, 170
Gilpin Lodge, Windermere, 218
Glasgow, 99
    Burrell Collection, 99
    Cathedral, 99
    Kelvingrove Art Gallery and Museum, 99
    One Devonshire Gardens, 250
    Pollok House, 99
    St. Mungo Museum of Religious Life and Art, 99
    Tenement House Museum, 100
    The People's Palace, 100
    Tourist Information Centre, 99
Glastonbury, 30
    Abbey, 30
Glebe House (The), North Berwick, 257
Glen Coe, 98
Glen Shee, 85
Glenapp Castle, Ballantrae, 229
Glenfiddich Distillery, 87
Glenfinnan, 94
Glenlivet Distillery, 88

Goring (The), London, 123
Grange, 57
Grange (The), Fort William, 248
Grange (The), York, 222
Grasmere, 57
    Dove Cottage, 56
    Wordsworth Museum, 56
Grassington, 76
Gravetye Manor, East Grinstead, 166
Great House (The), Lavenham, 178
Great Langdale, 56
Greywalls, Gullane, 251
Griffin (The), Felin Fach, 274
Grosmont, 74
Gullane
    Greywalls, 251
Gunnerside, 77

H

H.M.S. Victory, 44
Haddon Hall, 63
Hadleigh, 51
Hambleton
    Hambleton Hall, 171
Harrogate
    Vin (Hotel du), 172
Hartington, 62
    Cheese Shop, 62
Hartwell House, Aylesbury, 140
Hathersage, 67
    George (The), 173
Hawes, 77
    Wensleydale Creamery, 77
Hawkshead, 55
    Beatrix Potter Gallery, 55
Hay-on-Wye, 104

P

Peak Cavern, 66
Pelham Hotel (The), London, 130
Penmaenpool
    Penmaenuchaf Hall, 281
Penmaenuchaf Hall, Penmaenpool, 281
Pennine Way, 67
Penrhyn Castle, 105
Penshurst Place, 39
Penzance, 33
    Abbey Hotel (The), 195
Perth, 84
    Ballhousie Castle, 84
    Museum and Art Gallery, 84
    Museum of the Black Watch, 84
    St. John's Kirk, 84
Petworth, 43
    Petworth House, 43
Pheasant (The), Bassenthwaite Lake, 57, 144
Pilsey, 64
Pitlochry, 85
    Festival Theatre, 85
    Knockendarroch House, 259
    Tummel Dam Fish Ladder, 85
Plockton, 96
Plumber Manor, Sturminster Newtown, 206
Porlock, 31
    Oaks Hotel (The), 196
Porlock Weir, 31
Porthmadog, 108
Portloe, 34
Portmeirion, 109
Portpatrick
    Knockinaam Lodge, 260
Portree, 91
    Viewfield House, 92, 261

Portscatho, 34
Portsmouth, 44
    Navy Museum, 44
Prestonfield, Edinburgh, 243
Priory (The), Wareham, 214

Q

Queensberry Hotel (The), Bath, 146

R

Raglan Castle, 103
Ramsgill
    Yorke Arms (The), 197
Rannoch
    Finnart Lodge, 262
Reeth, 77
    Burgoyne Hotel (The), 77, 198
Reservations (Introduction), 13
    Fax, 14
    Letter, 14
    Telephone, 14
Rhayader, 104
Rhum, Isle of, 94
Riber Hall, Matlock, 186
Richmond, 78
    Castle, 78
Rievaulx Abbey, 74
Ripley
    Boar's Head Hotel (The), 199
Ripon, 75
Riverside House, Ashford-in-the-Water, 138
Robin Hood's Bay, 72
Rock
    St. Enodoc Hotel, 200
Romaldkirk
    Rose & Crown (The), 201

Y

Ynyshir Hall, Eglwysfach, 273
York, 71
    Betty's Bakery and Tearooms, 71
    Castle Museum, 72
    Clifford's Tower, 72
    Grange (The), 222
    Jorvik Viking Centre, 71
    Middlethorpe Hall, 223
    Minster, 71
    National Railway Museum, 72
    National Trust Shop, 71
    Treasurer's House, 71
Yorke Arms (The), Ramsgill, 197

KAREN BROWN wrote her first travel guide in 1976. Her personalized travel series has grown to 17 titles, which Karen and her small staff work diligently to keep updated. Karen, her husband, Rick, and their children, Alexandra and Richard, live in Moss Beach, a small town on the coast south of San Francisco. They settled here in 1991 when they opened Seal Cove Inn. Karen is frequently traveling but when she is home, in her role as innkeeper, enjoys welcoming Karen Brown readers.

JUNE EVELEIGH BROWN'S love of travel was inspired by the *National Geographic* magazines that she read as a girl in her dentist's office—so far she has visited over 40 countries. June hails from Sheffield, England and lived in Zambia and Canada before moving to northern California where she lives in San Mateo with her husband, Tony, their daughter Clare, their two German Shepherds, and a Siamese cat.

JANN POLLARD, the artist responsible for the beautiful painting on the cover of this guide, has studied art since childhood, and is well known for her outstanding impressionistic-style watercolors, which she has exhibited in numerous juried shows, winning many awards. Jann travels frequently to Europe (using Karen Brown's Guides) where she loves to paint historical buildings. Jann's original paintings are represented through The Gallery, Burlingame, CA, 650-347-9392 or *www.thegalleryart.net*. Fine-art giclée prints of the cover paintings are also available at *www.karenbrown.com*.

BARBARA MACLURCAN TAPP, the talented artist who produces all of the hotel sketches and delightful illustrations in this guide, was raised in Australia where she studied in Sydney at the School of Interior Design. Although Barbara continues with freelance projects, she devotes much of her time to illustrating the Karen Brown guides. Barbara lives in Kensington, California, with her husband, Richard, and daughter, Georgia.

Travel Your Dreams • Order Your Karen Brown Guides Today

Please ask in your local bookstore for Karen Brown's Guides. If the books you want are unavailable, you may order directly from the publisher. Books will be shipped immediately.

_____ *Austria: Charming Inns & Itineraries* $19.95

_____ *California: Charming Inns & Itineraries* $19.95

_____ *England: Charming Bed & Breakfasts* $18.95

_____ *England, Wales & Scotland: Charming Hotels & Itineraries* $19.95

_____ *France: Charming Bed & Breakfasts* $18.95

_____ *France: Charming Inns & Itineraries* $19.95

_____ *Germany: Charming Inns & Itineraries* $19.95

_____ *Ireland: Charming Inns & Itineraries* $19.95

_____ *Italy: Charming Bed & Breakfasts* $18.95

_____ *Italy: Charming Inns & Itineraries* $19.95

_____ *Mexico: Charming Inns & Itineraries* $19.95

_____ *Mid-Atlantic: Charming Inns & Itineraries* $19.95

_____ *New England: Charming Inns & Itineraries* $19.95

_____ *Pacific Northwest: Charming Inns & Itineraries* $19.95

_____ *Portugal: Charming Inns & Itineraries* $19.95

_____ *Spain: Charming Inns & Itineraries* $19.95

_____ *Switzerland: Charming Inns & Itineraries* $19.95

Name _____ Street _____

Town _____ State_____ Zip _____ Tel _____

Credit Card (MasterCard or Visa) _____ Expires: _____

For orders in the USA, add $5 for the first book and $2 for each additional book for shipment. Overseas shipping (airmail) is $10 for 1 to 2 books, $20 for 3 to 4 books etc. CA residents add 8.25% sales tax. Fax or mail form with check or credit card information to:

KAREN BROWN'S GUIDES
Post Office Box 70 • San Mateo • California • 94401 • USA
tel: (650) 342-9117, fax: (650) 342-9153, email: karen@karenbrown.com, www.karenbrown.com

Karen Brown Presents Her Own Special Hideaways

Karen Brown's Seal Cove Inn

Spectacularly set amongst wildflowers and bordered by cypress trees, Seal Cove Inn (Karen's second home) looks out to the distant ocean. Each room has a fireplace, cozy sitting area, and a view of the sea. Located on the coast, 35 minutes south of San Francisco.

Seal Cove Inn, Moss Beach, California
toll free telephone: (800) 995-9987
www.sealcoveinn.com

Karen Brown's Dolphin Cove Inn

Hugging a steep hillside overlooking the sparkling deep-blue bay of Manzanillo, Dolphin Cove Inn offers guests outstanding value. Each room has either a terrace or a balcony, and a breathtaking view of the sea. Located on the Pacific Coast of Mexico.

Dolphin Cove Inn, Manzanillo, Mexico
toll free telephone: (888) 497-4138
www.dolphincoveinn.com

England, Wales & Scotland Overview

- The Lake District
- Derbyshire Dales & Villages
- Wales
- Southeast England
- Scotland
- Southwest England
- Cambridge & East Anglia
- Dales & Moors of N. Yorkshire
- In & Around the Cotswolds

| 0 | 100 | 200 KM |
| 0 | 100 | 200 Mi |

ORKNEY ISLANDS

12

11

Glasgow

Edinburgh

13

9

10

8

Keswick

Isle of Man (U.K.)

York

IRELAND

4

5

7

Chester

Chesterfield

6

Cambridge

1

2

3

Oxford

Bath

London

Winchester

NETH.

BELGIUM

Exeter

FRANCE

Map 1

- ● Places to Stay
- — Southwest England

0   20   40 KM
0   20   40 Mi

Carmarthen

Swansea

M4

ATLANTIC
OCEAN

Selworthy

Porlock

Lynton   Oare

Barnstaple

Clovelly

A39

A361

A366

A377

Ashwater

Castle
Drogo   Exeter

Lewdown   Chagford
Lifton

Tintagel

Rock

A30

Tavistock
A390   Buckland   Widecombe
Abbey   in the Moor

Padstow

Lanhydrock   Cotehele   Buckfastleigh

Eden Project

Plymouth   A38   Torbay

Truro

Fowey   Talland

A30

Mevagissey

Veryan
Trelissick   Portscatho
St Just

Cape Cornwall

St Just   St Mawes

Salcombe

Lands End   St Michael's   Falmouth
Mount

ISLES OF
SCILLY

Mousehole   Penzance   Gillan

Map 2

- ● Places to Stay
- ── Wales
- ── Southeast England
- ── Southwest England
- ── In & Around the Cotswolds

0   20   40 KM
0   20   40 Mi

Pontiscill
Merthyr Tydfil
Tretower Court
Abergavenny
Raglan Castle
Monmouth
Gloucester
Woodstock
Aylesbury
A429
Burford
Witney
Oxford
Minster Lovell
Cirencester
A433
A419
Thames
A40
Henley
A404
Tintern Abbey
Swansea
Thornbury
A46
Moulsford
Newbury
Reading
M4
Cardiff
Bristol
Castle Combe
Lacock
A4
Bath
Avebury
A34
Bradford on Avon
M3
Trowbridge
Stonehenge
M5
Lynton
Porlock
Selworthy
Oare
Dunster
A39
Salisbury
A31
Winchester
Glastonbury
A36
Teffont Evias
A3
Taunton
Gillingham
Southampton
A361
A303
M27
M5
Sturminster Newton
Bournemouth
New Milton
A377
A35
Castle Drogo
Exeter
Beaminster
Wareham
Newport
Chagford
Dorchester
Bovey Tracey
Widecombe in the Moor
Buckfastleigh
A38
Torbay
English Channel
Salcombe

Map 3

● Places to Stay
━━━ Southeast England

| 0 | 20 | 40 KM |

| 0 | 20 | 40 Mi |

Map 4

- Places to Stay
- Wales

0   20   40 KM

0   20   40 Mi

Liverpool

M53

Holyhead

Isle of Anglesey

Beaumaris   Conwy Llandudno

A55

Llanfair

Bodnant Gardens

Chester

Llanddeiniolen

A494

Irish Sea

Caernarfon   Llanberis

Capel Garmon

Ruthin

Betws-y-Coed

A487

Blaenau Ffestiniog

A470

Llangollen

Porthmadog

Portmeirion

Bala

A5

Talsarnau

Llandrillo

A494

Dolgellau

Shrewsbury

M54

Penmaenpool

Dinas Mawddy

Severn

A458 Welshpool

Eglwysfach

A49   Norton

Aberystwyth

Llangurig

Ludlow

Rhayader

Leominster

Elan Valley

A470

Llangammarch Wells

Builth Wells

Hay-on-Wye

Felin Fach   Llyswen

Hereford

Newport Fishguard

Brecon

M50

Talybont-on-Usk

Pontiscill

Tretower Court

Carmarthen

Abergavenny

Merthyr Tydfil

Raglan Castle

Monmouth

Tintern Abbey

M5

Swansea

M4

Thornbury

Map 5

- ● Places to Stay
- ━━ Derbyshire Dales & Villages
- ━━ In & Around the Cotswolds

0   10   20 KM
0   10   20 Mi

Manchester
M62
M1   M18
Sheffield
Castleton
Hathersage
Tideswell   Eyam
Baslow
Buxton   Chatsworth
Ashford-in   Chesterfield
-the-Water
Monyash   Bakewell
A617
Hartington   Rowsley
Leek   Alstonfield   Matlock
Dovedale
M6   Tissington
Ilam
Ashbourne   M1
Stoke-   A1
on-Trent
Nottingham
Derby
A38
Stafford
Trent
M6
Leicester
M54
M42
M69
M42   Coventry   M6   M1
A340   A429
M6
A1

Map 6

- ● Places to Stay
- The Southwest
- In & Around the Cotswolds

0 10 20 KM
0 10 20 Mi

Norton
Birmingham
Coventry
Severn
M42
A429
M5
A340
Warwick
A40
Worcester
Stratford
M40
Hidcote
Banbury
Broadway
Chipping Campden
Broad Campden
Buckland
Moreton-in-Marsh
Ledbury
Snowshill
Stow-on-the-Wold
Winchcombe
Lower Swell
Cheltenham
U. Slaughter
Bourton
M50
L. Slaughter
Gloucester
Woodstock
Shurdington
Aylesbury
A429
Burford
Witney
Oxford
A46
Minster Lovell
M40
Cirencester
Thames
M5
A433
A419
M4
A404
Luckington
Moulsford
Henley
Thornbury
Grittleton
Nettleton
Castle Combe
Reading
Bristol
Lacock
A4
Bath
Avebury
A34
M3
Bradford on Avon

Map 7

● Places to Stay

— Cambridge & East Anglia

0   20   40 KM

0   20   40 Mi

North Sea

Holkham Hall

Morston

Wells-next-the-Sea

Holt

Cromer

Caley Mill

A148

Sandringham

Blickling Hall

A140

King's Lynn

Norwich

A1

A146

Stamford

Beccles

Hambleton

Southwold

Peterborough

A10

Walberswick

Dunwich

A11

A12

Bury St. Edmunds

Framlingham

Aldeburgh

A45

Snape

Cambridge

Lavenham

Kersey

Northampton

Long Melford

Ipswich

A1

Bedford

Hadleigh

East Bergholt

M1

M11

Dedham

Colchester

A12

Hertford

Aylesbury

M40

M25

Chelmsford

A404

M25

London

Thames

Map 8

Places to Stay
The Lake District
Dales & Moors of N. Yorkshire

0   20   40 KM
0   20   40 Mi

Bonchester Bridge

A7

Maften

Newcastle-upon-Tyne

M74

Brampton

A69

Blanchland

Durham

North Sea

A19

Penrith

A66

A1/M

Ullswater

Romaldkirk

Middlesbrough

Thirlmere

M6

Gunnerside

Reeth

Grosmont

Whitby

Grasmere

Ambleside

Troutbeck

Windermere

Bowness

Muker

Leyburn

Rievaulx Abbey

A169

Robin Hood's Bay

Scarborough

Hawes

Bolton Castle

Middleham

Lastingham

Sizergh Castle

Kettlewell

Woodale

Helmsley

Pickering

Levens Hall

Arncliffe

Ramsgill

Ripon

Kilburn

Malton

Malham

Kilnsey

Fountains Abbey

Castle Howard

Bridlington

Burnsall

Bolton Abbey

Ripley

A64

York

Harrogate

Kingston upon Hull

Blackpool

Preston

M621

Leeds

M62

Wakefield

M6

M62

A1

M16

M180

Grimsby

Manchester

M1

M18

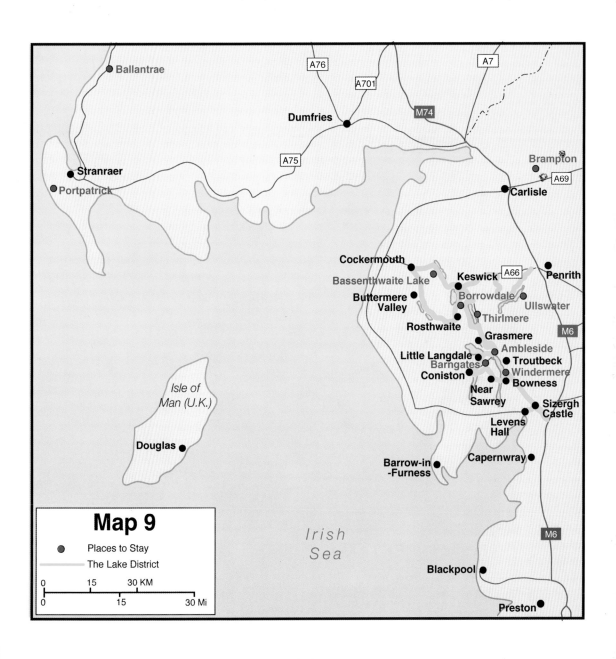

Map 9

- Places to Stay
- The Lake District

0   15   30 KM

0   15   30 Mi

Ballantrae

A76

A701

A7

Dumfries

M74

A75

Brampton

A69

Stranraer

Carlisle

Portpatrick

Cockermouth

Bassenthwaite Lake

Keswick

A66

Penrith

Buttermere
Valley

Borrowdale

Ullswater

Rosthwaite

Thirlmere

M6

Grasmere

Little Langdale

Ambleside

Barngates

Troutbeck

Coniston

Windermere

Near
Sawrey

Bowness

Isle of
Man (U.K.)

Sizergh
Castle

Levens
Hall

Douglas

Barrow-in
-Furness

Capernwray

Irish
Sea

M6

Blackpool

Preston

Map 10

- Places to Stay
- Scotland

0   15   30 KM
0   15   30 Mi

A9

A93

A90

Pitlochry

Kinclaven

Blairgowrie

Dunkeld

Dundee

Killin

A85

Perth

Saint Andrews

A84

Callander

Dunblane

M90

North Sea

Kirkcaldy

Stirling

North Berwick

Gullane

M9

A1

M74

M8

Edinburgh

Glasgow

Waren Mill

Tweed

Ettrickbridge

Jedburgh

A76

Bonchester Bridge

M74

A7

Map 11

Places to Stay
Scotland

0 — 15 — 30 KM
0 — 15 — 30 Mi

North Sea

Elgin
A96
A98
Nairn
Auldearn
Huntly
A92
Inverness
Cawdor Castle
Dufftown
Culloden
Rhynie
A95
Castle Fraser
Grantown-on-Spey
Alford
Kildrummy
Aberdeen
Craigievar Castle
A97
A93
Banchory
Ballater
A9
Braemar
Balmoral Castle
A93
A90
Pitlochry
Kinclaven
A85

Map 12

● Places to Stay

━━ Scotland

| 0 | 15 | 30 KM |
| 0 | 15 | 30 Mi |

Achiltibuie

Ullapool

Inverewe Gardens

A835

A832

Nairn

A96

Shieldaig

Torridon

Muir of Ord

Bunchrew

Inverness

Dunvegan

Colbost

Portree

Culloden

Tallisker

Isle of Skye

Kyle of Lochalsh

A82

Loch Ness

Sleat

Fort Augustus

A851

A87

HEBRIDES

Mallaig

Invergarry

A830

Glenfinnan

A9

Fort William

Strontian

Glencoe

Appin

A82